CREATING INTELLIGENT CONTENT WITH LIGHTWEIGHT DITA

Creating Intelligent Content with Lightweight DITA documents the evolution of the Darwin Information Typing Architecture (DITA) – a widely used open standard for structuring technical content. DITA has grown in popularity and features since its origins as an internal grammar for structuring technical documentation at IBM. This book introduces Lightweight DITA (LwDITA, which should be read as "Lightweight DITA") as a proposed version of the DITA standard that reduces its dependence on complex Extensible Markup Language (XML) structures and simplifies its authoring experience. This volume aims to reconcile discrepancies and similarities in methods for authoring content in industry and academia and does so by reporting on DITA's evolution through the lens of computational thinking, which has been connected in scholarship and media to initiatives for learning to code and programming.

Evia's core argument is that if technical communicators are trained with principles of rhetorical problem solving and computational thinking, they can create structured content in lightweight workflows with XML, HTML5, and Markdown designed to reduce the learning curve associated with DITA and similar authoring methodologies. At the same time, this book has the goal of making concepts of structured authoring and intelligent content easier to learn and teach in humanities-based writing and communication programs. This book is intended for practitioners and students interested in structured authoring or the DITA standard.

Carlos Evia is an associate professor in the Department of Communication at Virginia Tech. He teaches courses in professional communication and content management strategies. Carlos is also a voting member of the DITA technical committee and co-chair of the Lightweight DITA subcommittee at the Organization for the Advancement of Structured Information Standards.

ATTW Book Series in Technical and Professional Communication

Tharon Howard, Series Editor

Citizenship and Advocacy in Technical Communication
Godwin Y. Agboka and Natalia Mateeva

Communicating Project Management
Benjamin Lauren

Lean Technical Communication: Toward Sustainable Program Innovation
Meredith A. Johnson, W. Michele Simmons, and Patricia A. Sullivan

Scientific and Medical Communications: A Guide for Effective Practice
Scott A. Mogull

Plain Language and Ethical Action: A Dialogic Approach to Technical Content in the 21st Century
Russell Willerton

Rhetoric in the Flesh: Trained Vision, Technical Expertise, and the Gross Anatomy Lab
T. Kenny Fountain

Social Media in Disaster Response: How Experience Can Build for Participation
Liza Potts

For additional information on this series please visit www.routledge.com/ATTW-Series-in-Technical-and-Professional-Communication/book-series/ATTW, and for information on other Routledge titles visit www.routledge.com.

CREATING INTELLIGENT CONTENT WITH LIGHTWEIGHT DITA

Carlos Evia

Routledge
Taylor & Francis Group
NEW YORK AND LONDON

First published 2019
by Routledge
711 Third Avenue, New York, NY 10017

and by Routledge
2 Park Square, Milton Park, Abingdon, Oxon, OX14 4RN

Routledge is an imprint of the Taylor & Francis Group, an informa business

Library of Congress Cataloging in Publication Data
Names: Evia, Carlos, 1971- author.
Title: Creating intelligent content with lightweight DITA / Carlos Evia.
Description: [New York, New York] : Routledge, [2019] | Series: ATTW book series in technical and professional communication | Includes bibliographical references.
Identifiers: LCCN 2018034997| ISBN 9780815393825 (hardback) | ISBN 9780815393818 (paperback) | ISBN 9781351187510 (ebook)
Subjects: LCSH: Darwin Information Typing Architecture. | Technical writing—Data processing. | Writing—Automation. | Information organization—Computer programs.
Classification: LCC QA76.76.H94 E97 2019 | DDC 025.00285—dc23
LC record available at https://lccn.loc.gov/2018034997

ISBN: 9780815393818 (hbk)
ISBN: 9780815393825 (pbk)
ISBN: 9781351187510 (ebk)

Typeset in Minion
by Swales & Willis Ltd, Exeter, Devon, UK

To Jane and Sofia for being everything.
A mi papá (el original Dr. Carlos Evia), a mi mamá (que no es doctora pero de todo sabe), y a mis hermanos.

CONTENTS

FIGURES

PREFACE

In the summer of 2004, I was on my way to Blacksburg, Virginia, to start my new job as assistant professor of technical communication at Virginia Tech. Fresh out of graduate school at Texas Tech University, I was still in that period in which I thought it was my job to read and absorb everything and anything that was published or presented about technical communication. My new office only had a laptop computer on an otherwise empty desk when I started reading some of the just-published proceedings from the 2004 conference (now called the Summit) of the Society for Technical Communication.

The proceedings included a presentation titled "The Future of Technical Communication According to Those Who Teach It," by David Dayton – a fellow graduate (a couple of years ahead of me) of the PhD in Technical Communication and Rhetoric at Texas Tech University. Under the title of "Plate Tectonics of T-COM," Dayton's presentation included a slide that probably changed my academic life. Dayton's slide identified "two major fault lines (that) create tension, release continuous discourse" in the field of technical communication:

- Between academics and practitioners
- Among academics: literary/discourse focused versus social-science/technology focused.

As a somewhat naïve new PhD graduate, I was unaware of those fault lines. Probably it was because I came to the academic side of technical communication from industry (I was a practicing technical writer and rather clumsy interface designer when I decided to get a PhD). Or maybe it was because I was coming from a social sciences and computing systems background in another country. In Mexico, English departments (if they exist) focus on English as a second language and technical writing does not have a strong (any?) presence in literature or letters departments.

I remember calling my father and telling him about Dayton's presentation. I told him I was unsure about my affiliation on those divisions. As a new college professor, did I need to side more with academics? As a new professor in an English department, did I need to learn more about literary approaches and discourse?

My father's advice now sounds simple, but at the time was eye-opening and somehow unexpected. Why not do both? Why not build bridges and connect the seemingly separate camps?

Fifteen years later, this book represents my contribution to patching those fault lines. *Creating Intelligent Content with Lightweight DITA* is the work of an academic who has tried to keep an active presence in industry. It also attempts to connect discourse and writing principles to technological approaches for managing content.

Getting here has been a long trip, and this book was, at different points, a very different work. Initially, it was going to be a history of the computer manual. In that version, the book claimed that the obsolescence of the manual as the main genre of technical communication was one of the causes of the professional fault lines identified in Dayton's presentation. Some of that work survived and is present in Chapter 2. At another point, the book was going to be a guide for incorporating principles of computational thinking in technical writing courses aimed at students of computer science. That work influenced Chapters 7 and 8.

Nevertheless, my experience with the Darwin Information Typing Architecture (DITA) originally as a user, then as a professor teaching DITA in my classes, and eventually as a committee member and spec author, took the book in its final direction. Both original ideas for this book (the one about the history of the manual and the one about computational thinking in technical writing courses) somehow ended up in the same place: they proposed Lightweight DITA (LwDITA) as a solution to more than one problem affecting technical communication and content development. LwDITA represents the evolution of the computer manual and it provides a way to introduce computational thinking in writing courses.

When Taylor & Francis/Routledge circulated the prospectus and sample chapters for this book to anonymous reviewers, their feedback was on point: the book should be about Lightweight DITA. Since I had been breathing LwDITA in my teaching and research work at Virginia Tech, and in my committee contributions to OASIS since 2014, that sounded like an excellent idea. At the same time, it presented a very risky challenge: I had to write a whole book about a proposed standard for structuring information that had not been approved and will not yet be approved by the time the book is published. Therefore, this is not the ultimate LwDITA user guide, and the proposed content components and syntax details included in this book might change as the standard goes through the rounds of committee and general public approval enforced by OASIS. The history behind LwDITA, however, will not change. The need for a process or lifecycle that relies on simple markup structures and values the work of human authors to produce intelligent content will not change either. The evolution of DITA in a path that incorporates feedback from users, practices in writing instruction and communication that represent the bulk of this book will stay the same even if the LwDITA authoring formats look slightly different when the standard is finally approved.

Written from the hypocenter of the fault line between academia and industry in technical communication, I hope this book reaches its target audiences in both camps.

Reference

Dayton, D. (2004). The future of technical communication according to those who teach it. *Paper presented at the conference of the Society for Technical Communication.* May 10, 2004.

ACKNOWLEDGMENTS

This book reflects the hard work of the Lightweight DITA subcommittee at OASIS. We have been in conference calls for many years designing, evaluating, and revising the recommendations included in this book. I want to thank all active members of the subcommittee, but I need to specifically acknowledge the contributions and support of Rahel Anne Bailie, Bill Burns, Stan Doherty, Mark Giffin, Tim Grantham, Rob Hanna, Scott Hudson, and Keith Schengili-Roberts. In the early days of the subcommittee, Don Day, John Hunt, and Amber Swope made invaluable contributions to shape the proposed standard.

Kris Eberlein and Robert Anderson are also members of the subcommittee, but their guidance, leadership, and friendship as DITA spec authors deserve a special mention.

LwDITA would only be a theoretical experiment without the work of adventurous and generous developers like Jarno Elovirta, George Bina, and Radu Coravu. Bernard Aschwanden's interest in the proposed standard should take it to the next level in adoption and promotion. Sarah O'Keefe provided challenging and relevant feedback. JoAnn Hackos and Dawn Stevens made (and still make) room for LwDITA-related sessions in events of the Center for Information-Development Management that have promoted the proposed standard beyond the work of the dedicated subcommittee at OASIS.

Thank you to James Mathewson, Susan Carpenter, John Carroll, Jenifer Schlotfeldt, and all the former and current IBMers who shared with me their experiences about the past, present, and future of DITA and LwDITA.

My mentor and friend Carolyn Rude read all prototypes of this book, from the history of the manual to the LwDITA reference guide. Her feedback and vision as a pioneer explorer and bridge-builder of the technical communication fault lines has inspired me for decades. Rebekka Andersen, Tim Lockridge,

Kelly Pender (who actually knows a lot about LwDITA but probably won't admit it), and Russell Willerton helped finding sources, reading chapters, and keeping my disciplinary identity healthy. Allison Hutchison and Kelly Scarff brought their priceless graduate student eyes to the project. Allison's feedback, full of "I get it now!" moments, was a joy to read. Thank you to the dozens of undergraduate and graduate students in my courses who have been participating in my LwDITA experiments since 2014. Bernice Hausman and Joe Eska supported my DITA habit for many years.

Manuel Pérez-Quiñones, Ed Fox, Steve Sheetz, Patrick Fan, Chris Zobel, Deborah Tatar, and Steve Harrison have been at one point or another involved in my explorations for disrupting tradition and adapting principles of computational thinking to "traditionally non-computing" fields like writing and communication.

Tharon Howard believed in this project and encouraged me to write it in its current shape. "We have a good number of proposals in the series now," he said. "But nothing like yours."

Thank you to my brother Pedro Evia (the real Chef Pedro) and his business partner Eduardo Rukos for the *Sensei Sushi* materials.

Finally, if this book needed a co-author, that would be Michael Priestley – the original *ditaguy*. As the father of DITA and LwDITA, Michael has been an innovator and visionary in the world of content development. But above all things he has been a friendly collaborator, leader, and dad-joke generator. And if this book needed a substitute author, that would be my fact-checker, cheerleader, critic, and friend Alan Houser. An undisclosed percentage of this book's royalties might (or might not) go to a fund to buy a Vespa-themed Rolex for Alan.

Thank you to my wife and constant source of motivation Dr. Jane Robertson Evia. Thank you to Sofia Evia for being an awesome bebé. . . I mean, niña grande. Here's a link to Sofia's response to the question of "what is papá's book about?" https://youtu.be/MvPuw8XqOYs.

FOREWORD

Carlos Evia's book *Creating Intelligent Content with Lightweight DITA* is a most welcome addition to the ATTW Book Series in Technical and Professional Communication (TPC) because, as its title suggests, it is a book about building and maintaining content which is appropriate for users using an exciting new standard for Extensible Markup Language (XML) called "Lightweight DITA" or LwDITA. Like all the other books in the ATTW Book Series, *Creating Intelligent Content with Lightweight DITA* is solidly based on its author's comprehensive knowledge of the literature in the field and years of teaching TPC students to create content in DITA for industry clients. Balancing between his mastery of the academy and his practical industry experience as a voting member of the DITA technical committee and as co-chair of the Lightweight DITA subcommittee at the Organization for the Advancement of Structured Information Standards, Evia's book provides TPC students and practitioners with two valuable outcomes: 1) an introduction to a development model for creating digital content adapted for users, and 2) an accessible introduction to the new LwDITA standard.

Evia's work is firmly situated in what is starting to be called the shift from the "craftsman model" of Technical Communication to the "Component Content Management model." This shift has come about as a result of the ways that new technologies like XML DITA, single-source authoring environments, and Content Management Systems have changed the ways that technical writers deliver information to audiences (or what we would now call "users"). As Carlos explains in Chapter 2, the "craftsman" model made technical communicators responsible for the development and delivery of *entire* documents. Workplace practitioners wrote complete documentation sets, recommendation reports, marketing brochures, etc. And our curricula and textbooks are still based on the assumption that our students are being prepared as craft persons who will do this same sort of work in their careers. The Component Content Management paradigm shift—which Carlos describes in Chapter 2, which Tatiana Batova and Rebekka Andersen outline in their 2017 *IEEE Transactions* article on skills needed for Component Content Management, and which JoAnn Hackos describes in her 2015 ISO/IEC/IEEE 26531 standard on content management—has helped our field understand that in the digital era technical writers in the workplace don't "write" so much as they develop, delineate, and manage small content modules which they collect into information architectures. Today's technical communicators still have to write well, but now they also need a skill set which Carlos calls "computational thinking." They have to pull on their knowledge of content strategy, information architectures, and Rhetoric in order to produce usable documentation sets in digital environments.

The Component Content Management shift has tremendous implications for TPC pedagogies and curriculum development. As Filipp Sapienza observed in the *Journal of Technical Writing and Communication* back in 2002, it suggests that "technical communicators will probably face a day when all organizational documents are saved in XML format." As educators, we should prepare our students for that experience, but as Carlos observes in this book, the problem is that learning XML and its complicated DITA standard is really hard. Even academics familiar with XHTML and CSS can find DITA intimidating. But because the new Lightweight DITA standard Carlos and his colleagues have been developing is much less dependent on both XML and DITA, it's far more accessible to TPC students and practitioners new to coding. LwDITA is exciting because it enjoys the benefits of the semantic web and single-source authoring without the incredibly steep learning curve required for XML and DITA.

This book is an extremely timely and much needed introduction to the Component Content Management and computational thinking movement in TPC. As such, it's a pleasure to have it in the ATTW Book Series in Technical and Professional Communication.

Dr. Tharon W. Howard
Editor, ATTW Book Series in Technical
and Professional Communication
July 21, 2018

1

REVISITING THE FUTURE OF TECHNICAL COMMUNICATION

James Mathewson knows a thing or two about technical communication. In his role as Distinguished Technical Marketer at IBM, James, a graduate of the Master of Science in Scientific and Technical Communication from the University of Minnesota-Twin Cities, was looking for interns who could work in a structured authoring environment. James took to Twitter to express his frustration after coming back empty-handed from his search for interns.

> Yes. Writing reusable content is a rare skill. Would that they taught it in college. Essays from whole cloth is more the thing.
>
> (Mathewson, 2016)

When he talks about "reusable content," Mathewson is referring to the "practice of using content components in multiple information products" (Eberlein, 2016 p. 54). In many technical communication practices, "efficient content reuse does not involve copy-and-pasting; instead it uses *transclusion*, whereby content is authored in one location and used by reference in other locations" (Eberlein, 2016 p. 55). The "essays from whole cloth" reference is a nod to the book-oriented kind of writing using a word processor that most academic programs in technical communication and content development teach as standard practice.

It was not supposed to be like this.

In 2012, the Adobe Technical Communication Suite (TCS) team distributed on several social media channels a video titled "The Future of Technical Communication." The video used stop-motion animation and fast-draw techniques to summarize the features of "Adobe's Tools and Services" for technical communication. As a pair of rapidly animated hands assembles Lego pieces (Figure 1.1), the video's narrator describes that "for some, (the future of technical

FIGURE 1.1 Screen capture from the video "The Future of Technical Communication," by Adobe Technical Communication Suite. This specific frame displays the future of our profession as "more and more structured content and the ability to work faster and smarter with XML and DITA constructs."

communication) is all about more and more structured content and the ability to work faster and smarter with XML and DITA constructs." Approaching the end of its 2:30-minutes runtime, the video claims that "it is most certainly an exciting future to be in" (AdobeTCS, 2012).

The "future" of technical communication described in the Adobe video focuses on what Rebekka Andersen describes as "structured content that is highly adaptable and portable and can be configured on the fly in response to specific user requests" (2014, p. 116). Andersen adds that this type of content supported by topic-based information design "has been given various names, including intelligent content, nimble content, smart content, portable content, and future-ready content." Rockley, Cooper, and Abel describe intelligent content as "designed to be modular, structured, reusable, format free, and semantically rich and, as a consequence, discoverable, reconfigurable, and adaptable" (Rockley et al., 2015, p. 1). In academia, scholars have praised Extensible Markup Language (XML) as the foundation for information reuse, single sourcing, and, particularly, content management for more than a decade. Publications from the 2000s heralded that "technical communicators will probably face a day when all organizational documents are saved in XML format" (Sapienza, 2002, p. 156) and argued that "technical communicators should be able to write, edit, and manage XML documentation, including XML tags, document type definitions (DTDs), XML schemas, and Darwin Information Typing Architecture (DITA)" (Gesteland McShane, 2009, p. 74).

The future of technical communication, as seen from industry and academia, was supposed to cover the type of structured writing for reuse that James Mathewson was looking for.

It is not as though the academic side of technical communication is stagnant. On the contrary, scholars in the field have expanded the work of technical communication into domains and scenarios like healthcare, policy-making, and social justice, among others, that were closed to writing researchers in the recent past. James's tweet started a discussion about the many topics covered in courses and programs in technical communication. Researchers work with practitioners that include community partners, government officials, and medics. However, "many of the pedagogical concerns of academic instructors in professional and technical communication have changed little over the past decade, even as practitioner discourse has continued to spin off in the direction of content strategy and similar areas" (Clark, 2016, p. 19). Academic discussion related to the implementation and innovation of intelligent content has been slow, as evidenced by the titles and abstracts of presentations and publications from 2012 to 2018 in relevant conferences and journals, respectively.

Traditionally, and as mentioned in the Adobe video, intelligent content workflows for technical communication rely on structure provided by Extensible Markup Language (XML) and some of its specific grammars like DocBook, S1000D, and DITA (Cowan, 2010; Glushko & McGrath, 2008; Hackos, 2011, among others). Although the benefits of a well-planned and implemented intelligent content workflow built on XML or DITA are undeniable, this type of solution presents significant challenges that have repercussions in the academic and workplace facets of the profession.

Technical communication consultants and practitioners frequently report on success stories and challenge narratives from implementing and managing XML-based content projects in conferences like DITA/Content Management Strategies and LavaCon. Furthermore, blogs and social media postings from content professionals create and maintain an active online community of discussion and recommendations. Because of proprietary practices, it would be impractical to poll private companies, government agencies, and non-profit institutions worldwide to tally a number of DITA and XML users. Nevertheless, some attempts at quantifying and documenting usage figures do exist. For example, the website "DITA Writer" maintains a list of companies using DITA based on reports from social media channels. As of summer 2018, the list included 724 companies, excluding consulting and training firms (DITAWriter, n.d.).

Adoption numbers and success stories should not hide that the evolution of intelligent content takes place on a slightly rocky path; even in practitioner circles, there is pushback and criticism against XML and its relationship with technical communication. In blogs and social media exchanges, some practitioners have questioned the status of XML, and DITA, as the main markup language for information products. While acknowledging DITA's effectiveness as a replacement for large user manuals in complex industries, a few authors lament that "this form of structured content can feel cold and clinical, especially to those from the editorial or marketing side of content" (Wachter-Boettcher, 2012, p. 20). Others argue that in the world of computing code verbose languages are becoming obsolete, but intelligent content still relies on XML and its nested tag structures:

> What are we seeing? Simplification. Ease of use. A learning curve that gets less steep every time. Languages that drop features that aren't used, or aren't used often. And what has techcomm poured resources into? DITA. An arcane, overly complex language with a massive learning curve that requires specialized tools.
>
> (Kaplan, 2014)

Those are valid concerns. DITA, as it evolves as an open standard, needs to address them and learn from its users. This chapter presents an overview of the evolution of DITA – an XML-based "end-to-end architecture for creating and delivering modular technical information" (Priestley et al., 2001, p. 354). The future of technical communication still involves XML; therefore, the following sections include brief introductions to Extensible Markup Language and the Darwin Information Typing Architecture, providing examples of the main content and collection types included in the latter. Then, the chapter explains the need for a simplified version of DITA that allows authors to contribute to intelligent content ecosystems writing in markup languages that do not require complex XML structures. Lastly, the chapter focuses on strategies for adopting a DITA workflow in three simplified authoring formats, which are connected to principles of computational thinking and emphasize the importance of human abstraction before machine automation.

An Introduction to XML in Technical Communication

Although an author does not even need to be familiar with XML in order to create information products in the workflows introduced in this book, the ideas presented in *Creating Intelligent Content with Lightweight DITA* are rooted in DITA and XML. As a result, I cannot leave out working definitions and background for context when introducing the standard and its evolution as a problem-solving methodology for technical communication. This section will be especially useful to readers who have not ventured into standards and markup languages for intelligent content.

First, I define XML for the specific context of *Creating Intelligent Content with Lightweight DITA*. Definitions and descriptions of the Extensible Markup Language abound in academic and practitioner publications. A search for "XML" on amazon.com reveals more than 1,100 results under the "Books: Computers & Technology: Programming Languages" category. In the realm of rhetoric studies, Applen and McDaniel wrote an important text about XML and its implications for rhetorical work. In one of the contrasting moves of their definition, they posit XML as different from Hypertext Markup Language (HTML) and other typesetting and formatting syntaxes because it enables the processes of "identifying, separating, and recombining" content for different purposes (Applen & McDaniel, 2009, p. 42). Content in XML, for example, can be tagged as a product name, a procedure, a works cited entry, or any other part of a technical or professional document. Once those parts or components are tagged, they can be "assembled" in different ways for use in a variety of deliverables and media. New documents need not be written for each purpose, and one single change can be reflected accurately across all the information materials produced by a given company.

Let me introduce you here to Pedro, a chef and restaurateur who is going to be the main user-author in this book's examples. Chef Pedro has a background in marketing and culinary arts. He is comfortable with technology and social media, but he has never worked with any type of computer code. He is looking for a way to standardize the recipes used by his staff in the several kitchens he manages. As a franchise owner, he wants to ensure that the food in his restaurants is consistent, and his kitchen staff needs up-to-date documentation with recipes and techniques adopted in all of his restaurants. At the same time, the menus in his restaurants need to reflect some of that content, which is also featured on a website, mobile app, and an electronic book he sells describing the history and process of his restaurants. Chef Pedro, like many content owners in this world, has been using Microsoft Word for most of his information products, and the publications department in his company takes some of those Word files and, through long sessions of copy and pasting, produces menus and flyers in Adobe InDesign and maintains the restaurant's website using WordPress. When a change needs to be reflected in those information products (e.g., the kitchen introduces a new special or the office's telephone number should be updated), Chef Pedro makes the changes in his original Word files, and then the publications team has to manually update the menus, flyers, and website that borrow content from the Word master source.

Someone mentioned structured authoring with XML and that caught Chef Pedro's attention. The promise: a centralized content repository structured in XML can be the source for many user deliverables. And the production and update of those deliverables can be automated. No more copy and paste! Now, if Pedro were to open a text editor in his computer and start typing XML tags to structure his content, he probably would not know where to go after typing for a few minutes. To create information deliverables ready for human consumption, XML files need to go through a process of publishing that, according to O'Keefe, can involve the following roles, which "in a small group, one person may hold any or all" (2009, p. 14):

- Document architect, who defines and implements document structure
- Template designer, who establishes the look and feel of content deliverables
- Writer, who creates content
- Technical editors, who can focus on word choice, grammar, and overall organization
- Production editors, who will get involved in defining the transformation files that assign formatting based on structure.

For someone like Chef Pedro (and even for many of my technical writing students), creating the tags to structure content in XML can be an easy-to-learn task. On the other hand, producing information deliverables based on that structure (say, a webpage with a specific recipe) is not necessarily simple when implementing a custom XML content type. That's when a standard like DITA can help. Pedro could buy a software package to structure his recipes and create an online cookbook; however, in a previous stage of his career he was involved in a marketing project that depended on a commercial application. When the developer stopped updating the application and it became obsolete, Pedro's content was locked and required an expensive and time-consuming process of conversion to be rescued in another program. A chef might not be familiar with scholarship in writing studies, but authors like Karl Stolley, in his influential "The Lo-Fi Manifesto," have argued for the adoption of open standards over software packages, identifying it as the only way to ensure that "digital works should long outlast the software that played a role in their creation" (Stolley, 2008).

This kind of data tagging and manipulation that XML allows is at the heart of intelligent content. From the practitioner side of technical communication, O'Keefe points out that XML "defines a standard for storing structured content in text files" (2009, p. 15). O'Keefe's extended definition includes the following features of XML:

- It is a markup language, which means that content is enclosed by tags.
- Its element tags are enclosed in angle brackets (<element>This is element text</element>).
- It does not provide a set of predefined tags. Instead, authors define their own tags and their relationships. (O'Keefe, 2009, p. 15)

Additionally, O'Keefe provides a sample XML file that presents a recipe for making marinara sauce. (O'Keefe, 2009, p. 16) (Figure 1.2).

This process of tagging, commenting, and nesting data will look familiar to readers who have used HTML or another markup language. O'Keefe's recipe[1] features a main container element (<**Recipe**>), which includes several sub-elements (<**Name**>, <**IngredientList**>, and <**Instructions**>). Some of these sub-elements

```
<Recipe Cuisine="Italian" Author="Unknown">
    <Name>Marinara Sauce</Name>
    <IngredientList>
        <Ingredient>
            <Quantity>2 tbsp.</Quantity>
            <Item>olive oil</Item>
        </Ingredient>
        <Ingredient>
            <Quantity>2 cloves</Quantity>
            <Item>garlic</Item>
            <Preparation>minced</Preparation>
        </Ingredient>
        <Ingredient>
            <Quantity>1/2 tsp.</Quantity>
            <Item>hot red pepper</Item>
        </Ingredient>
        <Ingredient>
            <Quantity>28 oz.</Quantity>
            <Item>canned tomatoes, preferably San Marzano</Item>
        </Ingredient>
        <Ingredient>
            <Quantity>2 tbsp.</Quantity>
            <Item>parsley</Item>
            <Preparation>chopped</Preparation>
        </Ingredient>
    </IngredientList>
    <Instructions>
        <Para>Heat olive oil in a large saucepan on medium. Add garlic and hot
  red pepper and sweat until fragrant. Add tomatoes, breaking up into smaller
 pieces. Simmer on medium-
low heat for at least 20 minutes. Add parsley, simmer for another five minutes.
   Serve over long pasta.</Para>
    </Instructions>
</Recipe>
```

FIGURE 1.2 Sarah O'Keefe's sample recipe for marinara sauce in XML. The structured recipe keeps content organized and should help computers understand and manipulate elements and attributes. Human readers, however, still need to wait for a publishing process that will produce content deliverables that do not look like computer code.

hold actual content (e.g., **<Name>**), and others nest additional levels of elements and, eventually, content (e.g. the "parsley" **<Item>** inside **<Ingredient>** inside **<IngredientList>**). XML also uses attributes to present additional information about data and content (see the **@Cuisine** and **@Author** attributes in the main **<Recipe>** element). If you're unfamiliar with XML structures, don't worry; the relevant XML elements for this book will be discussed in detail in subsequent chapters. For now, just focus on the fact that XML uses tags to identify the types of rhetorical "moves" that the content on the page represents.

Just like Chef Pedro, who wants to create a structured template for all entries in his recipe guide, information developers at IBM started looking at XML in the late 1990s to organize technical content. One of the solutions that came out of those explorations at IBM was the Darwin Information Typing Architecture.

Much Ado About DITA

In an interview for the website "DITAWriter," Don Day, one of the original developers of the DITA standard, chronicled the origins of his XML experiments while working for IBM in the last decade of the 20th century as follows:

> With the advent of XML as a new markup standard in 1998, the Customer and Service Information (C&SI) group began adopting a Tools and Technology mantra under Dave Schell who was the strategy lead. By 1999, Dave was aware of my participation as IBM's primary representative with the XSLT and CSS standards activities at the World Wide Web Consortium, and I delivered a presentation at a formative meeting in California that forecast the possibility of XML to solve IBM's still-lingering problems with variant tools and markup usage.
>
> (Day, quoted in DitaWriter, 2016)

DITA consists of a set of design principles for creating "information-typed" modules at a topic level and for using that content in delivery modes such as online help and product support portals on the Web. (Day et al., 2001). Day explained that, when naming the standard, DITA "represented a great deal of messaging in a compact and memorable acronym:"

- **Darwin**: for specialization and how things could "evolve" from a base
- **Information Typing**: for representation of knowledge as typed units
- **Architecture**: a statement that this was not just a monolithic design but an extensible tool that could support many uses (Day, quoted in DITAWriter, 2016).

IBM eventually donated DITA as an open standard, which is currently maintained by the non-profit consortium OASIS. DITA, however, "has evolved substantially since that initial donation to encompass a very wide scope of requirements indeed" (Kimber, 2012, p. 6). At the OASIS DITA Technical Committee, the standard continually evolves with the purpose "to define and maintain the Darwin Information Typing Architecture (DITA) and to promote the use of the architecture for creating standard information types and domain-specific markup vocabularies" (OASIS Darwin Information Typing Architecture TC, n.d.). Hackos summarizes the key benefits of DITA for technical communicators as follows:

- A fully tested DTD or schema for XML-based authoring
- A community of developers investing in improvements to the DITA model
- An open source toolkit you can use to produce your own output in multiple media without having to invest in proprietary tools
- A thoroughly developed approach to information development originating with OASIS and now encompassing many other companies, large and small, that find value in a standards-based approach (2011, p. 9).

Additionally, from a perspective addressing the needs of managers and supervisors, Hackos presents a list of DITA's business advantages, which suggest that the standard will (promote) the reuse of information quickly and easily across multiple deliverables, reduce the cost of maintaining and updating information, enable continuous publishing, share information across the global enterprise, reduce the cost of localization, and reduce the technical debt caused by inadequate, incorrect, and unusable legacy information (Hackos, 2011, p. 10).

For Chef Pedro, adopting a standard like DITA simplifies the process of structuring content and producing information deliverables for human users. Instead of designing custom tags and depending on a publishing team to design templates and validation tools, he can use DITA's content types and take advantage of the benefits listed by Hackos. For an author, the main benefit from Hackos's list is in the "fully tested DTD or schema for XML-based authoring," which I discuss in the next section.

DITA Content Types: More than Templates

DITA's "fully tested DTD or schema for XML-based authoring" comes from the *Information Typing* part of its name. Content in DITA is presented as units or individual XML files that conform to pre-established types or models. Those pre-established content types are enforced by files that are commonly referred to as DTDs, although DTD is only one of the markup languages used to verify the structure of those files. XML, and as a consequence DITA, files can also be validated by XML Schema and RELAX NG (Regular Language for XML Next Generation) files.

If that validation process sounds a little too complicated, as an author all you need to know is that the content types enforced by the DITA standard create information topics. A topic is "a self-contained unit of information. An effective topic covers only one subject. Each topic is long enough to make sense on its own, but short enough to stick to one point without expanding into other subjects" (Bellamy et al. 2012, p. 8), and can be defined as "small independent piece of information on a single subject" (Baker, 2013, p. 71). Topic-based writing is described as "authoring an information set as a collection of discrete units called *topics*, rather than as a whole book or help system" (Baker, 2016 p. 52). This kind of writing is the basis of several technical communication and intelligent content practices and techniques, including component content management systems (CCMS), which are "a centralized system that helps organizations capture, manage, store, preserve, and deliver topic-based content (components)" (Kerzreho, 2016 p. 60), and single sourcing, which can be defined as the practice of "creating content once, planning for its reuse in multiple places, contexts, and output channels" (White, 2016 p. 56).

While authors certainly can work on a topic-based environment without DITA (see Baker, 2013), the term *topic* is frequently associated with this open standard, as explained in the following quote from Andersen & Batova:

> Content components are the building blocks of information products. While terms such as granules, modules, and units are commonly used to describe these blocks, the term topic has gained the most traction in the past few years, particularly in the trade literature. Topic derives from the widely adopted open content standard known as Darwin Information Typing Architecture (DITA), which defines a common structure for content that promotes the consistent creation, sharing, and reuse of content.
> (Andersen & Batova, 2015, p. 255)

The literature focuses on three topic types that "represent the vast majority of content produced to support users of technical information" (Hackos, 2011, p.7): concept, task, and reference, which Pringle & O'Keefe define succinctly as follows:

- Concept: contains background information and examples
- Task: includes procedures ("how to" information)
- Reference: describes commands, parameters, and other features (Pringle & O'Keefe, 2009, p. 235).

For authors of technical content, these foundational topic types provide constraints and structures beyond a presentation-oriented template. In DITA, authors can create consistent topics to assemble collections of information with elements that can be reused even at the phrase level. For example, a concept could be an introduction to the sauces section in Chef Pedro's recipe book, while tasks can provide recipes for specific salsas and condiments (he can write a step about dicing tomatoes once and reuse in all the recipes that need it!), and a reference topic can list common techniques and tools for preparing ingredients.

In practical terms, DITA's topic types include XML tags for content "moves" or strategies (such as a short description, steps, and examples) frequently used in technical publications. Pure XML (as we saw in the marinara sauce example) does not provide a defined set of tags, but DITA does offer a catalog of elements and attributes relevant for technical communicators. Although in Chapters 5 and 6 I will further analyze the DITA tags and attributes, for the scope of this introductory section, I structured and tagged O'Keefe's recipe for marinara sauce as a DITA task (Figure 1.3). You can download these code samples from the *Creating Intelligent Content with Lightweight DITA* GitHub repository (https://github.com/carlosevia/lwdita-book).

The recipe has a strong structure with visible sections. The **<task>** element opens the topic announcing "this is a task," and it contains elements like the following:

- **<shortdesc>** with a summary of the topic's contents
- **<prolog>** with some information about the recipe's author and category
- **<prereq>** with a list of the ingredients needed for the recipe
- **<steps>** with a collection of individual **<step>** elements containing a command (**<cmd>**) with an action verb.

```
<?xml version="1.0" encoding="UTF-8"?>
<!DOCTYPE task PUBLIC "-//OASIS//DTD DITA Task//EN" "task.dtd">
<task id="t-marinara">
    <title>Marinara Sauce</title>
    <shortdesc>Prepare a crowd-
pleasing red sauce for pasta in about 30 minutes.</shortdesc>
    <prolog>
        <author>Unknown</author>
        <metadata>
            <category>Italian</category>
        </metadata>
    </prolog>
    <taskbody>
        <prereq>
            <ul>
                <li>2 tbsp. of olive oil</li>
                <li>2 cloves of garlic, minced</li>
                <li>1/2 tsp. of hot red pepper</li>
                <li>28 oz. of canned tomatoes, preferably San Marzano</li>
                <li>2 tbsp. of parsley, chopped</li>
            </ul>
        </prereq>
        <steps>
            <step>
                <cmd>Heat olive oil in a large saucepan on medium</cmd>
            </step>
            <step>
                <cmd>Add garlic and hot red pepper and sweat until fragrant
</cmd>
            </step>
            <step>
                <cmd>Add tomatoes, breaking up into smaller pieces</cmd>
            </step>
            <step>
                <cmd>Simmer on medium-low heat for at least 20 minutes</cmd>
            </step>
            <step>
                <cmd>Add parsley</cmd>
            </step>
            <step>
                <cmd>Simmer for another five minutes</cmd>
            </step>
            <step>
                <cmd>Serve over long pasta.</cmd>
            </step>
        </steps>
    </taskbody>
    </task>
```

FIGURE 1.3 Marinara sauce recipe as a DITA task. The standard's "fully tested DTD or schema for XML-based authoring" includes commonly used elements or moves in technical publication. Thus, the recipe collector does not have to invent custom tags.

Hackos mentioned "an open source toolkit you can use to produce your own output in multiple media without having to invest in proprietary tools" (2011, p. 9). Using that toolkit, known as the DITA Open Toolkit (OT), or a software tool that uses the Open Toolkit, Chef Pedro can produce quick information deliverables. If a sous-chef needs a printable PDF version of the recipe, Pedro can produce it without hiring a template designer (Figure 1.4). And if a different member of the kitchen team requires a web version of the recipe, the DITA-OT also provides that option and allows the author to link to a Cascading Style Sheet (CSS) file for formatting and design (Figure 1.5). In this introductory chapter I will only present the results of transformations using the DITA-OT, but in Chapter 5 I will focus on specific steps for conducting those transformations.

Concept, task, and reference are, for many authors and their managers, essential to DITA. Yet, the big-picture ideas of topic-based information and component content management go beyond the actual topic types enforced by the DITA standard and DITA-aware tools. Although concept, task, and reference are still defined types in the DITA standard, the official specification for DITA 1.3 also includes topic types for troubleshooting, which "provides markup for corrective action information such as troubleshooting and alarm clearing" (2.7.1.6 Troubleshooting topic, 2016) and glossary, which "defines a single sense of one term" (2.7.1.7 Glossary entry topic, 2016). Actually, the all-inclusive edition of the DITA 1.3 standard has 26 document types (predefined document, or even genre, templates) and 621 element types (placeholders or structures for specific content moves). Even in its base edition, DITA 1.3 has 4 document types and 189 element types. And authors should not underestimate

Marinara Sauce

Prepare a crowd-pleasing red sauce for pasta in about 30 minutes.

- 2 tbsp. of olive oil
- 2 cloves of garlic, minced
- 1/2 tsp. of hot red pepper
- 28 oz. of canned tomatoes, preferably San Marzano
- 2 tbsp. of parsley, chopped

1. Heat olive oil in a large saucepan on medium
2. Add garlic and hot red pepper and sweat until fragrant
3. Add tomatoes, breaking up into smaller pieces
4. Simmer on medium-low heat for at least 20 minutes
5. Add parsley
6. Simmer for another five minutes
7. Serve over long pasta.

FIGURE 1.4 Marinara sauce DITA task transformed to a PDF deliverable. This simple output did not require a dedicated stylesheet or choices about pagination and typography.

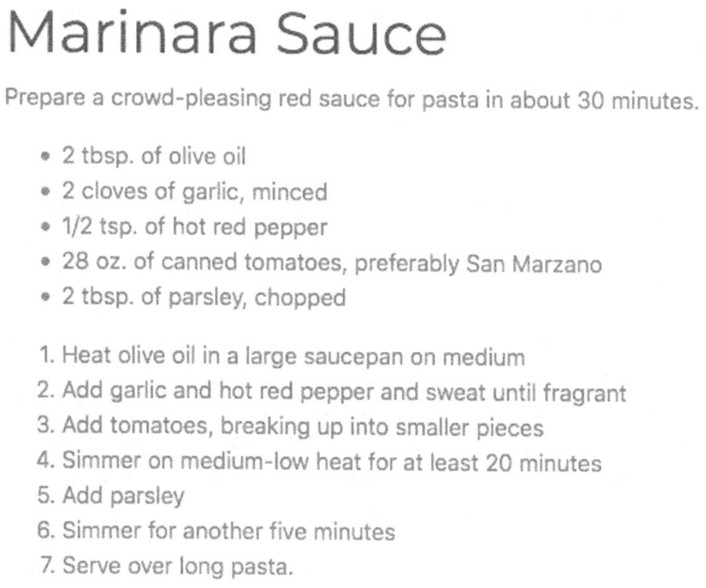

Marinara Sauce

Prepare a crowd-pleasing red sauce for pasta in about 30 minutes.

- 2 tbsp. of olive oil
- 2 cloves of garlic, minced
- 1/2 tsp. of hot red pepper
- 28 oz. of canned tomatoes, preferably San Marzano
- 2 tbsp. of parsley, chopped

1. Heat olive oil in a large saucepan on medium
2. Add garlic and hot red pepper and sweat until fragrant
3. Add tomatoes, breaking up into smaller pieces
4. Simmer on medium-low heat for at least 20 minutes
5. Add parsley
6. Simmer for another five minutes
7. Serve over long pasta.

FIGURE 1.5 Marinara sauce DITA task transformed to an HTML5 deliverable. This sample output includes a link to an external CSS file for formatting.

the importance of a generic topic, defined as "the basic unit of authoring and reuse" (2.2.1.1 The topic as the basic unit of information, 2016), which is the only information type included in the base edition of the DITA standard. The generic topic, with its simple tags for paragraphs and lists, can mark up a marketing blog post. A basic topic can also include a flexible procedure, or even provide pointers for a web-based product tour with some JavaScript processing, among many other applications. Additionally, the versatile task topic in DITA 1.3 can take the shape of a general task topic, a strict task, or a machinery task topic, depending on the context and purpose of usage. DITA 1.3 also includes topic types designed for learning and training projects: learning plan, learning overview, learning content, learning summary, and learning assessment.

If those pre-established topic types were not enough for a particular writer and context, DITA topics can be *specialized* to create information types unique to any intelligent content domain. At the topic level, and without getting too deep into the process of DITA specialization, just as **<concept>** and **<task>** are specialized from the original generic **<topic>**, **<task>** could specialize into **<recipe>**. For example, Chef Pedro is going to need to provide ingredients for his recipes, so he could create an ingredients specialization to include this specific element (i.e., **<ingredients>** as a specialization of **<prereq>** for pre-requisites). This exercise in markup flexibility is a direct application of both the extensible part of XML and the Darwin element in DITA: XML elements can be extended and DITA information types can evolve to accommodate diverse content and processing needs.

DITA Maps

Properly tagged DITA topics can create or join content collections ready for reuse of material, single-sourcing of whole topics or their elements, and filters as determined by a deliverable's audience or context. The process of assembling topic collections depends on DITA maps, which are defined as "the glue that binds your topics together, the driver for producing your output, and the information path for your users to follow" (Bellamy et al., 2012, p. 91).

In their textbook *DITA Best Practices*, Bellamy et al. recommend using DITA maps to create an information set that specify which topics should be included in a user deliverable produced from the map, define an information architecture with the navigation for a set of topics, and create relationships between topics (Bellamy et al., 2012).

The following scenario combines the examples I have presented so far: Chef Pedro has a website in which he critiques recipes. For this week's entry, he will critique the marinara sauce recipe from Figure 1.3. The web deliverable that Chef Pedro needs for this project should include the following sections:

- The marinara sauce recipe (structured as a DITA task)
- Chef Pedro's critique of the recipe (structured as a DITA concept)
- Chef Pedro's "about" page, with biographical and professional information (structured as a DITA concept).

Figure 1.6 shows a very basic DITA map for Chef Pedro's recipe critique website.

The DITA map has a **<title>** element for the whole project. Then, the map includes links (**<topicref>**) for the individual files needed for the website. Using the DITA-OT, which I will cover in more detail in Chapters 5 and 6, I transformed

```
<?xml version="1.0" encoding="UTF-8"?>
<!DOCTYPE map PUBLIC "-//OASIS//DTD DITA Map//EN" "map.dtd">
<map>
   <title>Chef Pedro's Recipe Critique</title>
   <topicref href="t-marinara.dita" />
   <topicref href="c-marinara-critique.dita" />
   <topicref href="c-about.dita" />
</map>
```

FIGURE 1.6 DITA map for Chef Pedro's recipe critique website. The map includes links (or topic references) to the marinara sauce recipe, Chef Pedro's critique of the recipe, and an "about" page with information about the author.

the map to a web deliverable. The DITA-OT automatically generated a navigation menu (figure 1.7) and took care of basic layout.

These features and benefits contribute to DITA's popularity and adaptability as an intelligent content solution for technical communication. Without a doubt, these features and benefits can also be intimidating for an author new to DITA. Although no author is expected to become an expert on all topic types and their relations, criticism in industry and, perhaps, the timid interest from academia stem from the long, and getting longer, list of types, tags, and their functions included in the DITA standard.

Let's go back to Chef Pedro, who is attempting now to structure some of his own recipes as tasks following specifications from the DITA 1.3 standard. The process sounds simple, and the content components in the DITA *task* document type seem just right for structuring a recipe. There can be some instances of the <**step**> element with a <**cmd**> for a command in each step, but things get quite complicated when Pedro looks at all the available elements in a task topic[2], which include the following: <**taskbody**>, <**prereq**>, <**context**>, <**steps**>, <**steps-informal**>, <**steps-unordered**>, <**step**>, <**stepsection**>, <**cmd**>, <**info**>, <**substeps**>, <**substep**>, <**stepxmp**>, <**choicetable**>, <**chhead**>, <**choptionhd**>, <**chdeschd**>, <**chrow**>, <**choption**>, <**chdesc**>, <**choices**>, <**steptroubleshooting**>, <**stepresult**>, <**tutorialinfo**>, <**tasktroubleshooting**>, <**result**>, and <**postreq**>. And that's just the task document type! Keep in mind that DITA 1.3 has 26 document types.

The next section introduces a DITA-based approach to intelligent content that has the potential of minimizing the standard's learning curve and promoting its adoption in small and medium scale information authoring and processing environments as well as classrooms.

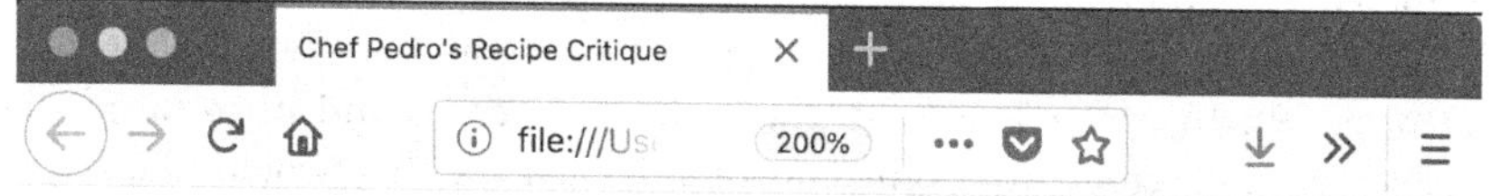

FIGURE 1.7 Navigation menu for a web transformation of Chef Pedro's recipe critique project. The DITA-OT generated the menu and took care of basic layout for this web deliverable.

DITA, Why Go Lightweight?

Michael Priestley, Senior Technical Staff Member and Enterprise Content Technology Strategist at IBM and known as one of DITA's "founding fathers" (Etheridge, 2016), defines Lightweight DITA (LwDITA, which should be read as "Lightweight DITA") as a simplified schema for structuring content, with fewer elements, tighter content models and a simplified specialization architecture to define new types compared to those of DITA XML. According to Priestley, "if there are three ways of doing things with full DITA, there will be only one way to do it with Lightweight DITA."

> That simplification makes it possible to implement DITA without XML – for example using Markdown, or HTML5. This brings the advantages of structured authoring to where people are already creating content, rather than trying to get every author onto one content platform. Lightweight DITA can be the glue that ties together many different authoring platforms across a company. It can also be an on-boarding ramp for full DITA. Lightweight DITA is particularly attractive to companies who need a faster ROI [return on investment] and an easier learning curve.
>
> (Priestley, quoted in Etheridge, 2016)

Creating Intelligent Content with Lightweight DITA introduces and analyzes LwDITA as an approach for developing intelligent content. It aims to address concerns and doubts about the adoption and evolution of DITA as a major standard for technical publications. Those concerns and doubts revolve around a major point of discrepancy in the world of technical communication: in industry, XML and DITA are widely used and some critics even see them as outdated and complex; in academia, "faculty are simply ignoring the subject, even though it has played a central role in the practitioner literature" (Clark, 2016, p. 19). In conversations at academic conferences and in social media exchanges, colleagues from other universities tell me they would like to try DITA in the future and make plans to contact me when they are working on their technical communication syllabus. I rarely get a second call and the conversation stays in the "someday/maybe" list. If XML and DITA are still seen as new tools by academics when some practitioners are already labeling them as arcane, then we are just writing a new chapter in the documented gap between research and practice in the field (Andersen, 2013; Rude, 2015; Lauren & Pigg, 2016, and others).

For an audience of curious but hesitant academics, this book demystifies the process of authoring and processing intelligent content. *Creating Intelligent Content with Lightweight DITA* shows structured authoring in practice without the need for sophisticated software tools. It also connects the rhetorical structures that drive the evolution of DITA as a standard for technical information to foundational concepts from the field's academic background and to common structures in computing education. For interested practitioners, this book presents the logical and computational essence of changes and improvements on a major documentation standard. For any reader, *Creating Intelligent Content with Lightweight DITA* places human authors at the center of intelligent content workflows, proposing that adopting LwDITA as a thought process and authoring schema will provide writers with some of the benefits associated with other information standards (DITA included) while **emphasizing thinking and abstraction over automation and machine processing**. This book is not about a specific tool or software platform: as an open standard in development, LwDITA does not depend on a vendor or "app." Hackos explains the importance of information standards for technical communicators with the following scenario, which also applies to LwDITA:

> What that means to information developers is that you can author a DocBook or DITA topic in one tool and open the topic in another tool without the loss of information or invalid markup. If the tool developers respect the standard, they allow for interoperability among tools.
>
> (Hackos, 2016, p. 29)

Based on the LwDITA proposed standard, the principles and strategies included in this book can be effective in a variety of authoring environments. I am aware, though, that some large content repositories with diverse user groups do need a robust environment built on DITA XML, and that strong component of the standard is not going away. I am a voting member of the DITA Technical Committee with the Organization for the Adoption of Structured Information Standards (OASIS), which is currently working on version 2.0 of the standard; DITA's present and future are necessary for the lightweight approaches discussed in this book. Therefore, this is unequivocally a book about DITA, but it is not a detailed introduction and how-to to the widely adopted XML-based DITA standard (for comprehensive introductory texts to DITA XML, see Hackos, 2011; Bellamy et al., 2012).

Creating Intelligent Content with Lightweight DITA does not have a reader prerequisite of experience with the DITA standard. However, I do assume that readers from industry and academia will have a technological curiosity about content development in workflows that go beyond a word processor or a "What You See Is What You Get" (WYSIWYG) web editor. Some experience with HTML or Markdown would also help, but the book provides enough context and information about those languages to understand and use the LwDITA proposed standard.

Computational Thinking and the Evolution of DITA

The theoretical axis of the evolution of DITA analyzed in this book is based on the concept of computational thinking, which is defined by their main proponents as follows:

> Computational thinking is the thought processes involved in formulating problems and their solutions so that the solutions are represented in a form that can be effectively carried out by an information-processing agent.
>
> (Cuny et al. 2010, quoted by Wing, 2011)

Computational thinking (CT) has been connected in scholarship and media to initiatives for learning to code and programming. In her seminal essay on this topic, Wing explains that computational thinking takes an approach to "solving problems, designing systems and understanding human behavior by drawing on concepts fundamental to computer science" (Wing, 2006, p. 33), and that it is more about conceptualizing than programming. She adds that "thinking like a computer scientist means more than being able to program a computer. It requires thinking at multiple levels of abstraction" (2006, p. 35). She succinctly defines abstraction as "the essence of computational thinking" (2008, p. 3717).

In the technical communication literature, the concept of abstraction has been linked to Johndan Johnson-Eilola's work to establish "common ground between academic and corporate models" of the profession. Johnson-Eilola's skills for rearticulating technical communication included abstraction, which "requires students not merely to memorize information but also to learn to discern patterns, relationships, and hierarchies in large masses of information" (Johnson-Eilola, 1996, p. 260). Johnson-Eilola adds that a "paradigmatic example of this skill can be found in one of the most common tasks in software documentation: rethinking a series of system commands so that it coincides with a user's task representation and context" (1996, p. 260). More than two decades after Johnson-Eilola's model was published, abstraction continues to be a desired skill in the training and work of technical communicators. Furthermore, his example is still relevant when thinking about LwDITA and computational thinking: an author needs to separate the layers of abstraction when creating a task topic for a specific audience and context. The tools might be different, but the principles are the same.

Abstraction allows authors of intelligent content to separate the "layers" of a particular problem, and work on each one individually without concern for the others. Then, as the layers are recombined, they work together to solve the problem at hand, much like an algorithm. In the case of a computational solution for intelligent content, abstraction is a combination of two elements: information representation and separation of concerns (layers of abstraction). Computing is concerned with automating these abstractions. In order for that automation to be successful, computational thinking requires understanding not only of the concepts that each layer of abstraction represents, but also of the relationships between the multiple layers behind a specific problem.

Some computing professionals will argue that the abstractions in computational thinking are mainly related to algorithms. Some technical communication practitioners share that opinion (Baker, 2016). In Wing's model, however, computing abstractions go beyond numerical abstractions and cover symbolic, algorithmic, and representational abstractions (Wing, 2008). Others will emphasize the role of automation even in Wing's definition of computational thinking. *Creating Intelligent Content with Lightweight DITA* does not have the purpose of minimizing the importance of computing automations, and by all means technical communicators should learn computing programming languages and workflows if given the chance. This book treats ambitious promises of computational thinking with caution, as "there is little evidence to believe that students are learning higher-order thinking skills by learning programming" (Guzdial, 2016, p. 50). Nonetheless, thinking in and planning abstractions are really the everyday tasks of technical authors in an intelligent content environment. Wing (2008) describes computing as a combination of "mental" tools (abstractions) and "metal" tools (automation). Authors are in charge of the abstractions behind the code and content that provides the backbone for intelligent content. Automation is then provided by software applications, be it a commercial product like Adobe FrameMaker or an open source implementation of DITA. Authors do not need special software tools to create content in DITA; however, they will need a software processor to transform DITA topics into deliverables for human users. I will describe those processing applications later in this chapter (and throughout the book). Authors can participate in automation by writing a script or application to filter content. However, that step is not necessary for applying principles of computational thinking in technical communication from an author's perspective. I have seen colleagues in technical communication who value computational thinking and literacy as core skills of a college education and, as a result, send their students to take an introductory class in programming in a Computer Science department. Before (or in addition to) taking, say, a Python course out of their disciplinary context, why not send technical communication students to a course covering the *mental* and *metal* tools that practitioners in their field value?

A core argument in this book is based on Wing's definition of computational thinking, previous research about abstractions in technical communication, the work I have conducted as co-chair of the Lightweight DITA subcommittee at OASIS, and my experience teaching DITA at the college level since 2006 and LwDITA since 2015. I argue that **if technical communicators are trained with principles of rhetorical problem solving and computational thinking, they can work in lightweight environments without the need of a robust XML solution.** This type of training will primarily enhance an author's understanding of the layers of abstraction and common argumentation moves behind an intelligent content solution. These layers of abstraction are not necessarily new to the field of technical communication (they include long-discussed concepts and principles like separating content from design, and planning for single-sourcing and content reuse, among others), but are essential building blocks of intelligent content solutions that are still not fully embraced in academia. Before LwDITA existed, I presented a preliminary list of those abstractions as they applied to my teaching of DITA XML (Evia et al., 2015). Chapters 7 and 8 present an analysis of the abstractions behind the computational thinking and rhetorical problem solving processes that generate intelligent content with LwDITA, but the next section focuses on the potential benefits of LwDITA for content developers who do not need the features of full DITA XML.

Structuring Intelligent Content with LwDITA

LwDITA is a topic-based architecture for tagging and structuring intelligent content using flexible markup options. Lightweight DITA aims to streamline the DITA authoring experience by presenting three formats for content creation:

- *XDITA*, an XML format with a subset of DITA elements that can be used for validated authoring and complex publishing chains
- *HDITA*, an HTML5 format that can be used for either authoring or displaying content
- *MDITA*, a Markdown[3] format with a subset of XDITA elements that can be used for maximizing input readability while maintaining structure in content.

You do not need to use all three "flavors" at the same time to adopt LwDITA. You can work in HDITA all the time and you would still be using LwDITA. You can live in an MDITA environment without XML or HTML tags and you would still be using LwDITA. All three LwDITA formats are compatible with each other and with DITA XML. For a team of authors with diverse technical backgrounds and communication skills, the different formats of LwDITA allow collaboration and content exchange in a centralized solution. For example, Pedro can hire a technical writer to create recipe topics in XDITA (based on XML) while a marketing professional writes a description of the cookbook's features in HDITA (based on HTML5), and an engineer uses MDITA (based on Markdown) to create a reference for a specific command from the kitchen's laboratory. All their topics are treated as DITA and can take advantage of the standard's reuse, filtering, and single-sourcing capabilities.

All code examples in this book will focus on the open standards for DITA and LwDITA, and automation-related discussions will be based on features and affordances from the open source DITA-OT and "raw" XML, HTML5, and Markdown code. Professional authoring tools can hide code in What You See

Is What You Get (WYSIWYG) options, but the rhetorical, pedagogical, and computational principles of *Creating Intelligent Content with Lightweight DITA* view and perceive LwDITA topics as code.

The idea of simplified DITA code that would reduce its learning curve has been a topic of discussion on the standard's technical committee with OASIS for a few years. In 2011, the technical committee planned to release a "limited DITA profile," which was still XML-based, but depended heavily on HTML tags (such as **<p>** for paragraph and **<li>** for list item) to simplify many semantic structures of DITA XML. As the concept of Lightweight DITA developed further, at one point it became an XML subset of DITA that included, for example, 27 possible elements inside a topic, whereas DITA XML includes a possible combination of 90+ elements. Originally, Lightweight DITA was planned as a component of the DITA 1.3 specification, but interest from members of the DITA technical committee, vendors, and researchers pushed it out of the main specification and into its own parallel and compatible standard. The purpose of LwDITA is not to replace DITA XML. Instead, LwDITA provides basic access to authors who do not need all the DITA standard's features but whose deliverables should be compatible with DITA XML.

Michael Priestley, from IBM, created the OASIS Lightweight DITA subcommittee in 2014 with the purpose of releasing LwDITA as an open standard related to but independent from DITA XML. I co-chair the Lightweight DITA subcommittee with Priestley, and I have published, alone and with Priestley, about the development of LwDITA (e.g., Evia & Priestley, 2016; Evia, 2017). While LwDITA is under development and not an approved OASIS standard at the time of this writing, feedback on our talks and papers about the new standard provides support for its development based on positive reactions and interest from partners in industry and academia. As lead editor of the LwDITA technical specification, I have attempted to combine the needs and resources of academic and industry content professionals, testing and implementing applied computational principles built on common concepts of genre and rhetorical theory.

As of this writing, LwDITA is a work in progress. This book reflects the structure of this proposed standard as it was presented in its initial introductory committee note (Evia et al., 2018). LwDITA details might change between the publication of this book and the actual release of the Lightweight DITA standard.

For a quick example of LwDITA in action (and I will analyze *more thoroughly* its formats later in the book), I coded O'Keefe's recipe for marinara sauce in LwDITA's different authoring formats. Figure 1.8 shows the recipe authored in XDITA – the LwDITA authoring format based on a simplified version of DITA XML.

The first major change is the topic type. In DITA XML (see Figure 1.3), the recipe was structured as a task and had predetermined elements that the DITA standard associates with a task (like **<steps>** and **<prereq>**). The simplified authoring experience of LwDITA, however, is based on a single topic type with elements common to most information units, including the following:

```
<?xml version="1.0" encoding="UTF-8"?>
<!DOCTYPE topic PUBLIC "-//OASIS//DTD LIGHTWEIGHT DITA Topic//EN"
"lw-topic.dtd">
<topic id="t-marinara">
    <title>Marinara sauce</title>
    <shortdesc>Prepare a crowd-
pleasing red sauce for pasta in about 30 minutes.</shortdesc>
    <prolog>
        <data name="author" value="Unknown"/>
        <data name="category" value="Italian"/>
    </prolog>
    <body>
        <section>
            <title>Ingredients</title>
            <ul>
                <li>
                    <p>2 tbsp. of olive oil</p>
                </li>
                <li>
                    <p>2 cloves of garlic, minced</p>
                </li>
                <li>
                    <p>1/2 tsp. of hot red pepper</p>
                </li>
                <li>
                    <p>28 oz. of canned tomatoes, preferably San Marzano</p>
                </li>
                <li>
                    <p>2 tbsp. of parsley, chopped</p>
                </li>
            </ul>
        </section>
        <section>
            <title>Preparation</title>
            <ol>
                <li>
                    <p>Heat olive oil in a large saucepan on medium</p>
                </li>
                <li>
                    <p>Add garlic and hot red pepper and sweat until fragrant
</p>
                </li>
                <li>
                    <p>Add tomatoes, breaking up into smaller pieces</p>
                </li>
                <li>
                    <p>Simmer on medium-low heat for at least 20 minutes</p>
                </li>
                <li>
                    <p>Add parsley</p>
                </li>
                <li>
                  <p>Simmer for another five minutes</p>
                </li>
                <li>
                   <p>Serve over long pasta.</p>
                </li>
            </ol>
        </section>
    </body>
</topic>
```

FIGURE 1.8 Marinara sauce recipe as an XDITA topic. The XML tags are still visible and the recipe looks like a DITA topic. However, it is no longer a task, since LwDITA's initial specification only includes one topic type.

- Title: A label that connotes the purpose of the content that is associated with it
- Short description: A brief depiction of the purpose or theme of a topic
- Prolog: A container for metadata about a topic (for example, author information or subject category)
- Body: A container for the main content of a topic. It might include several sections
- Section: An organizational division within a topic. It can have an optional title.

These common elements can be represented, with modifications to accommodate different authoring languages, in XDITA, HDITA, and MDITA. Figure 1.9 shows the same recipe as a topic tagged in HDITA, the LwDITA authoring format that uses HTML5.

The topic has commonly-used HTML5 elements like headings and lists, but an additional benefit of HDITA is that topics authored in this LwDITA format do not require a transformation process to generate a publishable outcome (Figure 1.10). Because the topics are HTML5 files, they can be rendered in any web browser, and publishers can customize the rendered format with a standard CSS stylesheet.

MDITA, the LwDITA authoring format that uses Markdown, can also be used to structure the recipe for marinara sauce (figure 1.11). In its core profile, MDITA provides structure for major elements present in DITA XML and Markdown (title, sections, lists, etc.). In its extended profile, MDITA allows a header authored in YAML[4] (the recursive acronym for *YAML Ain't Markup Language*) with metadata about the topic's author and some categories that we have been carrying since the original XML sample.

Regardless of its authoring format, when transformed with LwDITA-aware tools into information deliverables for human users, the topic for the marinara sauce recipe would pretty much look the same. That is a key feature of LwDITA: end users will not know the author's process and will just receive information products with consistent structure. Figure 1.12 shows a PDF version of the XDITA topic created with the DITA-OT.

An author trained in principles of structured authoring could use XDITA and take advantage of its DITA-like sections, elements, and constraints. XDITA provides some of the DITA mechanisms for reuse and single sourcing that could be essential for a technical communicator but probably distracting or confusing for a casual content contributor. HDITA can be less intimidating for collaborators with experience creating content in HTML5, while still including reuse and filtering options. Both XDITA and HDITA can be authored in WYSIWYG editors that keep code and tags hidden (permanently or temporarily, depending on the specific software tool) from the content creator. MDITA is a plain text variant for developers and authors who do not need advanced content reuse capabilities (but they still can use them with raw HDITA code fragments). All three formats, however, are compatible with each other and also with topics created according to the DITA XML standard. All three formats also incorporate fundamental actions of content authoring, like staging, coaching, and describing, which are essential moves of

```
<!DOCTYPE html>
<meta name="author" content="Unknown">
<meta name="keywords" content="Italian">
       <title>Marinara sauce</title>
      <body>
        <article id="t-marinara">
            <h1>Marinara sauce</h1>
            <p>Prepare a crowd-
pleasing red sauce for pasta in about 30 minutes.</p>
            <h2>Ingredients</h2>
            <ul>
                <li>
                    <p>2 tbsp. of olive oil</p>
                </li>
                <li>
                    <p>2 cloves of garlic, minced</p>
                </li>
                <li>
                    <p>1/2 tsp. of hot red pepper</p>
                </li>
                <li>
                    <p>28 oz. of canned tomatoes, preferably San Marzano</p>
                </li>
                <li>
                    <p>2 tbsp. of parsley, chopped</p>
                </li>
            </ul>
            <h2>Preparation</h2>
            <ol>
                <li>
                    <p>Heat olive oil in a large saucepan on medium</p>
                </li>
                <li>
                    <p>Add garlic and hot red pepper and sweat until fragrant
</p>
                </li>
                <li>
                    <p>Add tomatoes, breaking up into smaller pieces</p>
                </li>
                <li>
                    <p>Simmer on medium-low heat for at least 20 minutes</p>
                </li>
                <li>
                    <p>Add parsley</p>
                </li>
                <li>
                    <p>Simmer for another five minutes</p>
                </li>
                <li>
                    <p>Serve over long pasta.</p>
                </li>
            </ol>
        </article>
   </body>
```

FIGURE 1.9 Marinara sauce recipe as an HDITA topic. The topic is now an HTML5 article, and the elements' structure looks very similar to what can be accomplished with XML.

Marinara sauce

Prepare a crowd-pleasing red sauce for pasta in about 30 minutes.

Ingredients

- 2 tbsp. of olive oil
- 2 cloves of garlic, minced
- 1/2 tsp. of hot red pepper
- 28 oz. of canned tomatoes, preferably San Marzano
- 2 tbsp. of parsley, chopped

Preparation

1. Heat olive oil in a large saucepan on medium
2. Add garlic and hot red pepper and sweat until fragrant
3. Add tomatoes, breaking up into smaller pieces
4. Simmer on medium-low heat for at least 20 minutes
5. Add parsley
6. Simmer for another five minutes
7. Serve over long pasta.

FIGURE 1.10 HDITA recipe for marinara sauce seen on a web browser. An added benefit of HDITA is an instant presentation view that does not require processing or transformation to generate a basic publishable outcome.

```
---
id: t-marinara
author: Unknown
category: Italian
---
# Marinara Sauce
Prepare a crowd-pleasing red sauce for pasta in about 30 minutes.

## Ingredients
- 2 tbsp. of olive oil
- 2 cloves of garlic, minced
- 1/2 tsp. of hot red pepper
- 28 oz. of canned tomatoes, preferably San Marzano
- 2 tbsp. of parsley, chopped.

## Preparation
1. Heat olive oil in a large saucepan on medium
2. Add garlic and hot red pepper and sweat until fragrant
3. Add tomatoes, breaking up into smaller pieces
4. Simmer on medium-low heat for at least 20 minutes
5. Add parsley
6. Simmer for another five minutes
7. Serve over long pasta.
```

FIGURE 1.11 Marinara sauce recipe as an MDITA topic. The major change in this version is the absence of tags to represent elements.

technical communication (Eli Review, n.d.) that act as commonplace elements in the repertoire of an author. Chapter 3 will look at how those common moves of technical communication relate to content structures in DITA and LwDITA.

For processing purposes, a single DITA map can combine topics created in different LwDITA formats (Figure 1.13).

Deliverables created from the sample map in Figure 1.13 can include a print cookbook or an online recipe guide, based on the automation tools used by Chef Pedro and his team in a specific publishing scenario.

Computer Code for Human Authors

DITA and all three LwDITA formats are undeniably code. Calling them "computer code," however, could offend programmers and developers. Particularly for technical communication students and practitioners with backgrounds in writing and the Humanities, *this is* their computer code. They will probably not use advanced programming languages, but they work with XML, HTML5, and even Markdown code that for them requires a different kind of thinking than desktop publishing workflows involving long document files with a word processor. These are the skills that someone like IBM's James Mathewson expects from a technical communication graduate.

Authors using any combination of LwDITA formats do not need new technological skills. They will continue "the move away from a document-based to a

Marinara sauce

Prepare a crowd-pleasing red sauce for pasta in about 30 minutes.

Ingredients

- 2 tbsp. of olive oil
- 2 cloves of garlic, minced
- 1/2 tsp. of hot red pepper
- 28 oz. of canned tomatoes, preferably San Marzano
- 2 tbsp. of parsley, chopped

Preparation

1. Heat olive oil in a large saucepan on medium
2. Add garlic and hot red pepper and sweat until fragrant
3. Add tomatoes, breaking up into smaller pieces
4. Simmer on medium-low heat for at least 20 minutes
5. Add parsley
6. Simmer for another five minutes
7. Serve over long pasta.

FIGURE 1.12 PDF version of the XDITA topic for the marinara sauce recipe. Compare to the deliverable produced from a DITA XML task in Figure 1.4. The topic gained sub-headings because the <section> element replaced more specific moves associated with a task.

```
<?xml version="1.0" encoding="UTF-8"?>
<!DOCTYPE map PUBLIC "-//OASIS//DTD DITA Map//EN" "map.dtd">
<map>
    <title>Fantastic Cookbook</title>
    <topichead>
    <topicmeta><navtitle>Sauces and condiments</navtitle></topicmeta>
    <topicref href="t-tikkamasala.dita" format="dita" />
    <topicref href="t-mole.html" format="hdita" />
    <topicref href="t-marinara.md" format="mdita" />
    </topichead>
</map>
```

FIGURE 1.13 DITA map aggregating different LwDITA formats. The end users will see all the recipes with the same structure regardless of authoring process.

topic-based approach to developing, managing, and publishing content" (Andersen, 2014, p. 116) widely adopted in the field of technical communication. New knowledge will actually come in the form of abstractions that allow authors to identify rhetorical moves (e.g., staging with a **<shortdesc>**, guiding with **<steps>**, showing with **<example>**) that were strictly enforced in DITA XML but are not required in LwDITA. In DITA, for example, an author has strict tags for a short description element and hazard statements, whereas in some LwDITA formats those sections are just paragraphs. These thought processes follow the foundations of the skill set labeled as computational thinking in recent literature about computing education.

LwDITA is not for everyone. In a large organization with limited resources to train authors, the content integrity and structural consistency provided by DITA XML might be the best solution. Fortunately, DITA is still evolving and its technical committee at OASIS is at the time of this writing planning version 2.0 of this content standard. LwDITA does not have the objective of replacing DITA, which is still available for authors and teams who need its full capabilities. The abstraction tasks from this framework, however, will enable critical users to apply computational thinking and technical communication principles in a series of layers that reveal intelligent content structure beyond what a software tool allows.

The 2012 Adobe video described a future of technical communication that now is more like its present, or even its past. For some, technical communication is still about structured information and intelligent content that adapts to users' needs. However, complex XML code is only one way (and maybe approaching obsolescence) to get there. Simplified lightweight markup (or *markdown*) cannot be ignored because authors are creating topics directly on the online environments where they will be read; after all, not every publishing project needs advanced reuse and filtering. Furthermore, coding and automating content delivery is but a "metal" element in the complicated process behind authoring and publishing intelligent content. Human beings in charge of content creation need to move their "mental" focus to the abstraction thinking behind the rhetorical decisions that make content intelligent.

Before we move on to specific how-to and examples of creating intelligent content with LwDITA following principles of computational thinking, we need to revisit the origins of DITA XML and analyze how its content structures and discourse conventions (based on the archetypal computer manual) evolved into LwDITA, and those are the main themes of the next chapter.

Notes

1 I present the recipe in the source's original Pascal Case; all other code examples in this book will use lowercase, which is more commonly associated with DITA best practices.

2 http://docs.oasis-open.org/dita/dita/v1.3/errata01/os/complete/part2-tech-content/langRef/containers/task-elements.html#task2

3 "a plain text format for writing structured documents, based on formatting conventions from email and usenet," http://commonmark.org

4 http://yaml.org

References

2.2.1.1 The topic as the basic unit of information. (2016, October 25). Retrieved from http://docs.oasis-open.org/dita/dita/v1.3/os/part1-base/archSpec/base/topicdefined.html#topicdefined

2.7.1.6 Troubleshooting topic. (2016, October 25). Retrieved from http://docs.oasis-open.org/dita/dita/v1.3/errata01/os/complete/part3-all-inclusive/archSpec/technicalContent/dita-troubleshooting-topic.html#dita-troubleshooting-topic

2.7.1.7 Glossary entry topic. (2016, October 25). Retrieved from http://docs.oasis-open.org/dita/dita/v1.3/errata01/os/complete/part3-all-inclusive/archSpec/technicalContent/dita-glossary-topic.html#glossaryArch

AdobeTCS. (2012, July 16). *Future of TechComm.* [Video File]. Retrieved from https://youtu.be/dSdhnyDF0YY

Andersen, R. (2013). The value of a reciprocal relationship between research and practice. *Information Management News.* Retrieved from http://www.infomanagementcenter.com/publications/e-newsletter/may-2013/the-value-of-a-reciprocal-relationship-between-research-and-practice/

Andersen, R. (2014). Rhetorical work in the age of content management: Implications for the field of technical communication. *Journal of Business and Technical Communication*, 28(2), 115–157.

Andersen, R., & Batova, T. (2015). The current state of component content management: An integrative literature review. *IEEE Transactions on Professional Communication*, 58(3), 247–270.

Applen, J. D., & McDaniel, R. (2009). *The rhetorical nature of XML: Constructing knowledge in networked environments.* New York: Routledge.

Bacha, J. (2009). Single sourcing and the return to positivism: The threat of plain-style, arhetorical technical communication practices. In G. Pullman & B. Gu (Eds.) *Content management: Bridging the gap between theory and practice* (pp. 143–159). Amityville, NY: Baywood.

Baker, M. (2013). Every page is page one: Topic-based writing for technical communication and the web. Laguna Hills, CA: XML Press.

Baker, M. (2016, March 1). Algorithms: Separating content from formatting. Retrieved from https://techwhirl.com/algorithms-separating-content-from-formatting/

Bellamy, L., Carey, M., & Schlotfeldt, J. (2012). *DITA best practices: A roadmap for writing, editing, and architecting in DITA.* Upper Saddle River, NJ: IBM Press.

Clark, D. (2016). Content strategy: An integrative literature review. *IEEE Transactions on Professional Communication*, 59(1), 7–23.

Cowan, C. (2010). *XML in technical communication* (2nd ed.). Peterborough: Institute of Scientific and Technical Communication.

Day, D., Priestley, M., & Schell, D. (2001, March 1). *Introduction to the Darwin Information Typing Architecture.* Retrieved from http://www.ibm.com/developerworks/library/x-dita1/

DITAWriter (n.d.). Companies Using DITA. Retrieved June 19, 2018, from http://www.ditawriter.com/companies-using-dita/

DITAWriter. (2016, July 15). *Don Day and Michael Priestly [sic]* on the beginnings of DITA: Part 2. Retrieved from http://www.ditawriter.com/don-day-and-michael-priestly-on-the-beginnings-of-dita-part-2/

Eberlein, K.J. (2016). Content reuse. In R. Gallon (Ed.) *The Language of Technical Communication* (pp. 54–55). Laguna Hills, CA: XML Press.

Eli Review. (n.d.). The Essential moves of technical communication. Retrieved from http://elireview.com/content/curriculum/techcom/

Etheridge, A. (2016, May 17). Experts talk DITA & localization – Michael Priestley. Retrieved from http://www.whp.net/en/experts-talk-dita-localization-michael-priestley/

Evia, C. (2017). Authoring standards-based intelligent content the easy way with Lightweight DITA. *Proceedings of the 35th ACM International Conference on the Design of Communication.*

Evia, C., Sharp, M. R., & Perez-Quiñones, M. A. (2015). Teaching structured authoring and DITA through rhetorical and computational thinking. *IEEE Transactions on Professional Communication*, 58(3), 328–343.

Evia, C., & Priestley, M. (2016). Structured authoring without XML: Evaluating lightweight DITA for technical documentation. *Technical Communication*, 63(1), 23–37.

Evia, C., Eberlein, K., & Houser, A. (2018). *Lightweight DITA: An introduction.* Version 1.0. OASIS.

Gesteland McShane, B. (2009). Why we should teach XML: An argument for technical acuity. In G. Pullman & B. Gu (Eds.) *Content management: Bridging the gap between theory and Practice* (pp. 73–85). Amityville, NY: Baywood Pub.

Glushko, R. J., & McGrath, T. (2008). Document engineering: Analyzing and designing documents for business informatics and web services. Cambridge, MA: The MIT Press.

Guzdial, M. (2016). *Learner-centered design of computing education: Research on computing for everyone.* San Rafael, CA: Morgan & Claypool.

Hackos, J. T. (2011). *Introduction to DITA: A user guide to the Darwin Information Typing Architecture including DITA 1.2* (2nd edition). Comtech Services, Inc.

Hackos, J. T. (2016). International standards for information development and content management. *IEEE Transactions on Professional Communication*, 59(1), 24–36.

Johnson-Eilola, J. (1996). Relocating the value of work: Technical communication in a post-industrial age. *Technical Communication Quarterly*, 5(3), 245–270.

Kaplan, N. (2014, May 3). *The death of technical writing, part 1.* Retrieved from https://customersandcontent.com/2014/05/03/the-death-of-technical-writing-part-1/

Kerzreho, N. (2016). Component content management system. In R. Gallon (Ed.) *The language of technical communication* (pp. 60–61). Laguna Hills, CA: XML Press.

Kimber, E. (2012). *DITA for practitioners, volume 1: Architecture and technology.* Laguna Hills, CA: XML Press.

Lauren, B., & Pigg, S. (2016). Toward multidirectional knowledge flows: Lessons from research and publication practices of technical communication entrepreneurs. *Technical Communication*, 63(4), 299–313.

Mathewson, J. [James_Mathewson]. (2016, September 8). Yes. But writing reusable content is a rare skill. Would that they taught it in college. Essays from whole cloth is more the thing. [Tweet]. Retrieved from https://twitter.com/James_Mathewson/status/774044623840870400

O'Keefe, S. (2009). Structured authoring and XML. In O'Keefe, S. (Ed.) *The compass: Essential reading about XML, DITA, and Web 2.0.* Durham, NC: Scriptorium Publishing Services, Inc.

OASIS Darwin Information Typing Architecture (DITA) TC. (n.d.). Retrieved from https://www.oasis-open.org/committees/tc_home.php?wg_abbrev=dita

Priestley, M., Hargis, G., & Carpenter, S. (2001). DITA: An XML-based technical documentation authoring and publishing architecture. *Technical Communication*, 48(3), 352–367.

Pringle, A., & O'Keefe, S. (2009). Technical writing 101: A real-world guide to planning and writing technical content. Durham, NC: Scriptorium Press.

Rockley, A., Cooper, C., & Abel, S. (2015). *Intelligent Content: A Primer*. Laguna Hills, CA XML Press.

Rude, C. D. (2015). Building identity and community through research. *Journal of Technical Writing and Communication*, 45(4), 366–380.

Sapienza, F. (2002). Does being technical matter? XML, single source, and technical communication. *Journal of Technical Writing and Communication*, 32(2), 155–170.

Stolley, K. (2008). The lo-fi manifesto. *Kairos: A Journal of Rhetoric, Technology, and Pedagogy* 12(3). Retrieved from http://kairos.technorhetoric.net/12.3/

Wachter-Boettcher, S. (2012). Content everywhere: Strategy and structure for future-ready content. Brooklyn, N.Y: Rosenfeld Media.

White, L.W. (2016). Single sourcing. In R. Gallon (Ed.) *The language of technical communication* (pp. 56–57). Laguna Hills, CA: XML Press.

Wing, J. (2006). Computational thinking. *Communications of the ACM*, 49(3), 33–35.

Wing, J. M. (2008). Computational thinking and thinking about computing. *Philosophical Transactions of the Royal Society A: Mathematical, Physical and Engineering Sciences*, 366(1881), 3717–3725. https://doi.org/10.1098/rsta.2008.0118

Wing, J.M. (2011). Research notebook: Computational thinking – what and why? Retrieved from https://www.cs.cmu.edu/link/research-notebook-computational-thinking-what-and-why

2

BEFORE INTELLIGENT CONTENT, THERE WAS THE COMPUTER MANUAL

John M. Carroll is held responsible for some actions and decisions that have defined the academic and professional field of technical communication as we know it today. Carroll's work on applying principles of minimalism to technical documentation, presented chiefly in his book *The Nurnberg Funnel* (1990), still resonates with professionals advancing theory and practice related to procedural writing, delivery of instruction, and interface design. At the same time, and in a more tongue-in-cheek fashion, Carroll has also been labeled as "the man who killed the manual" (Svenvold, 2015). A casualty in the manual's demise, one could argue, was the main line of research that connected practitioners and academics in technical communication. As a proposed standard for authoring and publishing content that includes technical communication, Lightweight DITA shares a common ancestor with the computer manual of the past. Therefore, LwDITA can be described as a resource to mend some aspects of the research-to-practice loop in our discipline.

The title of Carroll's influential book refers "to the legendary Funnel of Nurnberg, said to make people wise very quickly" (1990, p. 10). Carroll used the term to describe approaches to self-instruction related to computing that expected that a user would consume content at their own pace and then come out competent, after returning to "varying levels of incompetence" (p. 4) in the use of a specific hardware or software system. Carroll's proposed approach was a commitment to "minimizing the obtrusiveness to the learner of training material — hence the term *minimalist*" (p.7, his emphasis). The three key aspects of Carroll's minimalist approach to instruction are the following:

1. Allowing learners to start immediately on meaningfully realistic tasks
2. Reducing the amount of reading and other passive activity in training

3. Helping to make errors and error recovery less traumatic and more pedagogically productive (p. 7).

In Svenvold's account of the events, the manual was doomed when Carroll applied those principles of minimalism to the production of that specific genre of technical communication.

> Short, succinct manuals allow the user to dive into many different tasks and to accomplish them quickly, thereby gaining a sense of control and autonomy that inspires further learning.
>
> (Svenvold, 2015)

The "death" of the manual as the default genre of technical communication has impacted the field in more than one way. Gone are the days when the manual was binding the academic and practitioner camps of technical communication as they worked towards the advancement of this common genre. At professional conferences, I occasionally engage in nostalgic conversations with colleagues who continue to state the claim that content developers *and their readers* lost something when the manual disappeared. A certain kind of colleague who still writes in a command-line environment using a text editor like Vim would promptly procure pseudo-evidence to build a case arguing that developers and users have lost the "itch" to tinker with software and hardware because the manual is no longer there to guide them and provide hundreds of reference points. That same colleague would also point out examples of independent software companies that still produce lengthy user manuals.

Except they did not. In John Carroll's opinion, today's developers and users have not really lost the itch to tinker with systems because the manuals disappeared. "A lot of things changed," Carroll said. "One thing is that back in the day, people had to be tinkerers because things didn't work and they were clunky and you had to know your Unix and not be scared of the command line blinking. We live in a much better world." Carroll pointed out that those early days of computing were dominated by data-processing professionals in a highly selective environment: "They were mostly white men, and now computers are used by everybody in the world" (J. Carroll, personal interview, 2015, May 28).

It was a warm day in May when I interviewed John Carroll at his office on the Penn State campus, and he looked more like a Jimmy Buffett concertgoer than the patron saint of technical communicators. We reminisced about the Virginia Tech Center for Human-Computer Interaction (CHCI), which Carroll founded in 1995. As I write this, I am a member of the CHCI executive committee and chair of its education-oriented strategic planning group. Yet, John Carroll and I never worked together, as he left Virginia Tech a few months before I arrived as an assistant professor in 2004. I insisted on the potential consequences of losing the flagship genre of technical communication, and Carroll painted a bigger picture:

"It's not just the manual, but the world has changed, and the software and documentation business model. We cannot afford the manual. Actually, the answer (for the manual's disappearance) is not minimalism, but money." Carroll explained that with computing systems like notebook computers and smartphones (which are considerably more affordable than their mainframe ancestors in the 1980s and earlier), "there's no way to economically produce definitive manuals that cheap. There's no business model for that."

Carroll admitted that, at a personal level, he shares the feeling of nostalgia over the missing manuals. "When I open a box, and I take something out and there's no manual, that's my first thought: Where's the manual?" For a moment, he acknowledged that readers lost something when the manual became an extinct genre: "The instruction manual was also a symbol of empowerment, almost democratic; that's another source of the nostalgia. If I have a manual, I am as good as the expert: I have the information and if I don't I have to call a help number and admit that someone else is in control." But then he hammered in the last nail in the manual's coffin: "All this being said . . . the manuals didn't work. People didn't read them. Even today, they still have the plastic on them in libraries. Nobody read them."

John Carroll Takes the Stand

We then moved on to the technical communication-related accusations that hang over John Carroll's head. How does Carroll plead when facing the accusation of killing the manual?

> I find it very flattering that anyone can think I can have that effect on anything. I honestly think it was much more a matter of a paradigm shift, a change in business model, changing populations, and the fact that the computer became a universal device instead of an elite device. Those were forces bigger than minimalism. I don't think an information model did it.
> (Carroll, personal interview, 2015, May 28)

Carroll added that the death of the manual is not the only factor responsible for the disconnect in interests and priorities between academia and industry in technical communication. He described that as a problem of scaling: when there were a handful of important tech companies, their research and development departments could work closely with academics, and those partnerships were reciprocal. Professors would benefit from knowledge applied in their courses and research projects, and practitioners operated under the idea that professors had something important to tell. Carroll identified the same pattern of disparities in computing-related fields: "People who build interfaces and build products don't go to ACM (Association for Computing Machinery) conferences like they used to. And when you go to practitioner events, you don't see professors."

In the 1990s, Carroll's work on minimalist documentation also influenced an IBM technical writer to architect the original DITA schemas for structuring content. That technical writer was Michael Priestley, who a few years later co-wrote (with JoAnn Hackos) the original technical specification for the DITA standard and is currently co-writing (with me) the spec for LwDITA. Priestley has mentioned on many occasions the impact and influence of Carroll's work on DITA and LwDITA. Therefore, Carroll is also "blamed" for the development of DITA. "John Carroll's work on minimalism was part of the context of DITA," Priestley told me.

> DITA just encoded some existing writing standards within IBM, for topic orientation and information typing. It wasn't until we went public with DITA and people started challenging those choices that I went back and tried to understand where they came from. Minimalism was one of the big influences on DITA, but I first received the influence filtered through guidelines written by others, including the editorial standards in the IBM publication Developing Quality Technical Information.
>
> (Priestley, personal communication, 2017, November 21)

Priestley remembers that, a few years ago, someone questioned on a practitioner's blog if DITA was indeed a product of minimalism applied to technical instruction. As a result, he went back to Carroll's original writing in *The Nurnberg Funnel* and found "the prototypical example, the user guide that Carroll used to test out the principles." He discovered that "you could write that user guide in DITA today. I was surprised and gratified by how close the match was, and by how resilient and persistent those principles have proved." That concept of applied minimalism is an undeniable engine behind the concept of intelligent content, which would not exist if authors were still writing print-based manuals with unstructured sections and chapters.

So, how does John Carroll plead when confronted with the claim of DITA ancestry?

> If DITA was inspired by my work, then thank you. However, that mostly happened after me (at IBM). This idea of adding metadata to facilitate modular reuse of text, I first encountered it with a (female) technical communicator at IBM, at the Raleigh lab in the early 90s. It was an interesting idea because people were talking back then about object-oriented software, modular units . . . all that kind of object-oriented thinking that was being applied to text in a pretty interesting analogy.
>
> (Carroll, personal interview, 2015, May 28)

I tried to identify the technical communicator from the IBM lab in Raleigh who introduced Carroll to DITA. Based on conversations with former and current IBM employees, I determined that the technical communicator could be

Susan Carpenter, who is now a senior manager of technical documentation at Red Hat and "led the first pilot of DITA with IBM WebSphere Application Server docs" (DITAWriter, 2016). Through an online introduction by Michael Priestley, I received the following reply from Carpenter:

> It was probably me. I was leading IBM's production pilot of DITA in 2001/2, and I definitely had contact with him (Carroll) during that time. I don't remember specifically talking about minimalism with him, but it was very much on my mind. We stripped a lot of bloated material out of inventory as part of our conversion to DITA.
>
> (Carpenter, personal communication, 2018, May 14)

A few weeks after I interviewed John Carroll, the influential technical communication blogger Tom Johnson talked to him at the Society for Technical Communication Summit. Johnson questioned if DITA was a product of minimalism in documentation.

> I had the opportunity to ask John Carroll what he thought of DITA, since many DITA people claim Carroll's minimalism as foundational to tech comm. Carroll said he's always elated to see people take his work and incorporate it into their approaches. At the same time, he said any system that traps you into a fixed pattern or template can be detrimental if the content doesn't fit that pattern or template.
>
> (Johnson, 2015)

Michael Priestley claims that the DITA content types of concept, task, and reference are an implementation of Carroll's idea behind the minimal manual. The fixed content types that have been a part of DITA XML since its origins at IBM have always been open to evolution: an author can write, for example, a task topic with the default elements and attributes included in the DITA standard. That same author could, with some tweaking of XML schemas or with help from an information architect, adapt the task topic to make the "fixed pattern or template" mentioned by Johnson into something that works for them. In Chapter 1, I mentioned an example of Chef Pedro, who could *specialize* elements of the DITA task content type into more meaningful components for his intended purpose (i.e., **<ingredients>** as a specialization of the default **<prereq>** for pre-requisites). This process of specialization is reflected in the "D" of DITA: topics and their elements can evolve in the Darwinian sense of the word. However, that process of evolution is not necessarily transparent for authors who do not want or do not know how to edit XML schemas. By simplifying the core "fixed pattern of template" of DITA, LwDITA embarks on a process of genre evolution that empowers entry-level users while keeping its tools to support our human obsession with order and rules.

Our Obsession with Order and Rules

The demise of the manual is an event that affects genre theory and technical communication, as this was the flagship format that the profession produced for decades and, for some, justified its existence as an academic subject and area of practice. Nobody navigates that crossroad of genre and technical communication like Carolyn Miller. Even after retirement from her faculty position at North Carolina State University, Miller continues her explorations on the human need for genres in culture, literature, and the sciences "to help us make sense of this blooming, buzzing confusion" of new forms of communication and interaction (Miller, 2015, p. 155).

Using Darwinian terminology that resonates with design principles of the DITA and LwDITA standards, Miller noted that "in trying to understand the process of genre change and the emergence of what seem to be 'new genres' in both new and old media, we have come to rely heavily on the concept of 'evolution'" (2015, p. 155). As she traced the use of evolutionary language when describing genre use in literature, architecture, music, and painting, Miller attributed this appropriation of language from biological sciences to an "obsession with order and rules" (2015, p. 162). That same obsession is behind the methodology of structured authoring of technical information, which is all about "capturing, guiding, and validating the content, order, and form of a piece of content" (Baker, 2013, p. 189). It is also behind the predetermined content types (e.g. concept, task, and reference) in the DITA standard. The obsession shaped the old flagship genre, as heavy computer manuals established rules for data processing, ordered sections according to product features, and forced readers to follow a specific instruction and consultation pattern.

Taken to its most dangerous extreme, this obsession with order and rules can lead to the standardization of cultural products that Theodor Adorno (1991) presaged. In contrast, taken to its most beneficial extreme, obsessing about order and rules can produce information schemas as revolutionary as those proposed by J.C.R. Licklider (1965) for cataloging library sources. For technical communicators creating intelligent content, the negative side of schemas (probably presented as XML files) is in the "perception that XML forces writers into creating cookie-cutter topics rather than useful technical information" (O'Keefe, 2010, p. 37). A positive side comes from the order and consistency in content that structured authoring methodologies enable.

> Therefore, structured writing is not the enemy of professional writers, but a natural and proper part of their professional tool chest. And for occasional writers – those whose main job is something else but who are sometimes called on to produce content – structured writing can be a godsend if implemented properly. It guides authors and lets them know what is required and when they have completed the task in a satisfactory manner.
>
> (Baker, 2013, p. 189)

The process of identifying, documenting, and implementing common structures to preserve order and rules in the content produced by technical and professional communicators follows a longstanding tradition of applied rhetoric in writing studies. For example, Linda Flower explored transferable tasks in professional writing through the use of schemas and writing plans, acknowledging that "many discourse conventions are, in fact, formalizations of rhetorical moves" (Flower, 1989, p. 34). Studies about rhetorical conventions in technical and professional communication genres have not disappeared, as Kim Sydow Campbell and Jefrey S. Naidoo showed on their study of structural moves in marketing white papers (Campbell & Naidoo, 2017). For a discourse community of technical communicators producing computer manuals before the dawn of minimalism in technical communication, those rhetorical conventions were documented and analyzed in computing-related publications – and those are the origins of LwDITA and intelligent content.

Common Structures in Technical Content Before Minimalism

The October 1975 edition of *Asterisk* (the "Systems Documentation Newsletter" from the Association for Computing Machinery) included a glimpse of a technical manual's rhetorical conventions. In the "Technical Writing" column, edited by Diana Patterson (she of the prestigious ACM SIGDOC Diana Award), Larry Wygant, of CAPONE – Chicago Area Programmers of Novas and Eclipses, recommended some sections for user manuals aimed at attracting the attention of a reader, who was expected to be male in the "highly selective environment" of old computing described by John Carroll earlier in this chapter.

> I feel very strongly that when one opens a manual, the first printed page to fall to the eye should be a very general explanation of exactly what the system is, what problem it was intended to attack, and the reasons for bothering to attack that problem at all. This is somewhat akin to the 'hook' at the opening of a novel; if the readers' attention is not captured immediately, he is likely to wander off on any number of tangents and end no better informed than he began.
>
> (Patterson, 1975, p. 8)

Wygant's analysis of a user manual then focused on the criteria behind the extent and cost of documentation: content, intent, and technique. When it came to content, he recommended to "(s)uit the complexity of the manual to the complexity of the subject, and don't belabor the obvious." He defined intent as the goal to cover the users' needs: "The documentation should be clearly aimed at the prospective user of the system. As many levels of documentation are required as there are levels of users." Technique was connected to the budget and quality of documentation: "Two elements of documentation are indispensable – integration with the system implementation and on-line machine-readable generation" (Patterson, 1975, p. 8).

A later issue of *Asterisk* included a more detailed "User Manual Outline," authored by Joe Rigo (he of the prestigious ACM SIGDOC Rigo Award). Rigo's outline was "designed mainly for a software vendor or equivalent system application. It is a manual of instructions on how to use the program or system. It assumes a batch, or similar non-interactive, application" (Rigo, 1976, p. 7). The sections identified in Rigo's outline provide a rich description of the genre's rhetorical conventions (or at least those identified by the author), which include the following:

Preface ("less than 1 page"). Should identify the system by name and state its purpose, intended audience ("by job title or profession") or special training prerequisites, hardware and software requirements, "(c)opyright restrictions, address for questions and comments, list of other directly relevant publications, etc." "None of these topics should extend beyond a single short paragraph. Some can be handled with a single sentence. The rest of the manual can be used to expand where necessary" (1976, p. 7).

Introduction. Should describe "the program or system as it will appear to the user. Identify its main functions and refer to an appropriate section later in the manual for detailed information." "The complete introduction should not be more than 1–3 printed pages. It is really not much more than a long-winded Topic Index" (1976, p. 7). The Introduction should also note any documentation conventions used in the manual (all caps means that words should be coded exactly as printed, lower case describes a user entry point, braces represent a mandatory choice, brackets represent optional parameters, etc.) Rigo added that if "the system does not function as described, users will quickly lose faith in the manual. On the other hand, they will accept almost any outrageous restriction if it is identified and described clearly" (1976, p. 7).

Basic requirements. Should include "any information that the user needs to determine whether he can run the system in his installation or use it for his application. This information may be moved to an appendix if it is more than 2–3 pages or is primarily technical in a manual that is intended for people with no programming experience" (1976, p. 8).

Basic functions. Should contain "step-by-step instructions for performing a task of primary interest to the user. It shows how different elements of the system are used together on an intermediate level" (1976, p. 8). This section "introduces new users to the system. Experienced users will refer directly to the reference material in other chapters. Do not assume that a person reading these sections knows anything about the system" (1976, p. 9).

Creating the data base (sic). "This section does not apply to all software packages (sic), and its contents are variable even when it does apply. It may be moved to an appendix if the process is performed only once for the entire installation" (1976, p. 9).

Processing and reporting. Should describe "all statements, commands, parameters, and options that a user must cope with" (1976, p. 9). In Rigo's outline, "each statement, command, option, parameter, or similar independent item" requires the name of the statement or command, a paragraph describing its function, a formal definition using the documentation conventions stated in the Introduction, examples of valid commands/statements, summary of rules, and additional examples as needed. Rigo closed this section stating that the "manual must then include a reference chart showing all command formats on a single page" (1976, p. 9).

Sample output. Should contain "little more than an annotated listing from a typical run." Rigo specified that this "section does not have to explain everything" (1976, p. 9) and it should advise the user "that this is all he needs to know about the subject unless he wants to become a computer programmer, in which case he should read some other book" (1976, pp. 9–10).

Complete examples. Should contain "at least one complete example." "Do not try to show off every bell and whistle in the system in a single example. This simply creates confusion" (1976, p. 10).

Error messages. "List each error message that a user may encounter. Explain what the user must do to eliminate the error condition. Be specific. No error message is self explanatory" (1976, p. 10).

Appendices. "An appendix is the purest, most usable form of computer system documentation. It is usually well defined and restricted to a single narrow topic. As a result, it becomes very easy for a user to find exactly the information that he is looking for" (1976, p. 10). Rigo concluded his ode to the appendix with the following: "Appendices are great. Use them" (1976, p. 10).

Supplemental. Should include a table of contents and an index. "A page of 'How to . . . ' references is also helpful. Glossaries are rarely worth the effort. I have never yet used one that provided the explanation that I needed. It is common to include a list of illustrations, but no one seems to use them very much" (1976, p. 10).

Rigo's proposed sections and moves establish a clear pattern or schema for composing an example of the technical manual as a genre of technical communication. The conventions he identified had the purpose of keeping the document's contents in order and make it easier to access for a reader.

Putting the Manual on Life Support

Joe Rigo's outline for a computer manual reflects a healthy and confident genre of technical communication in the 1970s. However, the manual started to lose genre power in the 1980s and was on life support even before John Carroll delivered the final uppercut with the concept of minimalism. Gerald Cohen and

Donald Cunningham, in the introduction to their 1984 book *Creating Technical Manuals: A Step-by-Step Approach to Writing User-Friendly Instructions*, already talked about a "crisis in manual writing." According to these authors, manual readers in the 1980s were "more sophisticated and liberated" than those from before 1970 and would not "tolerate a poorly conceived manual." Many of their recommendations urged the manual writer "to serve as an agent representing the reader." One of the greatest failures of manual writing, they wrote, is "the lack of representation from the reader needs" (Cohen & Cunningham, 1984, p.13). They provided the following causes behind the crisis in manual writing:

1. An "increasing reluctance to read instructions, whether they are on a product, on its packaging, or in a manual." They hypothesized that conditions like "the age of television we live in" or the bad reputation spawned by manuals of the past were to blame.
2. A more discerning audience, aware that users' "inability to understand a manual is *not* a reflection on them but on those who created and published the manual.
3. A need "to get the reader productive right away," claiming that a reader "cannot, and will not, spare the time for a long period of learning for a product or procedure that is supposed to be simple and easy to use or do, maintain, or repair" (Cohen & Cunningham, 1984, p.1).

Cohen (then a technical writer at IBM) and Cunningham (then a professor of technical and professional writing at Texas Tech University) were quite prescriptive when documenting rhetorical conventions of the manual. They advocated for the use of a series of plan sheets that functioned as the manual's blueprint: "Just as a house should not be built without a blueprint, a manual should not be created without a blueprint – not just an outline, but a blueprint" (1984, p.12). Their recommended plan sheets were to be initially completed by subject-matter experts (actually, the authors said that writers should "use" subject-matter experts, with awareness that the experts "are busy people"), who would provide information "in a form that is close to the coherent pattern you will use in writing the manual. With the completed plan sheets, you will be able to determine systematically and with reasonable completeness the information you need to write the parts of the manual" (1984, p.14). The plan sheets from Cohen and Cunningham covered the following conventions of the manual as a genre of technical writing:

- Naming the Product or Procedure
- Explaining What the Product or Procedure Does
- Translating Technical Facts

- Explaining the Distinguishing Characteristics of the Product or Procedure
- Illustrating the Old Product or Procedure
- Illustrating the New Product or Procedure
- Outlining the Task
- Detailing the Task
- Presenting the Alternatives Sheet
- Presenting the Troubleshooting Table (Cohen & Cunningham, 1984).

Although the recommendations from Cohen and Cunningham were focused on a manual that was to be presented as a book, they predicted an era "when advanced technology will enable us to use on-line documentation exclusively" (1984, p.146). They presented the possibility of online documentation as "a tool radically different from the traditional user's manual" that would require a new approach to composing prose.

Focusing on a different genre of technical writing, Carolyn Miller and Jack Selzer analyzed the structure and argumentation elements of technical reports by detailing their rhetorical conventions, or topical basis of discourse. They proposed three kinds of topics: "Those specific to a genre, those specific to an organization or institution, and those specific to a discipline" (Miller & Selzer, 1985, p. 311). Following their model, the rhetorical conventions of a technical manual presented by Cohen and Cunningham can be described as generic – they were specific to a genre (the technical manual). The authors did not present them as, say, the official rhetorical conventions for manuals at IBM. Jonathan Price, however, did move beyond the generic conventions and crossed into the organizational or institutional type of topical convention in his 1984 book *How to Write a Computer Manual: A Handbook of Software Documentation*. Price was a senior technical writer at Apple, and described the book as related to organizational practices,

> This book began at Apple Computer as a guide to the new employees and freelance writers working for the User Education group in the division that produces the Apple II family of computers.
>
> (Price, 1984, p. v)

Price's conventions and recommendations were presented with the ultimate goal of creating "friendly manuals," which the author posited as the antidote against bad manuals of the past. "Friendly manuals sell products, expand users' understanding of the extra features, and save everyone's time," he wrote (Price, 1984, p.7). In a meta application of his own recommendations, Price's description of the features in *How to Write a Computer Manual: A Handbook of Software Documentation* reflected the organizational patterns of the type of friendly manual promoted in the book.

1. A table of contents, which lists all the main sections at the beginning of the book. Also, the start of each chapter includes a table of contents.
2. Lots of headlines, which allow the reader to "skip to the part of the book you want."
3. Checklists of key points, which are presented at the end of every chapter and then collected at the end of the book.
4. A glossary, which defines terms mentioned in the book and is presented at the end of the book.
5. An index, which is organized alphabetically and also presented at the end of the book (Price, 1984).

Some of Price's recommendations transcended to the third kind of rhetorical convention proposed by Miller and Selzer, as they became disciplinary moves or commonplaces. Price's separation of a manual's text into content types establishes a distinction between tutorial ("offers step-by-step training focused on a particular activity") and reference ("offers procedures that users can apply in many different circumstances") writing conventions. Those moves advanced from the organizational realm (Apple Computer, in his case) and became disciplinary conventions: task and reference (along with concept) are the main content types associated with the DITA standard.

Price also included a whole chapter dedicated to "Creating Computer-Assisted Instruction." When he compared online documentation to its printed version, he claimed that "people find them friendlier (At least it can be friendlier. That's up to you)" (Price, 1984, p.100). He warned that creating online documentation generated new demand for skills in the technical writer's repertoire, including learning an authoring language or, "if you don't find an authoring language you enjoy," collaborating with a programmer. Price's discussion of online deliverables advanced the conversation on topic-based authoring that moved away from the traditional manual-as-book model that dominated the market in the 1970s and before. This move also planted the seed for disciplinary conventions, as topic-based authoring for online deliverable replaced the long print format of documentation.

Price's emphasis on task-orientation established some topical moves that still apply to tutorial/procedural content, with the overall recommendation of focusing on organization. Those moves included the following:

- Introduce each section
- Divide your material into short steps
- Show people how to get out
- Separate what to do from what it means
- Put in lots of displays
- Define your terms

- Put in pictures
- Anticipate variations
- Summarize
- Give people a break
- Allay anxiety
- Test it. Revise it. Test it again
- Tell people where to go next (Price, 1984).

Many of those moves are captured in the element types of the DITA 1.3 standard (e.g., a task is "what to do" and a concept is "what it means"). The element types in DITA also inherited generic, institutional, and disciplinary conventions from another title that was originally published in the 1980s: IBM's *Producing Quality Technical Information.*

Developing Quality Technical Information

When I tried to measure the impact of John Carroll's theory of minimalism on content development, I remembered that Michael Priestley has acknowledged in several occasions that minimalism, via the IBM publication *Developing Quality Technical Information* (*DQTI*), was one of the big influences on DITA. In a conversation we had after one of our presentations at a DITA North America conference organized by the Center for Information-Development Management, Priestley pointed out that IBM's *DQTI* was "all about DITA without mentioning DITA by its name."

Before *DQTI*, however, there was *PQTI*. The publication's original title was *Producing Quality Technical Information*, and it started as an internal IBM handbook of recommendations for content authors and evaluators. Published in 1983, *PQTI* was credited to Morris Dean and a long list of co-authors (or co-"preparers") and focused on a list of requirements of quality, presented under the principle of "technical information that meets all the requirements is quality information" (Dean et al., 1983, p. ii). The structure of *PQTI* is built around a list of quality requirements, and a standard pattern of presenting two examples when discussing each requirement: one showing a common error and the second illustrating a way to correct the error and "improve quality."

The original quality requirements from *PQTI*, organized in categories and specific actions under each category, were the following:

- Task orientation
  - Present information from the reader's point of view
  - Indicate a practical reason for information
  - Order the presentation to reflect the order of use
  - Devise titles and headings to reveal the task

- Organization
  - Reveal how the pieces fit together
  - Emphasize main points; subordinate secondary points
  - Don't force readers to branch unnecessarily
  - Present similar topics in a similar way
- Entry points
  - In introductory sections, reveal the order of topics to follow
  - Stock the index with predictable entries for the topics covered
  - Highlight key terms – including new terms being defined
  - Rarely run text for half a page without a heading
  - Rarely run a paragraph beyond a dozen lines
- Clarity
  - Present material so readers can understand it the first time
  - Pace the presentation to be neither too fast nor too slow
  - Write directly and economically
  - Use only technical terms that are necessary and appropriate
  - Define each term new to the intended reader
  - Provide appropriate examples to communicate effectively
- Visual communication
  - Attract and motivate your readers with graphic techniques
  - Employ visual techniques to communicate effectively
- Accuracy
  - Provide accurate technical information
  - Provide accurate references and other auxiliary information
  - Use correct grammar, spelling, and punctuation
  - Use sexually neutral terms, unless other terms are appropriate
- Completeness
  - Cover all the topics that readers need, and only those topics
  - Cover each topic in just as much detail as readers need
  - Include all standard parts and all promised information
  - Repeat information only when readers will benefit from it (Dean et al., 1983).

Some of Dean et al.'s recommendations reflected major changes for documentation from that period. These moves included advocating for task-oriented titles and headings in sections and the use of the term "topic" (years before the development of a DITA topic model) as a component in a "library" of information units that a writer used to assemble documentation deliverables. Other recommendations, however, were standard guidelines for technical writers. Table 1 shows a list of "weak verbs" and "roundabout expression" compared to "strong, precise verbs" and "concise terms" from the "Write directly and economically" recommendation under the requirement of "Clarity."

The combination of big-picture requirements and concrete recommendations responds to *PQTI*'s dual audience. Early in the document, the authors specified that "this book is to help writers produce quality technical information and to help reviewers judge the results" (Dean et al., 1983, p. ii). Therefore, identifying genre conventions in this text was not as direct as it was in other how-to titles about creating documentation.

In 1998, *PQTI* evolved into *DQTI* – the first edition of *Developing Quality Technical Information: A Handbook for Writers and Editors*, authored by Gretchen Hargis and published by IBM/Prentice Hall. Just as the original publication, *DQTI* focused more on recommendations than in specific topical conventions. However, in *DQTI* the quality requirements became "quality characteristics," presented as a "system for editing and evaluating technical information" (Hargis, 1998, p. xiii). Additionally, Hargis organized the characteristics "by their ability to make information" in the following groups: easy to use, easy to understand, and easy to find (Hargis, 1998, p. 2).

Hargis specified that the quality characteristics were not presented as generic conventions or, as she called them, "elements". She defined elements as "the units that physically make up technical information. An element can be as small as a word and as large as a tutorial" (1998, p. 3). She presented headings, lists, and tables as examples of those elements, indicating that whereas in works of

TABLE 2.1 Excerpt from the "Clarity" requirement of *Producing Technical Information*, which compares "weak verbs" to "strong, precise verbs" and "roundabout expressions" to "concise terms" (Dean et al., 1983, p. 24)

Weak Verbs	*Strong, Precise Verbs*
• has the capability • is capable • has a requirement • is in agreement • performs the printing • draws a conclusion • provides assistance	• can • requires • agrees • prints • infers • helps
Roundabout Expressions	*Concise Terms*
• at this (that) point in time • due to the fact that • in the event that	• now (then) • because • if

fiction a paragraph might be the main element, in technical information authors required "other means of differentiating information" (p. 3). The guidelines presented in *DQTI*, Hargis claimed, were "brief directives about what to do or not to achieve the characteristics of quality. These guidelines apply to the elements." Further describing the difference between characteristics and elements, Hargis noted that "writers cannot, for example, turn clarity on and off with a markup tag. Elements, however, do have recognizable limits and often have corresponding markup tags" (1998, p. 3).

Hargis also mentioned minimalism as a principle for writing technical information. In her discussion of the characteristic of completeness, she included the following paragraph:

> Writers have often created technical information that is too complete, including everything there is to know about a product. Today, the trend in technical writing is toward providing the user with far less information, an approach called minimalism. The minimalist approach not only yields a reduction in page count, but it also results in writing that doesn't get in the user's way. With a minimum of information, the user can independently explore a product after learning some basic concepts and tasks. (Hargis, 1998, p.49)

A second edition of *DQTI* came out in 2004, and it added a group of co-authors after Hargis's name. The second edition provided new details on the difference between the guidelines and the elements (topical conventions) that put those guidelines into practice.

- Guidelines are "brief directives about what to do or not to do to achieve the characteristics of quality. These guidelines apply to the elements."
- Elements are "the units that physically constitute technical information. An element can be as small as a word and as large as a tutorial" (Hargis et al., 2004, p. 5).

Gretchen Hargis passed away in 2005, and the third edition of *DQTI* was published in 2014, with some of the second edition's co-authors. According to its introduction, the 3rd edition of *DQTI* focused on,

- Greater emphasis on the embedded assistance in user interfaces
- The need to plan for information access from mobile devices
- The pervasiveness of Google and other search engines as users' preferred method for looking for information
- Video as a delivery medium for technical information (Carey et al., 2014, p. xviii).

The quality characteristics in all the available editions of *DQTI* follow the same structure. The definitions for some characteristics, however, have changed slightly over time. For example, task orientation was originally defined as: "A focus on helping users complete the tasks associated with a product in relation to their jobs," (Hargis, 1998, p. 2) and in the most recent edition is presented as: "In the context of a product, a focus on helping users do tasks that support their goals" (Carey et al., 2014, p. 14). The *DQTI* quality characteristics, which still show some resemblance to the requirements from *PQTI*, are,

Easy to use

- Task orientation
- Accuracy
- Completeness.

Easy to understand

- Clarity
- Concreteness
- Style.

Easy to find

- Organization
- Retrievability
- Visual effectiveness (Carey et al., 2014, p. 14).

Adding to the conversation about turning characteristics into elements or conventions, Carey et al. wrote the following on the 3rd edition of *DQTI*:

> You can apply the quality characteristics whether you're writing a book, a page, a paragraph, a sentence, or a single word in an interface. The quality technical information model of nine characteristics is flexible enough to support you as you develop ever smaller chunks of information to address the changing needs of users.
>
> (Carey et al., 2014, p. 14)

If the earlier versions of *Developing Quality Technical Information* were, as Michael Priestley said, "all about DITA without mentioning DITA by its name," that changed in the 3rd edition. In their analysis of the characteristic of "Style," under the category of "Easy to understand," the co-authors of *DQTI* asked readers to "use consistent markup tagging." A few of their specific recommendations for tagging elements focused on the generic, organizational, and disciplinary implementation of the characteristics into elements: DITA XML.

Implementation of Elements: DITA is Born

The quality guidelines for technical information that had been driving the work of authors, editors, and reviewers at IBM since the 1980s were put into practice in the content types and elements included in DITA XML. In Chapter 1, I gave a brief historical overview of the early DITA days at IBM, when the Customer and Service Information (C&SI), with work primarily conducted by Dave Schell, Don Day, and Michael Priestley started exploring XML as a language to create tags that would create templates for the genre conventions of commonly used content structures in the company's documentation. Going back to the Miller and Selzer taxonomy of topical conventions, that early work captured the generic structures of fixed types that included the classical DITA trio of concept, task, and reference. As those DITA fixed templates for topics and their structures at the section, paragraph, sentence, or even word level became widely used within IBM, the structures moved to the organizational or institutional category. In conference presentations and publications (Priestley et al., 2001; Priestley, 2001), members of that pioneer team were introducing DITA as the IBM way of authoring and publishing technical documentation. When other companies heard about DITA and tried to create their own architectures for authoring and publishing, the topical conventions moved to the disciplinary category, which started when IBM announced, on March 15, 2001 that they "were going public with an architecture for technical documentation using XML" (Priestley, 2001a), and then culminated with the release of DITA 1.0 as an open standard in 2005.

The transformation of *DQTI* guidelines into DITA elements was subtly documented in a 2001 article published in the "Technology Review" column of the journal *Technical Communication*. "DITA: An XML-Based Technical Documentation Authoring and Publishing Architecture" was authored by Michael Priestley, Gretchen Hargis, and Susan Carpenter, who have appeared previously as key players in this chapter.

The article started by acknowledging that XML "has gained popularity in the technical writing profession by offering us a logical and fairly straightforward framework for developing structured information" (Priestley et al., 2001, p. 352). Then, it warned readers about the pitfalls of implementing a custom XML solution or adopting a standard: "In other words, when you create a new markup language (using XML to define its markup and rules), you shut yourself off from interchange with the rest of the world; when you adopt a standard markup language, you lose the benefits promised by content-specific markup" (2001, p. 354).

Their proposed solution was, as we know by now, the Darwin Information Typing Architecture. The article emphasized that DITA was more than just an XML DTD (Document Type Definition) for structuring documents.

As presented in that introductory paper, a DITA-based solution for developing structured information consisted of the following three parts:

> Fix the content – Authors need to rethink how to write content to thoroughly separate form from content.
>
> Fix the design – Architects need to rethink how to classify and design information, to reduce the cost of upfront analysis and ongoing maintenance for content-specific markup.
>
> Fix the process – Programmers need to rethink how to create transforms and processes, to allow content-specific information to be exchanged, and to make it easier to create and maintain specialized processes.
>
> (Priestley et al. 2001, p. 354)

The implementation of quality characteristics into actual XML elements and conventions is all over those three parts, but it is mainly represented in the work to be performed by authors as part of their work to "fix the content" by categorizing topics by type of information. Priestley and his co-authors addressed the evolution of the manual as it became a collection of topics with "fine-grained" moves to signal or tag specific conventions:

> When writing software manuals, technical writers have historically distinguished task-based instructions (guidance information) from reference information. The content and organization of a user's guide, for example, is different from the content and organization of a reference manual. By writing topics, however, you can make finer-grained distinctions about the type of information that a user can expect than just at the level of the whole document.
>
> (Priestley et al. 2001, p. 355)

In the specific case of the task topic type, some of those moves included a rationale for the task ("why or when a user would want to perform this task"), prerequisites for the task ("what a user should do before performing this task"), responses to the actions ("what the user should see as a result of doing the action"), examples ("examples of what information to enter or what to do"), and post-requisites for the task ("what to do next after this task is completed") (Priestley et al. p. 356). This highly structured task topic reads like a smoothie that came out of a blender combining generic, organizational, and disciplinary conventions and commonplaces from Carroll, Price, and Hargis and her co-authors, and others who attempted to capture the essence of technical documentation.

To illustrate some of those moves, which were present in the early DITA task topic and are still part of the standard, consider the marinara sauce recipe from Chapter 1 (Figure 2.1). I added some extra elements (in bold font) to implement the information types mentioned by Priestley et al. in the previous paragraph.

```
<?xml version="1.0" encoding="UTF-8"?>
<!DOCTYPE task PUBLIC "-//OASIS//DTD DITA Task//EN" "task.dtd">
<task id="t-marinara">
    <title>Marinara Sauce</title>
    <shortdesc>Prepare a crowd-
pleasing red sauce for pasta in about 30 minutes.</shortdesc>
    <prolog>
        <author>Unknown</author>
        <metadata>
            <category>Italian</category>
        </metadata>
    </prolog>
    <taskbody>
        <prereq>
            <ul>
                <li>2 tbsp. of olive oil</li>
                <li>2 cloves of garlic, minced</li>
                <li>1/2 tsp. of hot red pepper</li>
                <li>28 oz. of canned tomatoes, preferably San Marzano</li>
                <li>2 tbsp. of parsley, chopped</li>
            </ul>
        </prereq>
      <context>Prepare this sauce in the summer for an Italian-inspired
afternoon</context>
        <steps>
            <step>
                <cmd>Heat olive oil in a large saucepan on medium</cmd>
            </step>
            <step>
                <cmd>Add garlic and hot red pepper and sweat until fragrant
</cmd>
            </step>
            <step>
                <cmd>Add tomatoes, breaking up into smaller pieces</cmd>
            </step>
            <step>
                <cmd>Simmer on medium-low heat for at least 20 minutes</cmd>
            </step>
            <step>
                <cmd>Add parsley</cmd>
      <stepxmp>Sprinke the parsley all over the saucepan</stepxmp>
       </step>
  <step>
         <cmd>Simmer for another five minutes</cmd>
      <stepresult>The Marinara should be thicker than regular tomato
sauce</stepresult>
                  </step>
            <step>
                <cmd>Serve over long pasta.</cmd>
            </step>
        </steps>
      <postreq>Don't forget to clean the kitchen after dinner</postreq>
</taskbody>
</task>
```

FIGURE 2.1 Expanded version of the marinara sauce recipe as a DITA task. Elements in bold type emphasize some of the moves of interacting with users that the DITA creators had in mind when developing the document types.

The rationale for the task is in the **<context>** element; it represents the conventional move of telling the user when or why to complete the procedure/recipe. The prerequisites were already present in the example from Chapter 1, in the **<prereq>** element, which includes an unordered list (**<ul>**) with list items (**<li>**) for all the ingredients the user would need to complete the recipe. The element **<stepresult>**, which is a child of the element **<step>**, provides possible responses to the actions conducted by users. Another child of the **<step>** element, **<stepxmp>**, gives an example of how to conduct a specific command or action. Lastly, the **<postreq>** element can provide one or more actions that need to be conducted after the core steps of this specific task topic.

Those conventions, or content commonplaces, specific to the genre of task identified by the DITA architects, created quite the strict template that came with many of the benefits I have mentioned in previous chapters. One of the many approaches I have adopted to introduce the DITA standard in a humanities-based Professional and Technical Writing curriculum is to present those elements as rhetorical conventions of our specialized discourse community. This approach also helped during the process of designing the content and element types of LwDITA, but it all started with understanding the different meanings of the term *topic* for the proposed standard's intended audiences of practitioners and academics.

A Topic by Any Other Name . . .

In the world of DITA XML, "a topic is the basic unit of authoring and reuse" (2.2.1.1 The topic as the basic unit of information, 2016). The technical specification for the DITA standard defines topic as follows:

> DITA topics consist of content units that can be as generic as sets of paragraphs and unordered lists or as specific as sets of instructional steps in a procedure or cautions to be considered before a procedure is performed. Content units in DITA are expressed using XML elements and can be conditionally processed using metadata attributes.
>
> (2.2.1.1 The topic as the basic unit of information, 2016)

In the world of rhetoric that defines discourse in most academic programs teaching technical communication in the United States, a topic would actually be one of those content units, and not necessarily the whole "DITA topic." Confusing? Imagine being a student in Professional and Technical Writing and reading the books *Topic-Driven Environmental Rhetoric* and *DITA – the Topic-Based XML Standard* for different courses on the same semester. The *topics* from the first book are not the same *topics* in the second book. Or are they?

The origins of DITA introduced the topic as a chunk of information with the following characteristics:

- One subject, signified by the title
- Wording that is independent of any other topic
- Appropriate length to treat the topic adequately yet not require lots of scrolling (Priestley et al., 2001, p. 355).

Trying to define the concept of topic in rhetoric is not that easy. Derek Ross warns readers about the deceptive simplicity of the terminology for topics in Aristotelian-inspired discourse:

> Aristotle's lack of definition is perhaps not surprising given the seemingly simple concept of "topic." Even today we think we readily understand what is meant by a "topic": We know that the "topic" of a conversation, for example, is that thing upon which the conversation hinges. Similarly, to some extent, we understand the idea of a commonplace without much prompting: A commonplace idea is one which is, quite literally, common to a particular place. The perception is that little explanation is needed.
>
> (Ross, 2017, p.6)

Ross summarizes the discussion by suggesting that topics are shared places common to all debate, which allow rhetors to shape viable argument, and that is where the rhetorical concept of topic meets the DITA topic. The rhetorical topics are the moves/elements inside a DITA topic: the element of, say, **<prereq>** for prerequisites in a task topic suggests a shared model common to all tasks and procedures that allows authors to produce viable how-to information. A definition of topic from Lawrence Prelli further supports this overlap. Prelli explains rhetorical *topoi* as "headings or topics that identify lines of thought." He adds that "some of these lines of development are relevant to virtually all discussion within a culture; others are peculiar to specific subjects and fields of inquiry" (Prelli, 1989, p. 185). Some DITA XML elements, like **<p>** for paragraph or **<li>** for list item, are relevant for any type of information and are present in HTML – the *lingua franca* of the web. Other elements, like **<lcObjective>** for a single learning objective or **<lcDelivery>** for delivery method of educational content, are peculiar to the DITA learning and training specialization.

William Hart-Davidson was an early DITA adopter in academia. His WRA 420: *Advanced Technical Writing* course at Michigan State University had students using the DITA standard to structure and publish information more than a decade before I started writing this chapter. Some of Hart-Davidson's work has focused on that overlap of the topic as content unit and the topic as commonplace element (Hart-Davidson & Omizo, 2017). Particularly, the course content he developed for the ELI Review modules on *The Essential Moves of Technical Communication* (Eli Review, n.d.) is based on common traits of technical communication genres. In a conversation we had a few years ago when he

TABLE 2.2 Attempt to map the essential moves of technical communication from the ELI Review curriculum to content elements from the DITA standard

Essential move of technical communication	*DITA element*
Staging: explaining the goal to be achieved	<shortdesc>
Staging: explaining conditions necessary to begin	<context> <prereq>
Coaching: describing steps in a process	<steps>
Coaching: describing success conditions	<stepresult>
Alerting: helping users avoid unwanted outcomes	<info> <note> <hazardstatement>

visited the Virginia Tech campus to give a talk precisely on rhetorical topics and commonplaces, Hart-Davidson linked those traits or moves to elements from the DITA standard, which I tried to capture in Table 2.

The overlap, despite apparent and actual differences, in the DITA XML and rhetorical discussion of topics and commonplaces highlights the practical applications of topics, and also their perceived limitations. Miller and Selzer analyzed rhetorical topics as repetitive but useful patterns of speech in the following paragraph:

> Topics can thus be conceived, alternatively, as pigeonholes for locating already existing ideas or as patterns of thought or methods of analysis that can be called on in the construction of arguments. In practice, these alternative versions are conjoined: by learning a mechanical system of pigeonholes, one masters patterns of thought that then become habitual and spontaneous.
>
> (Miller & Selzer, 1985, p. 311)

In DITA XML, that "system of pigeonholes" (the standard's elements and content types) allows authors to master specific forms of communication that enable the type of intelligent content discussed in this book. The next section focuses on the number of elements included in the DITA standard across its releases. It includes some examples showing the useful potential of those tags while setting the exigence for LwDITA's simplified content model.

An Element for Every (Content) Occasion

One could point out that the number of XML tags available in the DITA standard is the result of years of committee-based development with active members representing different sectors and industries with unique content-structuring needs. However, DITA was born a heavy spec. Even in its version 1.0, the standard had a total of 193 element types. Some of those original element types are now deprecated, but the specification for DITA 1.0, edited by Michael Priestley and JoAnn Hackos, included the following elements and categories:

- Topic elements: 11, including **<dita>, <topic>**, and **<title>**
- Concept elements: 2, consisting of **<concept>** and **<conbody>**
- Reference elements: 12, including **<reference>**, **<refbody>**, and **<refsyn>**
- Task elements: 25, including **<task>**, **<taskbody>**, and **<steps>**
- Body elements: 29, including **<ol>**, **<p>,** and **<ul>**
- Table elements: 11, including **<table>**, **<row>**, and **<entry>**
- Typographic elements: 6, including **<b>**,**<i>**, and **<u>**
- Programming elements: 25, including **<codeblock>**, **<apiname>**, and **<syntaxdiagram>**
- Software elements: 8, including **<varname>**, **<userinput>**, and **<systemoutput>**
- User interface elements: 5, including **<wintitle>**, **<menucascade>**, and **<screen>**
- Utilities elements: 4, including **<imagemap>**, **<area>**, and **<shape>**
- Miscellaneous elements: 5, including **<draft-comment>**, **<fn>**, and **<indexterm>**
- Prolog elements: 27, including **<audience>**, **<author>**, and **<platform>**
- Related links elements: 5, including **<link>**, **<linkinfo>**, and **<linktext>**
- Specialization elements: 6, including **<boolean>**, **<no-topic-nesting>**, and **<required-cleanup>**
- Map elements: 10, including **<map>**, **<navref>**, and **<topicref>**
- Map group elements: 2, consisting of **<topicgroup>** and **<topichead>**

The original DITA 1.0 technical specification is still available on the DITA Technical Committee website[1]. The spec is a well-organized document that presents details and examples of common topic and element types without overwhelming the readers with a force-feed of its 193 XML tags.

For version 1.3 of the DITA spec, the Technical Committee actually separated the standard's 621 available elements in three editions: base (with 189 elements), technical content (including the elements from the base edition and 251 additional elements), and all inclusive (including the elements from base, technical content, and 181 additional elements). This separation responds to the expanded audiences of the standard. DITA 1.0 was faithful to the IBM original and was intended mainly as a grammar to structure software documentation. DITA 1.3, in contrast, has users in diverse industries that share a need for structured information and versatile publishing, but do not have a clear need for concept, task, and reference as core content types.

The DITA Technical Committee at OASIS released a white paper/committee note titled DITA 1.3: Why Three Editions? that emphasizes "that topic and map are the base document types in the architecture" (Eberlein et al., 2015, p. 7). Therefore, those are the only content types present in the base edition. The technical content edition adds the technical communication content types (concept, task, reference) that defined DITA in its origins at IBM, and adds the content types of glossary entry, glossary group, and troubleshooting. The all-inclusive edition incorporates content types from the DITA learning and training specialization (learning assessment, learning base, learning content, learning overview, learning plan, and learning summary). The DITA Technical Committee describes the three editions as follows:

- "The base edition is designed for application developers and people who need only the most fundamental pieces of the DITA framework"
- "The technical content edition is designed for authors who document complex applications and devices, such as software, hardware, medical devices, machinery, and more"
- "The all-inclusive edition is designed for authors and publishers who develop and deliver well-structured, modular instructional materials. It provides a framework for using a learning objects approach to organize and sequence content as a learning deliverable" (Eberlein et al., 2015, pp. 10–17).

Providing a detailed explanation or tutorial of the content and element types included in DITA 1.3 is way beyond the scope of Creating Intelligent Content with Lightweight DITA. Some helpful titles that thoroughly describe and explain the standard have already been published (Hackos, 2011; Bellamy et al., 2012). Additionally, the website Learning DITA[2] from Scriptorium is a free and solid resource for novice-to-advanced users who need to learn about DITA and its content structuring and publishing capabilities. However, to put the three editions in context I include here some examples of representative topic types. Going back to the story of Chef Pedro from Chapter 1, a topic type from the base edition would look as Figure 2.2, which includes biographical information on Chef Pedro. The topic works as a simple template that separates content from presentation and leaves it ready to join a topic collection and be integrated into information products.

The topic's first line is the XML declaration that, as I tell my students, announces to the computing processors that the topic is an XML file and should be treated as such. The second line points out that the topic is not just a regular XML file, but that is complies with the structuring rules described in the document type definition (DTD) of "topic" from the DITA standard. This means that if an author decides to include an XML tag that does not belong in the DITA topic DTD, the file will not validate and will report an error when processed. The third line opens the actual topic (with the required attribute for a unique identifier value: "pedro-bio" in this case). And then the file has a few moves/genre conventions of the introductory topic: a short description (**<shortdesc>**),

```
<?xml version="1.0" encoding="UTF-8"?>
<!DOCTYPE topic PUBLIC "-//OASIS//DTD DITA Topic//EN" "topic.dtd">
      <topic id="about">
       <title>About Chef Pedro</title>
       <shortdesc>Executive Chef, Yucatec-International Fusion Alchemist,
Marketing Architect.</shortdesc>
       <body>
      <p>Self-taught and persistent in the kitchen and marketing aspects of
the restaurant business, Chef Pedro has established himself a key player in
the new scene of Mexican gastronomy, particularly in the tradition of dishes
and flavors from the Yucatan peninsula.</p>
      <p>From an early age, Pedro learned the craft in the always-open
kitchen of his mother, Doña Raquel, among aromas of truly mestizo gastronomy.
Original top notes of condiments and herbs mixed with traditional Spanish
middle notes of saffron and olive oil built on ancient Yucatec base notes of
roasted tomato and hot peppers salsa inspired him to experiment with his own
style of cooking.</p>
       </body>
      </topic>
```

FIGURE 2.2 DITA topic including biographical information about Chef Pedro. The topic's elements include simple structures like a title, a short description, and a body containing paragraphs.

the topic's body (<**body**>), and some paragraphs (<**p**>). When placed with other topics in a collection and processed by a DITA-aware software tool (I will talk more about tools in Chapter 5), this biographic introduction can inherit any formatting rules and become a page or section in a print magazine or book, a page or blurb on a website, and many other end-user deliverables depending on the author's publishing goals.

For the technical content edition, a task topic can provide an example. Earlier in this chapter, Figure 2.1 included a modified version of the marinara sauce recipe from Chapter 1. Similar to the generic topic from Figure 2.2, the task's first line of code announces to the computing processors that the topic is an XML file and should be treated as such. The second line points out that the topic is not just a regular XML file, but that is complies with the structuring rules described in the document type definition (DTD) of "task" from the DITA standard. Then, some of the topical conventions included in the XML tags are equivalent to the essential moves of technical communication from Table 2, including <**shortdesc**> as a staging move and <**step**> as a coaching move.

The DITA Technical Committee explained that separating the DITA 1.3 spec in three editions sets "the stage for future developments: Lightweight DITA and DITA 2.0" (Eberlein et al., 2015, p. 9). LwDITA, thus, can be a truly minimalist version of the standard, giving authors the structuring and publishing capabilities of DITA 1.3 in a reduced set of tags. LwDITA also makes DITA publishing workflows more inclusive and accessible, as it accommodates non-XML authoring formats to address the needs of authors outside of the traditional technical documentation audience of DITA 1.0. Those are strong selling points that drive the next chapter.

Notes

1 https://www.oasis-open.org/committees/tc_home.php?wg_abbrev=dita#technical
2 http://www.learningdita.com

References

2.2.1.1 The topic as the basic unit of information. (2016, October 25). Retrieved from http://docs.oasis-open.org/dita/dita/v1.3/os/part1-base/archSpec/base/topicdefined.html#topicdefined

Adorno, T.W. (1991). *The culture industry: Selected essays on mass culture*. London: Routledge.

Baker, M. (2013). *Every page is page one: Topic-based writing for technical communication and the web*. XML Press.

Campbell, K.S. & Naidoo, J.S. (2017). Rhetorical move structure in high-tech marketing white papers. *Journal of Business and Technical Communication*. 31(1) 94–118.

Carey, M. et al. (2014). *Developing quality technical information: A handbook for writers and editors*. 3rd Ed. Upper Saddle River, NJ: IBM Press.

Carroll, J.M. (1990). *The Nurnberg funnel: Designing minimalist instruction for practical computer skill*. Cambridge, MA: M.I.T. Press.

Closs, S. (2016). *DITA – the topic-based XML standard: A quick start*. Switzerland: Springer.

Cohen, G. & Cunningham, D.H. (1984). *Creating technical manuals: A step-by-step approach to writing user-friendly instructions*. New York, NY: McGraw-Hill.

DITAWriter. (2016, July 13). Don Day and Michael Priestley on the beginnings of DITA: Part 1. Retrieved from http://www.ditawriter.com/don-day-and-michael-priestley-on-the-beginnings-of-dita-part-1/

Eberlein, K.J., Harrison, N., Hunt. J., & Swope, A. (2015). *DITA 1.3: Why three editions?* OASIS.

Eli Review. (n.d.). The Essential moves of technical communication. Retrieved from http://elireview.com/content/curriculum/techcom/

Flower, L. (1989). Rhetorical problem solving: Cognition and professional writing. In M. Kogen (Ed.), *Writing in the business professions* (pp.3–36). Urbana, IL: NCTE.

Hargis, G. (1998). *Developing quality technical information: A handbook for writers and editors*. Upper Saddle River, NJ: Prentice Hall.

Hargis, G. et al. (2004). *Developing quality technical information: A handbook for writers and editors. 2nd Ed.* Upper Saddle River, NJ: Prentice Hall.

Hart-Davidson, W. & Omizo, R. (2017). Genre signals in textual topologies. In L. Walsh & C. Boyle (Eds.), *Topologies as techniques for a post-critical rhetoric* (pp. 99–123). New York, NY: Palgrave Macmillan.

Johnson. T. (2015, June 29). Slides, notes, and lessons learned at the STC summit 2015 in Columbus, Ohio. [Blog post]. Retrieved from http://idratherbewriting.com/2015/06/29/lessons-learned-at-the-stc-summit-2015/

Licklider, J.C.R. (1965). *Libraries of the future*. Cambridge, MA: M.I.T. Press.

Miller, C. R. (2015). Genre change and evolution. In N. Artemeva & A. Freedman (Eds.), *Genre studies around the globe: Beyond the three traditions* (pp. 154–185). Lexington, KY: Trafford.

Miller, C.R. & Selzer, J. (1985). Special topics of argument in engineering reports. In L. Odell & D. Goswami (Eds.), *Writing in non-academic settings*. New York: Guilford.

Dean, M. et al. (1983). *Producing quality technical information*. San Jose, CA: IBM.

O'Keefe. S. (2010). XML: The death of creativity in technical writing? *Intercom*, (February), 36–37.

Price, J. (1984). *How to write a computer manual: A handbook of software documentation*. Menlo Park, CA: Benjamin Cummings.

Ross, D. (Ed.). (2017). *Topic-driven environmental rhetoric*. New York: Routledge.

Svenvold, M. (2015, January 26). The disappearance of the instruction manual. *Popular Science*. Retrieved from https://www.popsci.com/instructions-not-included

Patterson, D. (1975). Technical writing: User manuals. *Asterisk*, 2(5), 8–9.

Prelli, L. (1989). *A rhetoric of science: Inventing scientific discourse*. Columbia, SC: University of South Carolina Press.

Priestley, M. (2001). DITA XML: A reuse by reference architecture for technical documentation. *Proceedings of the 19th annual international conference on computer documentation*, 152–156.

Priestley, M. (2001a). XML and the Darwin Information Typing Architecture (DITA). *Communication Design Quarterly Review*, 2(2), 3–4.

Priestley, M., Hargis, G., & Carpenter, S. (2001). DITA: An XML-based technical documentation authoring and publishing architecture. *Technical Communication*, 48(3), 352–367.

Rigo, J. (1976). User manual outline. *Asterisk*, 2(8), 7–10.

3

HOW DITA EVOLVED INTO LwDITA

chapter provides a behind-the-scenes look at the process of developing the proposed LwDITA standard for structuring and publishing content. If you are more interested in workflows and recommendations for producing content than in LwDITA history, this chapter may feel like "inside baseball" accounts of who did what in the DITA technical committee and the Lightweight DITA subcommittee with the Organization for the Advancement of Structured Information Standards. Nevertheless, I have interacted with many users, observers, and critics who are quick to ask "How come DITA does not have this or that feature?" or "Who came up with this idea in DITA or LwDITA?" This chapter, then, has a goal of reminding readers that the DITA and LwDITA standards are designed, tested, and revised over years by working groups comprised of mostly volunteers who follow strict guidelines and protocols. That makes the committees human and fallible, but also open to feedback and input on their constant process of revision and improvement.

The official definition of Lightweight DITA, which is included in the OASIS committee note/white paper titled *Lightweight DITA: An Introduction* that I co-edited with Kris Eberlein and Alan Houser, is as follows:

> Lightweight DITA (LwDITA) is a simplified version of the Darwin Information Typing Architecture (DITA). In comparison to DITA 1.3, LwDITA has a smaller element type and attribute set, stricter content models, and a reduced feature set. LwDITA also defines mappings between XML, HTML5, and Markdown, enabling authoring, collaboration, and publishing across different markup languages.
>
> (Evia et al., 2018, p. 5)

For readers already familiar with the DITA standard, a concise version would say that LwDITA is "like DITA but with fewer XML tags." A publishing workflow based on LwDITA can benefit from many of the popular content reuse and structuring mechanisms available in DITA, but without the long catalog of element structures (or pigeonholes, as Chapter 2 described them) that has given the DITA standard a reputation for being overwhelming to authors – particularly those who are new to structured authoring.

The development of LwDITA is a process of evolution. The concept of evolution, and particularly themes related to Darwin's Theory of Evolution, has been a component of DITA terminology since its origins at IBM. The *D* for *Darwin* is the first letter in the standard's acronym, and some additional Darwinian terms appear in the *Technical Communication* article from 2001 that introduced DITA to the world outside IBM. When describing the process of topic specialization, for example, Michael Priestley and his co-authors noted in that article that "specialization also lets you manage groups of related types by making changes to their common ancestor, instead of maintaining each instance separately" (Priestley et al., 2001, p. 358)

In the world of scientific and technical communication, DITA and structured authoring are not alone in using concepts of evolution to describe genre change. Carolyn Miller noted that evolution is not seen "as a mere metaphor or handy analogy for the process of genre change but as a set of ideas that has been central to thinking about cultural change as about biological change" (Miller, 2015, pp. 156–157). In using terminology from evolution to describe how genres change (or *evolve*) in society, Miller does not "want to be understood as suggesting that our understanding of cultural change must borrow from biology. Rather, I'm suggesting that evolution is a model of change more general than either biology or language, one that applies equally but differently to both" (2015, p. 178).

DITA terminology has been rich in metaphors and analogies about evolution since its development. Nevertheless, evolution can also be an appropriate way to describe how the DITA technical committee reacted to society and industry demands and spawned, at least in one of the standard's evolutionary branches, LwDITA. And this mention of "at least one evolutionary branch" is an important one: the OASIS DITA technical committee remains focused on the core evolutionary branch, with DITA 2.0 in development at the time of this writing.

One of the most notorious characteristics of LwDITA in its initial release is that it does not include the document types of concept, task, and reference that many users associate with the Darwin Information Typing Architecture. Looking, for example, at the 17 document types and 440 element types available on the technical content edition of the DITA 1.3 standard, I couldn't stop hearing the voice of John Carroll from the interview I reported on Chapter 2: "All this being said, the manuals didn't work. People didn't read them. Even today, they still have the plastic on them in libraries. Nobody read them." All this being said, and without data from every company that has adopted DITA in the world, how many of those 17 document types and 440 element types still have virtual plastic on them in the DITA specification for technical content? LwDITA aims to simplify the DITA authoring and publishing experience with the minimum number of content components that were useful for the sectors and industries studied by members of the Lightweight DITA subcommittee. This bold decision of decoupling a version of DITA from its popular document types is supported by claims that can be summarized in the following three points:

1. LwDITA **does not have existing DITA users as its primary audience**. Professionals already using DITA to create and architect content most likely learned about the standard in training sessions that emphasized the semantic benefits of the several document and element types in DITA 1.3. These professionals work in environments that depend on the separation of content in concept, task, reference, and other types. These professionals are welcome to try LwDITA as a content-creation alternative; however, they are not the intended audience for the proposed simplified standard. The LwDITA ideal user is someone who already works in HTML or Markdown and could adopt (or not) a simple XML grammar that does not contain hundreds of element types. At one point, Michael Priestley talked about an audience of people who have an aversion to XML or existing DITA workflows. These users can be casual content contributors (e.g., a subject matter expert who authors short topics that a technical author will later integrate into a larger DITA collection) or authors who are not working with DITA XML (e.g., marketing professionals creating intelligent content for multichannel publishing, or even technical writers who prefer to write in HTML or Markdown). Chapter 4 identifies additional user types for the three initial authoring formats of LwDITA.
2. LwDITA **does not have the purpose of replacing DITA XML**. As I write this chapter, the DITA Technical Committee at OASIS is working on the release of DITA 2.0 as a new standard parallel to LwDITA. The evolution of DITA is taking shape after several branches, with LwDITA as one of those possible paths for growth. In conference presentations, we frequently reassure DITA users that the standard, as they know it in its robust XML form, is not going away. Furthermore, LwDITA will maintain its compatibility with future releases of DITA XML, which preserves the simplified proposed standard as both an independent way to structure and publish content and a potential on-ramp for individuals and teams who start with LwDITA and then decide to explore the enhanced capabilities of DITA.
3. LwDITA, like DITA XML, **can be specialized into custom document and element types** based on the needs of specific users. Although it probably will

not be part of a LwDITA user's daily routine, the proposed standard allows document and element type specialization (the *Darwin* part of DITA) for information architects interested in creating custom structures. In Chapter 1, I mentioned that Chef Pedro probably needed a DITA-based content model that allowed authors to specialize a **<task>** into a **<recipe>**. That process of specialization, with some limitations in HDITA and MDITA, is allowed in LwDITA. Chef Pedro, or most likely an information architect or XML professional working for him, can still specialize the LwDITA **<topic>** into a **<recipe>**. Additionally, the Lightweight DITA subcommittee with OASIS is exploring the possibility of releasing a template-based mechanism for specialization that would make the customization of topics and elements more accessible to authors who are not familiar with XML schema or document type definitions.

Before describing the LwDITA topical conventions and tracking how they evolved from DITA 1.3 elements and produced their own offspring in the LwDITA three core authoring formats, the following section looks at the evolution of DITA as documented in the OASIS public email list and meeting minutes archive.

The Slow and Methodical Development of LwDITA

The popular John Godfrey Saxe quote, commonly misattributed to Otto von Bismarck, says that "laws, like sausages, cease to inspire respect in proportion as we know how they are made." Web designer Jeffrey Veen, in his podcast titled *Presentable*, added standards to that list (Veen, 2017). Everybody likes standards, laws, and sausage, said Veen, but nobody wants to know how they are made.

Information development and content management standards, like DITA and LwDITA, can be good examples of that description, as the process behind their releases can be complicated, and the consensus-driven nature of standards development takes time. JoAnn Hackos explained that "standards development is deliberately slow and methodical." According to Hackos:

> The slow pace ensures that representatives from the larger community worldwide have time to review and comment, adding their perspectives and concerns and, as a consequence, improving the standard.
>
> (Hackos, 2016, p. 25)

That sure has been the case with LwDITA as an evolution of DITA XML. Michael Priestley and I are working on the Lightweight DITA technical specification, and we have the goal of having it officially released in 2019. This is a long process of evolution that started in 2012. Actually, the OASIS email list archives mention a DITA "profile for modest needs" that sounds similar to Lightweight DITA on a message sent by Don Day (member of the original DITA development team at IBM), who then chaired the DITA Technical Committee, on April 4, 2011.

> I've been discussing this idea with several vendors and it seems to have traction. In short, some new users (and particularly those who are not tech writers by trade) do not necessarily need to experience the full extent of DITA capability. If we can agree on what a lowered profile of expectation and need is, there are several benefits: 1. Existing tools can provide UI masking of features that can be enabled later on (license upgrade, etc.) 2. New tools can enter the market providing function up to that level, and compete evenly in that space. 3. Users perceive lower cost, lower complexity at the range of use they expect, and can move up as requirements dictate (basically playing to progression of needs and investments in the DITA Maturity Model). Win/win.
>
> (LimitedDitaProfile, 2011)

The limited DITA profile was presented as an on-ramp for DITA users who were casual content contributors and did not need all the standard's features. That message was followed, on March 20, 2012 by the first Lightweight DITA proposal, also known as proposal 13076, presented by Michael Priestley to the OASIS DITA Technical Committee. Priestley introduced the proposal by saying that:

> The goal is to create a lightweight DITA framework that can ease adoption for casual, contributing, or non-technical authors. We want to make both editing and specialization easier for vendors to support by limiting options and choice points.
>
> (Priestley, 2012)

In that initial proposal, which was still depending on XML as its only authoring language, the simplified topic content model included the following elements or topical conventions:

- <**topic**> contains <**title**>, <**shortdesc**> (short description), <**body**>
- <**shortdesc**> contains <**ph**> (phrase) or text (directly written inside the tags)
- <**body**> contains <**section**>
- <**section**> contains <**p**> (paragraph), <**ul**> (unordered list), <**ol**> (ordered list), <**simpletable**>, <**image**>
- <**p**> contains <**ph**>, <**xref**> (cross reference), or text
- <**ph**> contains <**ph**> or text
- <**xref**> contains text

- **<ul>**/**<ol>** contain **<li>** (list item)
- **<li>** contains **<p>**
- **<simpletable>** contains 1 **<sthead>** (simple table header; optional), **<strow>** (simple table row)
- **<sthead>**/**<strow>** contain **<stentry>** (simple table entry or data)
- **<stentry>** contains **<p>**, **<ul>**, **<ol>**
- **<image>** contains **<alt>** (alternate text)
- **<alt>** contains text.

Priestley's proposal emphasized that the lightweight topic only included 16 elements, and that all attributes, with the exception of **@id** on **<topic>**, were optional. The simplified map content model included the following elements:

- **<map>** contains **<title>**, **<topicref>** (topic hyper-reference)
- **<title>** contains **<ph>** or text
- **<ph>** contains **<ph>** or text
- **<topicref>** contains **<topicmeta>** (topic metadata) or a new version of **<topicref>** including **<title>** as option before **<topicmeta>**
- **<topicmeta>** contains **<navtitle>** (navigation title)
- **<navtitle>** contains **<ph>** or text.

Priestley pointed out that the simplified map had 6 elements (5 if the **<topicref>** element was modified to include a title).

After receiving feedback from the DITA Technical Committee, Priestley revised the proposal and, in the summer of 2012, updated the list of topical elements to include 27 XML tags (**<object>**, **<note>**, and elements related to definition lists were among those added to the original proposal). The revised topic type depended on a series of constraint declarations that would give instructions to DITA processors. Priestley's basic topic appears on Figure 3.1.

```
<topic id="mini" domains="(lwdita-c)(no-nesting-c) (no-sections-c)">
<title>Mini topic</title>
<body>
<p>No sections allowed, no nested lists allowed, no conditional processing,
no conref, etc.</p>
</body>
</topic>
```

FIGURE 3.1 Prototype of an early LwDITA topic created by Michael Priestley in the summer of 2012. The values for the domains attribute, in bold, give constraining instructions to processors. In this case, they specify that the topic is Lightweight DITA and not full DITA XML, that it should not allow nested lists, and that it should not allow the inclusion of sections inside the topic. Incidentally, this is the first written instance of the LwDITA (or "lwdita" in this case) acronym for Lightweight DITA.

LwDITA and Information Mapping®: The Merger that Wasn't

A couple of months after he introduced the first LwDITA topic prototype, which he called the "strawman proposal," Michael Priestley made an announcement that surprised more than one DITA user or developer: the Information Mapping® (IM) content types would be available in the LwDITA catalog of content templates. IM, developed by Robert Horn, is a methodology for structuring content that has been used in instructional technology, technical writing, and many other industries since the late 1960s. The Information Mapping website gives the following historical description of the method (and company):

> In 1965, Robert E. Horn initiated the research into and design of the Information Mapping® method, initially developed as both a way of visually presenting information and a method for analyzing information to make it easier to communicate. 40 years later, The Method has been embraced by hundreds of thousands of individuals in 40 countries, standing the test of time and technological evolution.
>
> (The Information Mapping® Method, n.d.)

If that sounds like a commercial, it is because the company behind the method emphasizes its copyright. In 1969, Horn and his co-authors released a report introducing the method as an approach for structuring and organizing training content, which included the following definition:

> Information mapping is a system of principles for identifying, categorizing, and interrelating the information required for learning-reference purposes. The system can be applied to production of books for self-instruction or to the specification of data bases for computer-aided instruction. Most of the research and development work described in this report was concerned with information-mapped books.
>
> (Horn et al., 1969, p. 3)

The Information Mapping website now simply defines it as "a research-based method for writing clear and user focused information, based on the audience's needs and the purpose of the information" (About, n.d.). Like DITA, Information Mapping structures content in specific types or templates. Whereas the traditional topic types associated with DITA XML are concept, task, and reference, Information Mapping's core six information types are principle, process, procedure, concept, fact, and structure.

After years of fielding the question "Is DITA related to Information Mapping?", the Information Mapping company released a white paper, in 2011, titled "Information Mapping® and DITA: Two Worlds, One Solution." The white paper had the objective of explaining "why it does not make sense to move from Information Mapping® to DITA, or vice versa," and it posited that "Information Mapping® and DITA both have their strengths and weaknesses, and combining them may lead to the best results for an organization" (2011, p. 2). The 12-page white paper dedicated some 70 words to describe some "strengths" of DITA (increase in content reuse, reduction in localization costs, and reduction in desktop publishing costs). Eventually, it called for a combination of Information Mapping and DITA for structuring and publishing content. However, many of its claims were based on an *us-before-them* trope, which included sentences like "Before you start your DITA project, train your writers in Information Mapping®," or "Becoming familiar with Information Mapping® is a necessary first step towards a successful DITA implementation" (2011, p. 10). The IM white paper implied that authors had to "learn hundreds of DITA tags and attributes to structure the content correctly. This requires some technical background as well as training and coaching" (2011, p. 8).

Therefore, it was a surprise when Priestley sent a message to the DITA Technical Committee on October 23, 2012 announcing a merger of sorts between DITA and Information Mapping for the Lightweight DITA proposal.

> This builds on the lightweight model being proposed in 13076. I wanted to share my thoughts on how the lightweight model could be used to provide starting points for DITA users. One of the key developments here is the result of ongoing discussions with Information Mapping, who are now at the point of contributing their information type definitions to the DITA TC (technical committee) for inclusion in the lightweight proposal. The IM types correspond to section types in DITA, and so match perfectly with the lightweight model's focus on creating topic types by assembling predefined section types.
>
> (Priestley, 2012a)

Priestley's revised catalog of lightweight topics expanded from the one "strawman" topic and in the revised version included the following:

- Basic topic types
  - Lightweight topic: basic topic with default content models (sections, conditional attributes, list nesting enabled)
  - Superlightweight topic: lightweight topic with constraints applied (no list nesting, no attributes, no sections)
  - Specialization topic: topic specifically designed for defining lightweight specializations
- DITA classic topic types: concept, task, and reference, constrained to lightweight topic model
- Information Mapping topic types: common topic types made up of IM section types (Priestley, 2012a).

The LwDITA topic type (still a prototype at this stage) was moving away from the 27 XML tags promised in the summer of 2012. Embracing the six content types of Information Mapping, the Lightweight DITA prototype wrapped up 2012 with a total of 12 potential content types and the many tags or generic conventions associated with them.

Michael Priestley reiterated this expanded collection of lightweight topics at a presentation during the DITA North America/Content Management Solutions in Providence, Rhode Island. At that session on April 16, 2013 Priestley's slides for the talk "Lightweight DITA: A preview of the DITA 1.3 feature" included the 12 content types and quietly foretold the merger of content types from Information Mapping and DITA in LwDITA.

And then, the conversation about an Information Mapping and DITA merger ended, and in an updated version of that presentation, Priestley did not include any mention of Information Mapping and its trademarked content types (Priestley, 2013a). Instead, the conversation moved to the idea of separating LwDITA from the DITA standard. The standard was being split into three different versions for its 1.3 release: base, technical content, and all-inclusive, which were called "packages" or "packaging" in discussions before their official release. The recorded minutes of the DITA Technical Committee call held on October 8, 2013 include the following exchange between Priestley (MP) and Nancy Harrison (NH), from Infobridge Solutions, who is currently the Technical Committee's secretary:

MP: So when people say "DITA is too complex," we want to be able to reply, "which DITA?" We have a base, which is fairly simple, and others, which have more functionality.

NH: I thought the answer to that question was "look at lightweight DITA."

MP: Actually, there need to be 2 different answers to that question. One is Lightweight DITA, one is packaging (DITA Technical Committee, 2013).

Besides the idea of releasing LwDITA as a standard separate from the three versions of DITA 1.3, Priestley was also looking at the possibility of breaking DITA's dependence on XML as its sole language.

LwDITA Expands Beyond XML

The proposal for a lightweight version of the DITA standard crossed an important border in the spring of 2014. In a blog post titled "Overview of Lightweight DITA (XDITA and HDITA)," Michael Priestley introduced an idea to liberate the DITA standard from its longstanding dependence on the Extensible Markup Language (XML). The revised proposal of April 2014 had the goal "to align a lightweight DITA profile in XML with an equivalent markup specification based on HTML5" (Priestley, 2014). Feedback from audiences to conference presentations about LwDITA, and comments from members of the DITA Technical Committee, introduced potential applications for the simplified standard outside of the traditional DITA domain of technical documentation. Some of those applications were based around the needs of authors (e.g., creating marketing content, writing pharmaceutical information, or structuring books for a publishing house) who had no experience with XML. At the same time, HTML5 had been released with enhanced semantic tags and capabilities for extended attributes that could replicate fundamental structuring and publishing features of DITA XML.

According to Priestley, possible solutions would include 1) simplifying XML models, "as seen with many of the lightweight DITA tools that have come to market over the last few years," or 2) rebasing on an HTML5 model, "as seen with O'Reilly and more recently Pearson" (2014). Priestley proposed a combination of those solutions:

> This proposal suggests a third way – defining both a lightweight XML model based on DITA that can be used for validated authoring and complex publishing chains, and a lightweight HTML5 model that can be used for either authoring or display.
>
> (Priestley, 2014)

These authoring models, which Priestley named XDITA (based on XML) and HDITA (based on HTML5), were "designed for full compatibility with each other as well as conformance with the OASIS DITA and W3C HTML5 standards" (Priestley, 2014). For a generic topic type, "HTML5 and DITA are now close enough to achieve a reasonable and semantic mapping with the application of a few simple constraints" (Priestley, 2014). The XDITA and HDITA introductory blog post, however, still included specialized structural types for concept, task, and reference, which relied on HTML5 custom data attributes.

Instead of summarizing Priestley's blog post, I will focus here on how this proposal made the basic LwDITA topic from the summer of 2012 evolve into two branches based on its authoring language: XDITA for XML and HDITA for HTML5. Table 3.1 reproduces the simple topic/article that Priestley included in that introductory blog post:

Priestley's blog post from 2014 still included specializations for concept, task, and reference in XDITA (the XML-based version of LwDITA). In HDITA (the HTML5-based version of LwDITA), those specialized elements were "generic article or section elements with a custom attribute that uses a simplified form of the DITA class syntax." Table 3.2 reproduces the table of specialized structural elements that enabled the representation of concept, task, and reference in XDITA and HDITA.

The XDITA/HDITA proposal added two elements to the LwDITA catalog (**<address>** and **<aside>**). However, Priestley did not offer a count of total elements and instead focused on the expansion capabilities of including HTML5 as an authoring format for DITA-equivalent topics.

TABLE 3.1 Sample LwDITA topic, from Michael Priestley's blog post "Overview of Lightweight DITA (XDITA and HDITA)." The XDITA topic on the left column includes elements from the revised LwDITA proposal presented to the DITA Technical Committee in 2012. The HDITA version on the right column replicates those conventions with HTML5 tags.

XDITA	*HDITA*
<topic>	<article>
<title>The point of it all</title>	<h1>The point of it all</h1>
<shortdesc>I can sum it up here</shortdesc>	<p>I can sum it up here</p>
<body>	<p>I can say some more stuff</p>
<p>I can say some more stuff</p>	<section>
<section>	<h2>Stuff</h2>
<title>Stuff</title>	<p>And so on</p>
<p>And so on</p>	<ul>
<ul>	<li><p>This</p></li>
<li><p>This</p></li>	<li><p>Is</p></li>
<li><p>Is</p></li>	<li><p>A List</p></li>
<li><p>A List</p></li>	</ul>
</ul>	<section>
<section>	<h2>And more stuff</h2>
<title>And more stuff</title>	<p>With its own explanation</p>
<p>With its own explanation</p>	<dl>
<dl>	<dt><p>This</p></dt>
<dlentry>	<dd><p>Is explained</p></dd>
<dt><p>This</p></dt>	<dt><p>This</p></dt>
<dd><p>Is explained</p></dd>	<dd><p>Is also explained</p></dd>
</dlentry>	</dl>
<dlentry>	</section>
<dt><p>This</p></dt>	</topic>
<dd><p>Is also explained</p></dd>	
</dlentry>	
</dl>	
</section>	
</body>	
</topic>	

In the spring of 2014, I was teaching a section of the course ENGL 3814: *Creating User Documentation* at Virginia Tech. That course included a few modules on DITA, and some of my students who were new to XML had previous experience with HTML. We discussed in class the possibility of using an expanded HTML grammar as a DITA replacement. Therefore, Priestley's proposal immediately caught my attention. As soon as I read the blog post introducing XDITA and HDITA, I implemented Priestley's ideas on a couple of sample topics that I shared with my students. After that, I decided to contact Priestley and invite him to collaborate on a research project about the XDITA

TABLE 3.2 Specialized structural elements in XDITA and their equivalents in HDITA, which use custom data attributes to modify elements in HTML5. Note that this proposal included the addition of HTML5 tags (<address> and <aside>) in XDITA to have them available in both authoring formats.

XDITA	*HDITA*
<concept>	<article data-hd-class="concept">
<task>	<article data-hd-class="task">
<reference>	<article data-hd-class="reference">
<example>	<section data-hd-class="topic/example">
<context>	<section data-hd-class="task/context">
<prereq>	<section data-hd-class="task/prereq">
<steps-informal>	<section data-hd-class="task/ steps-informal">
<postreq>	<section data-hd-class="task/postreq">
<refsyn>	<section data-hd-class="reference/refsyn">
<address> (from section)	<address>
<aside> (from section)	<aside>

and HDITA author perspective: As a college professor, I had access to a population of novice content creators who were familiar with HTML but did not know XML. What could happen if we introduced my students to a DITA-like environment without starting with XML?

I had not interacted with Priestley before, although we followed each other on Twitter based on common friends and our shared interest on DITA, and one of my students conducting a research study had interviewed him in 2012 (and I incorporated some of his comments into my syllabus). We scheduled a phone call on April 30, 2014 that started our ongoing collaboration, but that also introduced a third authoring format for the proposed LwDITA standard.

Does DITA Need Tags?

The second half of 2014 marked the real genesis of the LwDITA standard. Although the concept of a simplified version of DITA XML had been around since 2011, before the spring of 2014 it all had been pretty much a side project of Michael Priestley, one of DITA's founding fathers, who still had a full-time position at IBM doing non-DITA work. Priestley and I started a research project that introduced Virginia Tech students to a DITA-like authoring and publishing environment without XML. Our work with the preliminary HDITA format was eventually published as the article "Structured Authoring without XML: Evaluating Lightweight DITA for Technical Documentation" in the journal *Technical Communication* (Evia & Priestley, 2016). In May of 2014, Priestley presented the XDITA/HDITA proposal in a webinar titled "Does DITA Need XML?" That month, he also submitted a formal proposal to the DITA Technical

Committee asking for the creation of a dedicated Lightweight DITA subcommittee. However, as audiences and study participants were exposed to the possibility of creating DITA content without XML, many were replying with the same question: if we can use HTML5 to represent DITA topics and elements, can we use Markdown as well?

Markdown is a "text-to-HTML conversion tool for web writers. Markdown allows you to write using an easy-to-read, easy-to-write plain text format, then convert it to structurally valid XHTML (or HTML)" (Gruber, 2004). The CommonMark initiative, which aims to propose a Markdown standard, adds that it is a "plain text format for writing structured documents, based on formatting conventions from email and usenet" (CommonMark, n.d.).

My initial conversation with Priestley from April of 2014 started on the topic of evaluating the effectiveness of HDITA as a non-XML introduction to the structuring and publishing capabilities of the DITA standard. We made a plan for a research study and then the conversation moved to the possibility of using Markdown as an authoring language in LwDITA topics. Priestley had been working with a group from the IBM Cloud project (then called Bluemix), which used Markdown for its documentation and needed to implement DITA-like reuse and transclusion features. In my introductory technical writing courses, my students were using Markdown as a shorthand form for web writing. I told him that I would develop some sample topics in HDITA and, a term we created at that moment, "MarkDITA" – a Markdown-based authoring format of LwDITA.

A few days after my initial call with Priestley, the topic of including Markdown as a component of the LwDITA proposal appeared in the minutes of the DITA Technical Committee call from May 10, 2014. Priestley is quoted saying: "In IBM, some folks hate DITA, and they don't even want to use (Microsoft) Word, but (prefer) simple web forms or Markdown syntax." He added that including Markdown in Lightweight DITA could open up "opportunities in both directions, (as it) provides (an) integration point against (the) whole corporate content spectrum" (DITA Technical Committee, 2014).

I scheduled a follow-up call with Priestley, who invited Jenifer Schlotfeldt – Senior Content Strategist at IBM who was working on the Bluemix documentation project. I shared with them a small collection of HDITA sample topics that incorporated some of the elements from Priestley's blog post but added the possibility of content reuse and single-sourcing with new HTML5 custom data attributes. My samples included a hastily assembled "MarkDITA" topic prototype that used a combination of HDITA tags with Markdown syntax to recreate a DITA task (Figure 3.2). After that, the conversation focused entirely on the "MarkDITA" prototype, which emphasized that there was an actual need for a Markdown-based LwDITA authoring format.

Priestley and I continued collecting data for our HDITA authoring research project. We decided to move the conversations about the Markdown-based

```
# How to have an academic summer

<section data-hd-class="task/context">
Be sure to do this only during the summer.
</section>

<section data-hd-class="task/prereq">
- Be done with the spring semester
- Check the calendar
</section>

<section data-hd-class="task/steps-informal">
1. Manage your time
2. Write a lot
3. Have some fun
</section>
```

FIGURE 3.2 Early "MarkDITA" topic prototype that I shared with Michael Priestley and Jenifer Schlotfeldt in May of 2014. The topic includes some HDITA snippets taken from Priestley's introductory blog post, which created a sense of structure for generic moves in the Markdown syntax.

version of LwDITA, now renamed MDITA, to the official DITA Technical Committee.

The Lightweight DITA Subcommittee

On May 27, 2014 Michael Priestley submitted the following proposal to the DITA Technical Committee asking for the creation of a dedicated Lightweight DITA subcommittee with OASIS:

Statement of purpose: To develop a specification for a lightweight DITA architecture that can ease implementation by vendors and adoption by users. The architecture will provide:

- Easy out of the box authoring for common topic types
- Out of the box mappings and specifications for authoring these topic types in other formats, such as HTML5 or markdown
- Easy assembly of new specializations from existing section types
- Easy creation of new specializations by generation from a topic type designed for specifying specializations
- Deliverables:
  - Analysis of lightweight DITA related personas, scenarios, and requirements
  - Lightweight authoring profiles for topic, concept, task, reference, potentially others
  - Lightweight specialization architecture

- Specialization authoring format
- Analysis of lightweight DITA implementation options in other formats, including HTML5 and markdown
- Implementations of lightweight DITA that allow for roundtripping with constrained versions of other formats (Priestley, 2014a).

The subcommittee was approved by the OASIS leadership on July 22, 2014 and Priestley was appointed as chair. The Lightweight DITA subcommittee had its first teleconference call on September 15, 2014. The recorded minutes show that the following individuals were in attendance: Mark Giffin, Tim Grantham, Stan Doherty, Kris Eberlein, Tom Comerford, Chris Nitchie, Mark Poston, Adrian Warman, Michael Priestley, Don Day, and Joe Pairman. John Hunt and Amber Swope joined the committee shortly after the first meeting. My daughter Sofia was born on September 12, 2014 and I couldn't join the subcommittee in time for its call.

Some of the early conversations during the Lightweight DITA subcommittee calls included selecting the right name for the proposed standard. Priestley questioned if including DITA in the name would be "a help or a hindrance for adoption" (Priestley, 2014b). Some alternatives briefly considered were acronyms like CAKE (Content Authoring for the Knowledge Ecosystem), PAF (Portable Authoring Framework), XFAS (Cross-format Authoring Specification), or a one-word evocative name, like Helium, Portable, Adapt, or Evolve. During the spring of 2015, some members of the subcommittee seriously considered the DITA-related name of FINCH (Fully Intelligent New Content Hierarchy). However, the subcommittee finally decided to stay with Lightweight DITA, stylized in an acronym as LwDITA. The "lightweight" adjective in the proposed standard's name does not imply a direct equivalency to lightweight markup languages. As Priestley's original proposal from on March 20, 2012 established, that adjective was applied to the framework that presented LwDITA as a lighter option compared to full DITA XML. Furthermore, there is no markup language called Lightweight DITA, as the markup languages included in this framework are called XDITA, HDITA, and MDITA.

Other lines of discussion in the early months of the subcommittee focused on the authoring formats to include in an initial release of the LwDITA standard. XDITA and HDITA were confirmed. MDITA was also considered a requirement. The subcommittee considered mappings to AsciiDoc, reStructuredText, EPUB3, Microsoft Word, and JSON. In April 2015, Priestley and I, along with metadata expert Lu Ai (former project manager at IBM and currently with Pearson) gave a presentation titled "Does DITA Need Tags?" at the DITA North America/CMS conference in Chicago, IL. Priestley opened with a general introduction to LwDITA and XDITA, I followed with some HDITA examples and usage scenarios, and Ai showed a preliminary approach for creating DITA-like content in JSON. However, the subcommittee did not find a champion to continue the work on JSON, and the proposed standard continued with three initial authoring formats: XDITA, HDITA, and MDITA. Some members of the subcommittee focused on researching the compatibility and exchange among the three authoring formats and the DITA 1.3 standard. How could content types created in XML, HTML5, and Markdown really speak the same language and represent established DITA conventions and structures?

A major task with the subcommittee was the creation of working groups in charge of developing user personas and usage scenarios for the LwDITA authoring formats. The groups were organized around the categories of learning and training, machine industries, software development, and marketing. Each group had the charge of developing profiles and establishing the essential DITA content and element types required for each industry or sector represented.

The subcommittee's work was also influenced by the independent release of an open source tool that allowed the processing of Markdown files as DITA topics. The Markdown DITA plugin for the DITA Open Toolkit[1], developed by the Finland-based programmer Jarno Elovirta, was released on February 2015 and made possible some of the ideas that Priestley and I, and then the whole subcommittee, had been proposing for integrating Markdown into DITA publishing workflows. Elovirta, who is the lead developer of the DITA Open Toolkit, generously contributed many open source hours to incorporating changes and suggestions that Priestley and I requested for our demos and conference presentations. And that became our *modus operandi*: we would boast about the potential benefits of LwDITA in conferences and webinars, developers and managers would show interest and ask for a demo, we requested plugin updates from Elovirta and offered a new demo . . . all increasing expectation about the proposed standard but working to the detriment of the subcommittee's actual purpose of developing the technical specification for an open standard and not software applications or industry-specific workflows.

In October 2016, Kris Eberlein (chair of the DITA Technical Committee) requested a formal deliverable from the subcommittee: a committee note/white paper that would work as a proposal for the LwDITA standard. To focus on this deliverable while also keeping an eye on future spec development, the subcommittee appointed me as its co-chair and also appointed Keith Schengili-Roberts as secretary. The committee note, titled "Lightweight DITA: An Introduction," was edited by me, Eberlein, and Alan Houser, former president of the Society for Technical Communication, who joined the LwDITA subcommittee in 2017.

LwDITA Topical Conventions

After a few years of preparing prototypes and drafts, receiving audience feedback and managing anticipation, LwDITA started 2017 with the official format that would be documented on the first formal deliverable of the Lightweight DITA subcommittee at OASIS. The proposed standard focused on only two content types for its initial release: topic and map. The LwDITA topic and map can be represented, with some limitations and substitutions, in three authoring formats: XDITA (based on a simplified grammar of DITA XML), HDITA (based on HTML5), and MDITA (based on Markdown). Topics and maps authored in XDITA are fully compatible with content created according to the DITA 1.3 standard. Additionally, the XDITA and HDITA content models were designed to be functionally equivalent to each other, while MDITA was introduced as a compatible subset.

Following reports from its working groups, which included a collection of personas and usage scenarios across diverse sectors and industries, the Lightweight DITA subcommittee at OASIS determined that a generic topic could represent most content structures needed across potential implementations. Additionally, the reports emphasized the need for components that would allow the inclusion of multimedia content in LwDITA topics. The DITA 1.3 technical specification, released in 2015, did not include element types to represent audio and video content natively in DITA tags (vendors and users developed their own solutions with the **<object>** tag or with HTML5 code snippets). Thus, although LwDITA had the primary objective of reducing the number of content components included in the DITA standard, the subcommittee proposed 9 new components to represent multimedia content to replicate common structures available in HTML5.

The committee note *Lightweight DITA: An Introduction* explains that the LwDITA topic includes a subset of conventions or components (the pigeonhole structures mentioned in Chapter 2) that were "carefully chosen to include only the most basic constructions that are needed to structure information effectively." To select those components, the subcommittee "considered the needs of diverse industries and sectors (including education, engineering, healthcare, and marketing)" (Evia et al., 2018, p. 10).

In DITA, each content *component* corresponds to an *element* in XML (e.g., a paragraph is a **<p>** and a short description is a **<shortdesc>**). In LwDITA, however, XML is not the only authoring language; therefore, these components should not be seen exclusively as XML elements. Some components are self-explanatory, but others require a definition. I have added a simple definition, sometimes redundant, to each generic convention, which I adapted from the LwDITA technical specification.

Basic Topic Components

- **Topic**: a coherent unit of content that conveys information.
- **Title**: a label that connotes the purpose of the content associated with it.
- **Short description**: the purpose or main point of a topic.
- **Body**: a container for the main content of a topic.

Body Components

- **Alternate text**: a textual description of an image that can be read or displayed in place of the image. This is commonly used to create text alternatives for readers or systems that cannot view the original image.
- **Definition list**: a list of terms and corresponding definitions.
- **Definition list entry**: an entry groups a term and its definition.
- **Definition term**: the text that is defined in a list entry.
- **Definition value**: text that provides the description for a term in a list entry.
- **Description**: a statement that describes or contains additional information about an object.
- **Figure**: a container for a variety of objects, including artwork, images, code samples, equations, and tables.
- **Footnote**: text that annotates content with notes that are inappropriate for inline inclusion. It is also used to indicate the source for facts or other material used in content.
- **Image**: a link to a graphic to be included in the content.
- **List item**: a single entry in an ordered or unordered list.
- **Ordered list**: a series of items sorted by sequence or order of importance.
- **Note**: information that expands on or calls attention to a particular point.
- **Paragraph**: a unit of text that expresses a single main idea.
- **Phrase**: a piece of text that is associated with a specific purpose.
- **Preformatted text**: content that includes line breaks and spaces that should be preserved when rendered.
- **Section**: an organizational division within a topic. It can have an optional title.
- **Unordered list**: a series of items in which the order is not significant.
- **Cross reference**: a labeled link to a piece of information.

Table Components

- **Table**: a collection of rows and entries to present organized content.
- **Table header**: an optional single heading row at the beginning of a table.
- **Table row**: a single row within a table.
- **Table entry**: a single cell within a table.

Highlighting Components (available in both topic and map)

- **Bold**, which is used to draw a reader's attention to a phrase without otherwise adding meaning to the content.
- **Italics**, which is a way to emphasize key points in a printed text or, when quoting a speaker, a way to show which words the speaker stressed.
- **Subscript**, which is a letter, number, or figure that is printed lower than the line. It is frequently used in chemical and mathematical formulas.

- **Superscript**, which is a letter, number, or figure that is printed above than the line. It is frequently used in chemical and mathematical formulas; it also is used for footnotes.
- **Underline**, also called an underscore, which is a more or less horizontal line immediately below a portion of writing.

Metadata Components

- **Prolog**: contains information about a file, for example, author information or subject category. This information might be entered by an author or maintained by an application.
- **Data**: a generic component for metadata.

Map Components

- **Map**: a component that describes the relationships among a set of resources, such as LwDITA topics.
- **Data**: a generic component for metadata.
- **Navigation title**: provides an alternate title for a topic that becomes a part of navigation resources or tables of contents in deliverables.
- **Key definition**: defines a variable at the map level.
- **Link text**: provides a label for a link or resource.
- **Phrase**: a piece of text that is associated with a specific purpose.
- **Topic metadata**: defines the metadata that applies to a topic when it appears in a map.
- **Topic reference**: identifies and links to a topic or external content source.

Multimedia Components

- **Audio**: a link to sound to be included in the content.
- **Autoplay**: determines if a multimedia component should play automatically on a deliverable.
- **Controls**: enables user interfaces for video playback and volume in web-aimed transformations.
- **Loop**: determines if a multimedia component should play constantly.
- **Muted**: determines if a multimedia component should have audio by default or not.
- **Poster**: a link to an image or static video frame.
- **Source**: a link to media resources of audio or video content.
- **Track**: a link to time-based text data relevant to audio or video content.
- **Video**: a link to an audiovisual product to be included in the content.

Does this mean that authors who want to give LwDITA a try have to memorize and use all those content components? Not at all. Sometimes a basic topic with a title and a couple of paragraphs is all a content situation requires. After teaching and researching how to create intelligent content with DITA for more than a decade, I have seen how the majority of my students can adapt the generic DITA topic to a variety of information structures and projects. Even when concept, task, reference, and the other document types from the DITA 1.3 specification are available for more rigorous structure, the generic topic can be powerful for users trained to *think* about structured content before writing.

In separate conversations with colleagues in academia (including Bill Hart-Davidson from Michigan State University) and industry (like Radu Coravu, from the Romania-based Syncro Soft), we have had unisonous affirmations of "structure starts in your head." For a specific type of user, the structure of a simple topic can be in their head as they go through the tasks related to the creation of intelligent. The LwDITA topic, even without specialization, can be all that these users need to structure and publish information. That generic LwDITA topic can also accommodate enough components and attributes to create content that sticks to the requirements of "modular, structured, reusable, format free, and semantically rich and, as a consequence, discoverable, reconfigurable, and adaptable" presented by Rockley et al. (2015, p. 1). For any case that requires stricter structured models, the DITA standard will be there as an alternative or a next-level solution. Additionally, the Lightweight DITA subcommittee will continue working on new releases of the proposed standard, which can include more content types based on user feedback and interest.

The LwDITA topic is also a versatile content unit that can be created in more than one markup language. The combination of XML, HTML5, and Markdown in the initial LwDITA authoring formats enhances the diversity of authors in a DITA-like environment, but it also represents challenges for compatibility and equivalency of models and structures. The next chapter focuses on the features and limitations of XDITA, HDITA, and MDITA – the initial LwDITA authoring formats.

Note

1 https://github.com/jelovirt/org.lwdita

References

About. (n.d.). Retrieved from https://www.informationmapping.com/en/information-mapping

CommonMark. (n.d.). CommonMark. Retrieved from http://commonmark.org/

DITA Technical Committee. (2013, October 8). October 8, 2013 Phone meeting. Archived at https://markmail.org/message/rzexlutrvecucxty

DITA Technical Committee. (2014, May 10). May 10, 2014 Phone meeting. Archived at https://markmail.org/message/zanoxhojqycwbbkn

Evia, C., & Priestley, M. (2016). Structured Authoring without XML: Evaluating Lightweight DITA for Technical Documentation. *Technical Communication*, 63(1), 23–37.

Evia, C., Eberlein, K., & Houser, A. (Eds.) (2018). *Lightweight DITA: An introduction.* Version 1.0. OASIS.

Gruber, J. (2004, December 17). *Markdown.* Retrieved from https://daringfireball.net/projects/markdown/

Hackos, J. T. (2016). International standards for information development and content management. *IEEE Transactions on Professional Communication*, 59(1), 24–36.

Horn, R.E. et al. (1969). *Information mapping for learning and reference.* United States Air Force.

Information Mapping. (2011). Information Mapping® and DITA: Two worlds, one solution [White paper]. Retrieved from http://www.writec.com/Media_public/WP-dita-white-paper.pdf

LimitedDitaProfile. (2011, April 4). In OASIS DITA Wiki. Retrieved from https://wiki.oasis-open.org/dita/LimitedDitaProfile

Miller, C. R. (2015). Genre change and evolution. In N. Artemeva & A. Freedman (Eds.), *Genre studies around the globe: Beyond the three traditions* (pp. 154–185). Lexington, KY: Trafford.

Priestley, M. (2012, March 20). Lightweight DITA proposal - 13076. Message archived at https://markmail.org/message/rydwna45z4yln7xe

Priestley, M. (2012a, October 23). DITA starter sets proposal – 13051. Message archived at https://markmail.org/message/lpmjxf5zigre2qf5

Priestley, M. (2013, April 16). Lightweight DITA: A preview of the DITA 1.3 feature. Paper presented at the *Content Management Strategies/DITA North America Conference*. Providence, RI.

Priestley, M. (2013a, December 10). A lightweight DITA update. Retrieved from https://www.slideshare.net/mpriestley/a-lightweight-dita-update

Priestley, M. (2014, April 11). Overview of Lightweight DITA (XDITA and HDITA). Retrieved from http://dita-archive.xml.org/blog/overview-of-lightweight-dita-xdita-and-hdita

Priestley, M. (2014a, May 27). Proposal for Lightweight DITA subcommittee. Message archived at https://markmail.org/message/cutgxe627wodz2ca

Priestley, M. (2014b, September 15). Strawman deliverables list. Message archived at https://markmail.org/message/jjb6z2n5dkgia2bd

Priestley, M., Hargis, G., & Carpenter, S. (2001). DITA: An XML-based technical documentation authoring and publishing architecture. *Technical Communication*, 48(3), 352–367.

Priestley, M., Evia, C., & Ai, L. (2015, April 20). Does DITA need tags? Paper presented at the *Content Management Strategies/DITA North America Conference*. Chicago, IL.

Rockley, A., Cooper, C., & Abel, S. (2015). *Intelligent Content: A Primer*. Laguna Hills, CA: XML Press.

The Information Mapping® Method. (n.d.). Retrieved from https://www.informationmapping.com/en/?option=com_content&view=article&id=50&Itemid=400

Veen, J. (Host). (2017, August 8). *Everything you know about web design changed last march* [Audio podcast]. Retrieved from https://www.relay.fm/presentable/28

4

THE LwDITA INITIAL AUTHORING FORMATS

In most of our conference presentations and webinars about LwDITA, Michael Priestley and I have described the authoring formats of this proposed content standard as ice cream flavors. The ice cream flavors analogy indicates the variety of offerings from LwDITA for authors, who no longer have to depend on XML structures to create topics of information that can be transformed into intelligent content and multichannel deliverables for users.

Even before we started using the term "authoring formats" (which came from Eliot Kimber – the ultimate expert on XML for technical communication and a vital member of the DITA Technical Committee), in the Lightweight DITA subcommittee the analogy of flavors drove the development of mappings to represent DITA components in diverse markup languages. The subcommittee evaluated the possibility of presenting several ways to represent the most useful DITA components for broader categories of authors. A simplified version of DITA XML (XDITA) was the original LwDITA flavor and, for a few months after Priestley proposed this new standard, the only one.

The flavors mapping DITA components to HTML5 and Markdown (HDITA and MDITA, respectively) followed, but the committee also considered mappings to JSON, AsciiDoc, reStructuredText, and even Microsoft Word. The three authoring formats, or flavors, included in the initial release of LwDITA are not definitive and could expand to include additional lightweight markup languages based on audience feedback and interest from current or future members of the subcommittee. LwDITA is a work in progress. Please note that details might change between this writing and the actual release of the Lightweight DITA standard.

The ice cream analogy also implies that authoring content is the fun part of a LwDITA-based publishing workflow. Students in Professional and Technical Writing courses from the Virginia Tech Department of English have fun creating content using the LwDITA flavors. Even before LwDITA existed, when my courses were based on full DITA XML, authoring was the "easy" part.

Which leads us to an important distinction in DITA (or LwDITA)-based workflows. In a 2015 teaching case based on the work I did with some colleagues for the course ENGL 3814: *Creating User Documentation*, we mentioned that whereas "basic XML syntax and tags are relatively easy to teach and learn, the automation of deliverables via XSLT and the DITA Open Toolkit is much more complicated" (Evia et al. p. 329). The same can be said about LwDITA work: creating content using the available authoring flavors is easy and even fun. However, in contrast to desktop-publishing workflows, automating and formatting deliverables (topics that I will cover in future chapters) are not necessarily ice cream parties, but those are not routine tasks for most content authors.

In this chapter, I give an overview of each of the three LwDITA flavors (XDITA, HDITA, and MDITA). I provide background information and identify the intended audiences for the three initial authoring formats of the LwDITA proposed standard. Then, I emphasize an important rule that affects some common content components in XDITA and HDITA. Lastly, I discuss the tools support available, and in progress, for authors who want to create and structure content with LwDITA.

XDITA

In March of 2012, when Michael Priestley officially proposed the development of a "lightweight framework for representing DITA topics," it was a given that Lightweight DITA would be based on XML. After all, XML-based DITA had been quite successful at IBM since the late 1990s and then became an internationally-adopted standard for structuring and publishing content in 2005. Priestley's original proposal responded to complaints about the "many tags" included in the standard, but a non-XML version of DITA was not yet a part of those early conversations. Two years after that initial proposal, Priestley started working on the idea of an HTML5-based version of the lightweight framework for representing DITA topics; however, LwDITA does not hide its origins in the XML language.

Michael Priestley created the acronym XDITA in 2014, and until then all Lightweight DITA prototypes resembled what we now know as XDITA. It was not until Priestley's blog post of April 2014 that Lightweight DITA became an umbrella term for different authoring formats – initially XML and HTML5, and then Markdown.

XDITA is similar to DITA XML by design. At its core, XDITA is a simplified version of DITA, with a limited set of elements (tags) and options but similar capabilities for content structure, reuse, and publication. Content structured with XDITA is also compatible with DITA; i.e., all XDITA topical components share syntax conventions with DITA, and collections of DITA topics can include XDITA files.

Intended Audiences for XDITA

Undeniably, DITA XML has an audience that has made the standard a very popular approach for structuring information. XDITA opens structured authoring and automated publishing workflows to a greater number of organizations. XDITA targets authors who are probably not DITA experts but could benefit from the structuring and publishing mechanism of a DITA-like workflow. Some current DITA users may find XDITA to be appropriate, but the XDITA authoring format of LwDITA is primarily aimed at content creators who either do not know about DITA or perceive the standard as too robust for their information needs. In sum, XDITA was designed for users who could benefit from a DITA-like experience for content creation and publication, but who do not need (or want) the full power of DITA.

When we were designing the XDITA content and collection components, the Lightweight DITA subcommittee at OASIS developed user personas and scenarios based on the following intended audiences:

- Information developers who use an XML editor but want a smaller set of elements and attributes (compared to DITA) with which to work
- Departments who want to reduce the cost of developing and maintaining style sheets
- Authors who want their XML content to be subsumed by a content set based on HTML5 or Markdown
- Technical writers with some XML experience
- Current XML (or DITA) users
- Structure purists
- Adventurous novice content creators.

HDITA

HDITA is the authoring format of LwDITA that uses HTML5 to structure information. At its core, HDITA uses some HTML5 elements and attributes (particularly custom data attributes) to reproduce some of the content structuring, reuse, and publishing capabilities of DITA without depending on XML.

In the committee note *Lightweight DITA: An Introduction* we point out that the "XDITA and HDITA content models are designed to be functionally equivalent to each other" (Evia et al., 2018, p. 9). As a result, every content component available in XDITA has a counterpart in HDITA. DITA and XDITA topic collections can include HDITA topics, and vice versa.

Because the HDITA content components represent a subset of all the available elements in the HTML5 standard[1], not all tags that are valid HTML5 are allowed in HDITA (e.g., there's no **<h3>** element to express a level-three heading in HDITA, although it exists in the HTML5 standard). That means that including an HTML5 element that is not allowed in HDITA, like **<aside>** or **<details>**, would produce a validation error in LwDITA-aware tools. One of the greater challenges to the Lightweight DITA subcommittee, as it develops the LwDITA technical specification, is to define how LwDITA tools should handle the presence of non-LwDITA HTML5 tags.

Intended Audiences for HDITA

Over the years, since Michael Priestley developed the original idea for HDITA in 2014, the Lightweight DITA subcommittee at OASIS has identified the following potential users for an HTML5-based version of the proposed standard:

- Marketing writers who want to contribute to DITA-based product documentation without using an XML editor
- Software developers who want to contribute to documentation using HTML-authoring tools
- Teachers and trainers who want to create course content for a web site or learning management system (LMS)
- Bloggers and content strategists who want to be able to create and edit content using mobile devices
- Authors who want to write simple content for the web that does not require a transformation process
- Non-English-speaking content creators who are comfortable with HTML5 semantic elements.

MDITA

In Chapter 1 I briefly introduced MDITA, the LwDITA authoring format based on Markdown, and its two content-development profiles – core and extended. In the OASIS publication *Lightweight DITA: An Introduction*, we define the MDITA core and extended profiles as follows:

> In its core profile, MDITA aligns with the GitHub Flavored Markdown specification. In its extended profile, MDITA can incorporate YAML front matter headers and HDITA elements and attributes to overcome Markdown limitations as a language for authoring structured and reusable content.
>
> (Evia et al, 2018, p.9)

Because the MDITA components represent a subset of the GitHub Flavored Markdown (GFM) syntax[2], not all moves that are valid in GFM or another Markdown flavor are allowed in MDITA extended profile (e.g., there's no ### syntax to express a level-three heading in MDITA extended profile, although it exists in most Markdown flavors). That means that including a Markdown component that is not allowed in MDITA extended profile, like the level-three heading I mentioned earlier, would produce a validation error in LwDITA-aware tools. The Lightweight DITA subcommittee at OASIS is, as of this writing, working on recommendations for handling instances of non-MDITA Markdown structures in MDITA core profile.

Intended audiences for MDITA

MDITA is designed for users who want to write structured content with the minimum of overhead, but who also want to take advantage of the reuse mechanisms associated with the DITA standard and the multi-channel publishing afforded by standard DITA tooling.

Potential users of MDITA include the following:

- Software developers who want to contribute to DITA-based product documentation without using an XML editor
- Developers and writers in charge of documenting application programming interfaces (APIs) that need to share content with technical publications or marketing content
- Individuals authoring content using a platform, such as a mobile device, that does not support an XML editor
- Individuals authoring content quickly that must be later refactored as structured content
- Non-English-speaking authors who want to take advantage of DITA reuse and publishing without depending on XML tags written in English
- Content curators who receive occasional contributions from developers written in Markdown
- Technical editors who need to incorporate Markdown files in DITA or XDITA topic collections
- Content developers familiar with DITA or XDITA who want to use Markdown as an authoring language on devices that do not support XML editors
- Developers who perceive XML as too verbose or even obsolete.
- Plain-text aficionados
- Casual content contributors.

Whereas XDITA and MDITA were designed to be functionally equivalent to each other, MDITA was created as a compatible subset that allows authors to represent basic DITA-like components in Markdown syntax.

Before getting into the specific tools and rules for creating content, the next section addresses an important authoring difference between DITA XML and some of the LwDITA authoring formats.

An Important Rule About "Mixed Content" in LwDITA

In this section, I explain an authoring requirement that affects the LwDITA formats based on XML and HTML5. While this requirement initially surprises some authors, it provides benefits for both authors and LwDITA stylesheet developers, and is an important foundational feature of LwDITA

When I introduce LwDITA in university courses and industry workshops, many authors who have previous experience with DITA XML, and even some who are not familiar with DITA but have worked with HTML, are initially confused by the "minimize mixed content" rule that defines some components in this proposed standard. The W3C XML recommendation states that an "element type has mixed content when elements of that type may contain character data, optionally interspersed with child elements" (W3C, 2008). In DITA 1.3, for example, a list item can have mixed content (e.g., child elements like a paragraph combined with non-whitespace character data like text). Figure 4.1 shows a very brief DITA 1.3 topic with three list items: one with mixed content, one with just character data, and one with a child element without character data.

A similar syntax structure would be valid in HTML5[3]. Figure 4.2 shows a file that reproduces the list items from Figure 4.1 in valid HTML5 syntax.

The simplified structures in LwDITA have the intention of minimizing authorial decisions when creating content. Thus, if in DITA 1.3 and HTML5 an author had to decide if their components should include character data, child elements, or a combination of those, in some of the LwDITA authoring formats there is only one valid way t create certain elements. For example, in XDITA and HDITA only a handful of elements allow character data. In XDITA and

```
<?xml version="1.0" encoding="UTF-8"?>
<!DOCTYPE topic PUBLIC "-//OASIS//DTD DITA Topic//EN" "topic.dtd">
<topic id="mixed-content">
    <title>A DITA topic with mixed content</title>
    <body>
        <ul>
            <li>I have a child <p>paragraph</p></li>
            <li>I am just character data (text!)</li>
            <li><p>I am just a child paragraph</p></li>
        </ul>
    </body>
</topic>
```

FIGURE 4.1 Sample DITA topic showing the difference among elements with mixed content and those with just character data or just child elements. The sample topic includes an unordered list (<**ul**>) that contains three list items (<**li**>). The first list item mixes character data with a child element (a paragraph in this case). The other list items do not mix character data with elements. All three list items are valid in DITA 1.3.

```
<!DOCTYPE html>
    <head>
        <title>An HTML file with "mixed content"</title>
    </head>
    <body>
        <ul>
            <li>I have a child <p>paragraph</p></li>
            <li>I am just character data (text!)</li>
            <li><p>I am just a child paragraph</p></li>
        </ul>
    </body>
```

FIGURE 4.2 Sample HTML5 file with a combination of list items including character data and child elements. The sample file includes an unordered list (<**ul**>) that contains three list items (<**li**>). The first list item mixes character data with a child element (a paragraph in this case). The other list items do not mix character data with elements. All three list items are valid in HTML5

HDITA, the **paragraph** element (<**p**> in both cases) can contain the following child elements:

- Bold
- Italics
- Phrase
- Superscript
- Subscript
- Underline.

This restriction of mixed content in block elements has the intention of simplifying LwDITA processing in software tools that will need to combine XML, HTML5, and Markdown topics to produce LwDITA deliverables. The "minimize mixed content" rule also relaxes the content reuse mechanisms of DITA XML: In DITA, for example, content from a command (<**cmd**>) inside a task step (<**step**>) can only be reused in another command inside a step, but in XDITA and HDITA a command is expressed as a simple paragraph (<**p**>) that can be reused wherever paragraphs are allowed.

Here I go back to the initial reaction of some authors that encounter this rule when they are introduced to LwDITA. In DITA 1.3 and HTML5 (the markup foundations for XDITA and HDITA, respectively) the following ordered list is valid:

```
<ol>
<li id="first">First item</li>
<li id="second">Second item</li>
</ol>
```

In XDITA and HDITA, the same list must be represented as follows:

```
<ol>
<li><p id="first">First item</p></li>
<li><p id="second">Second item</p></li>
</ol>
```

Authors with previous DITA or HTML experience question why the list item must include a paragraph to hold its content. More than once, I have received feedback, on the initial minutes of training after introducing this rule, saying that this rule is "slightly annoying," but authors can see its benefits once they reuse the paragraph with the identifier of "first" in any other place where paragraphs are allowed, and not just where list items are allowed. However, one person's annoyance is another's enjoyment: Patrick Bosek, co-founder of the *easyDITA* component content management solution, once told me that, in his opinion, the "minimize mixed content" rule is one of the best features of XDITA.

Is there a LwDITA App?

For years, some technical communicators in academia and industry have seen DITA as a tool, and some perceive it as an alternative to software applications like Microsoft Word or Adobe FrameMaker. In reality, DITA is a tool as much as HTML is a tool: as open standards, they can have tools built based on them, but the standards are not the tools. The standards set guidelines and rules for structuring and processing content or information. LwDITA, likewise, is not a piece of software and does not come with an official "app," and *Creating Intelligent Content with Lightweight DITA* does not require a specific software platform. However, authors need to use software tools to create and process LwDITA content.

You can create LwDITA content in any text editor, but probably should avoid using a word processor or a desktop publishing solution (because those embed behind-the-scenes code for format and layout that an author cannot control). For introductory experiments like the marinara recipe from Chapter 1, Notepad for Windows or TextEdit in macOS (be sure to select *Format/Make Plain Text* before saving your files) can work.

An advanced option is the commercial editor Oxygen XML Editor, from Syncro Soft. I am not affiliated with Syncro Soft and my recommendation is based on Oxygen's relative affordability for academic audiences (compared with enterprise-level editors with similar capabilities) and their developers' genuine interest and attention for the development of LwDITA as an open standard. The Lightweight DITA subcommittee at OASIS expects that after the standard is released more tool developers will incorporate LwDITA workflows and templates into existing platforms for writing in XML, HTML5, and Markdown (who knows . . . a WordPress plugin for HDITA or a GitHub-based MDITA processor for GitHub Pages?). The subcommittee maintains a wiki page with a growing list of LwDITA-aware tools (i.e., tools that can validate and enforce the syntax guidelines and rules presented in this book and/or include templates for creating content in the LwDITA authoring formats)[4].

Once you have created content units in any LwDITA authoring format, you will need a software processor to transform those LwDITA topics into deliverables for human users. Most LwDITA-aware tools, including Oxygen XML Editor, should take care both of the editing and processing tasks. Without a LwDITA-aware editor, you probably would need to use the open source DITA Open Toolkit, as Chef Pedro did in Chapter 1, to process LwDITA content and produce end-user deliverables. In her *Introduction to DITA*, JoAnn Hackos described the DITA Open Toolkit as follows:

> The DITA Open Toolkit (DITA-OT) is an implementation of the OASIS DITA Technical Committee's specification for DITA DTDs and schemas. The Toolkit transforms DITA XML source content into deliverable formats such as PDF, HTML, and help systems. Although the DITA-OT is closely associated with the DITA specification, it is not a standard approved by the OASIS DITA Technical Committee and therefore should be considered as only one option for transforming DITA content.
>
> (Hackos, 2011; p. 325)

The DITA DTDs (Document Type Definitions) and schemas mentioned in Hackos's description are files that validate (i.e., verify that a topic conforms with the DITA syntax rules) content created according to the DITA standard. The DITA-OT is not maintained by the DITA technical committee at OASIS, and it has its own governance structure with an international group of volunteers. The OT includes DITA and LwDITA validating schemas and DTDs combined with scripts that automate the production of deliverables. The DITA-OT, however, is a command-line application that does not have a built-in graphical user interface (GUI). When introducing the DITA-OT to undergraduate technical communication students who have never seen a command line program, I have found some good resources in the Software Carpentry curriculum for "The Unix Shell,"[5] which describes the command-line as follows:

> The heart of a command-line interface is a **read-evaluate-print loop** (REPL) called so because when you type a command and press Return. The shell reads it, executes (or "evaluates" it), prints the output, prints the prompt and waits for you to enter another command.
>
> (Software Carpentry, 2018)

Those same students tend to sigh collectively in relief when they find out that some LwDITA-aware tools like Oxygen XML Editor include a version of the

DITA-OT. Some tools also provide a GUI that with a few mouse clicks allows the transformation of DITA and LwDITA topics into end-user documents ready for print or online delivery.

I included some sample LwDITA topics and maps in Chapter 1, and I also showed how those files would look when processed and transformed into PDF and HTML deliverables. In the following chapter, I focus on the specific components of content collection used in LwDITA maps, and I provide a quick tutorial on processing LwDITA files using the DITA Open Toolkit and Oxygen XML.

Notes

1 https://www.w3.org/TR/html5/
2 https://github.github.com/gfm/
3 For some HTML5 communities, however, "mixed content" means something different: it is a concept that describes how a web browser should manage secure content requests, as explained by the W3C (Mixed Content, 2016, https://www.w3.org/TR/mixed-content/).
4 The wiki page with a list of LwDITA tools and resources can be accessed at https://wiki.oasis-open.org/dita/LightweightDITASubcommittee/lwditatools
5 http://swcarpentry.github.io/shell-novice/

References

Evia, C., Sharp, M. R., & Perez-Quiñones, M. A. (2015). Teaching structured authoring and DITA through rhetorical and computational thinking. *IEEE Transactions on Professional Communication*, 58(3), 328–343.

Evia, C., Eberlein, K., & Houser, A. (Eds.) (2018). *Lightweight DITA: An introduction.* Version 1.0. OASIS.

Hackos, J. T. (2011). *Introduction to DITA: A user guide to the Darwin Information Typing Architecture including DITA 1.2* (2nd edition). Comtech Services, Inc.

Software Carpentry (2018). Introducing the shell. Retrieved from http://swcarpentry.github.io/shell-novice/01-intro/index.html

W3C (2008, November 26). Extensible Markup Language (XML) 1.0 (Fifth Edition). Retrieved from https://www.w3.org/TR/xml/

5

THE LwDITA MAP COMPONENTS

One of the major features and advantages of DITA, and LwDITA, is the ability to specify and generate arbitrary collections of topic content. The document type of map enables this grouping of topics. Just as LwDITA defines a subset of DITA features for topics, it also defines a subset for the DITA map. And, as with LwDITA topics, you can specify a LwDITA map in XDITA, HDITA, or MDITA, as well as possible future authoring formats. This chapter provides an overview, with examples, of LwDITA maps.

The descriptions and examples featured in this chapter (and in Chapter 6) are based on work that I have conducted as lead author of official OASIS publications, which include the committee note *Lightweight DITA: An Introduction* (Evia et al., 2018) and the LwDITA technical specification, which I am currently editing with Michael Priestley. Because LwDITA has not been approved as an official OASIS standard as of this writing, the components presented in these chapters might change. However, their current format has already been approved by members of the DITA Technical Committee, and the general public, through our introductory committee note. Chapters 5 and 6 include separate sections for each authoring format; nevertheless, any LwDITA map can reference any LwDITA topic regardless of authoring format. A key feature of LwDITA is cross-format collaboration and compatibility.

I acknowledge that, as a whole, these chapters contain plenty of dense reference material, and I have attempted to include examples of the most common topical conventions available in LwDITA, with emphasis on frequent structures used by content creators. This chapter does not have the purpose of replacing or mirroring the technical specification (which will contain information and details for developers and information designers) for the proposed LwDITA standard. The LwDITA technical specification is the authoritative source for producing and processing content across the LwDITA authoring formats.

In Chapter 3, I introduced the content and collection components of LwDITA, which can be represented in the three initial authoring formats of the proposed standard. The information contained in Chapters 5 and 6 does not aim to be a complete tutorial on XML, HTML5, or Markdown. I assume that readers interested in LwDITA will already be at least slightly familiar with XML, HTML5, or Markdown. However, before I talk about the specifics of the LwDITA map, I need to bring back the DITA map from Chapter 1.

Revisiting the DITA Map

Bellamy et al. describe the DITA map as "the glue that binds your topics together, the driver for producing your output, and the information path for your users to follow" (Bellamy et al., 2012, p. 91). In Chapter 1 I included some examples of DITA maps and promised that I will show you how to process them with DITA-aware tools and generate end user documents. Now it's the time to fulfill that promise. In this section, I will use a software tool to process the DITA map, from Chapter 1, that Chef Pedro created for his recipe critiques website. Figure 5.1 shows the recipe critiques DITA map, which you can save as *marinara-critique.ditamap*.

The first topic reference in the DITA map from Figure 5.1 is the DITA task version of the marinara sauce recipe from Chapter 1 (Figure 5.2).

The second topic reference is the actual critique of the marinara sauce recipe, which can be structured as a DITA concept and look as Figure 5.3.

The third topic reference is the "about" page with Chef Pedro's information, which I introduced in Chapter 2 and reproduce in Figure 5.4.

If you have never interacted with the DITA Open Toolkit, and if you are not familiar with command-line based applications, I recommend a couple of introductory videos developed by Scriptorium as part of their free "Learning DITA" curriculum[1]. The video tutorials "Installing the DITA Open Toolkit"[2] and "Testing the DITA Open Toolkit"[3] provide enough information to follow the examples included in this book. You can download the DITA-OT from the website https://www.dita-ot.org/download. Be sure to download the latest version, because the developers are constantly updating the Toolkit and, among other things, improving

```
<?xml version="1.0" encoding="UTF-8"?>
<!DOCTYPE map PUBLIC "-//OASIS//DTD DITA Map//EN" "map.dtd">
<map>
   <title>Chef Pedro's Recipe Critique</title>
   <topicref href="t-marinara.dita" />
   <topicref href="c-marinara-critique.dita" />
   <topicref href="c-about.dita" />
</map>
```

FIGURE 5.1 DITA map for Chef Pedro's recipe critique website. The map includes links (or topic references) to the marinara sauce recipe, Chef Pedro's critique of the recipe, and an "about" page with information about the author.

```
<?xml version="1.0" encoding="UTF-8"?>
<!DOCTYPE task PUBLIC "-//OASIS//DTD DITA Task//EN" "task.dtd">
<task id="t-marinara">
    <title>Marinara Sauce</title>
    <shortdesc>Prepare a crowd-
pleasing red sauce for pasta in about 30 minutes.</shortdesc>
    <prolog>
        <author>Unknown</author>
        <metadata>
            <category>Italian</category>
        </metadata>
    </prolog>
    <taskbody>
        <prereq>
            <ul>
                <li>2 tbsp. of olive oil</li>
                <li>2 cloves of garlic, minced</li>
                <li>1/2 tsp. of hot red pepper</li>
                <li>28 oz. of canned tomatoes, preferably San Marzano</li>
                <li>2 tbsp. of parsley, chopped</li>
            </ul>
        </prereq>
        <steps>
            <step>
                <cmd>Heat olive oil in a large saucepan on medium</cmd>
            </step>
            <step>
                <cmd>Add garlic and hot red pepper and sweat until fragrant
</cmd>
            </step>
            <step>
                <cmd>Add tomatoes, breaking up into smaller pieces</cmd>
            </step>
            <step>
                <cmd>Simmer on medium-low heat for at least 20 minutes</cmd>
            </step>
            <step>
                <cmd>Add parsley</cmd>
            </step>
            <step>
                <cmd>Simmer for another five minutes</cmd>
            </step>
            <step>
                <cmd>Serve over long pasta.</cmd>
            </step>
        </steps>
    </taskbody>
</task>
```

FIGURE 5.2 Marinara sauce recipe as a DITA task.

its support for LwDITA topics and maps. Once you have downloaded the file that corresponds to your computer's operating system, extract or decompress the file to a directory where you want to install the Open Toolkit.

According to the DITA-OT documentation, the command that builds DITA (and LwDITA) deliverables from topics and maps from a Terminal or Command Prompt window looks like Figure 5.5

HTML5 is only one of the many core transformations included in the DITA-OT. The DITA-OT documentation website[4] includes a list of the output formats supported by the toolkit.

```
<?xml version="1.0" encoding="UTF-8"?>
<!DOCTYPE concept PUBLIC "-//OASIS//DTD DITA Concept//EN" "concept.dtd">
      <concept id="about">
       <title>Marinara Sauce Recipe Critique</title>
       <shortdesc>This could be the best, and easiest, marinara sauce recipe
ever written!</shortdesc>
       <conbody>
      <p>Delicious marinara sauce recipe with fresh tomatoes. I give it five
thumbs up.</p>
       </conbody>
      </concept>
```

FIGURE 5.3 Marinara sauce recipe critique as a DITA concept.

To generate an HTML5 version of the marinara recipe critique, you would enter the command (one single line) on a command-line environment *inside the directory or folder where you installed the DITA-OT* shown in Figure 5.6.

The command has the reference to the built-in (*bin*) subdirectory and the *dita* executable program, with the *marinara-critique.ditamap* file as input, and *html5* as the delivery format. The value for the *--input* argument directs the DITA-OT to the specific folder where you stored the *marinara-critique.ditamap* file (the *path-to-file* section of the command, which you should replace with the actual path to the file in your computer). As the Scriptorium video "Testing the DITA Open Toolkit" shows, the easiest way to record the correct file location or path is to drag and drop the file into the command line interface immediately after the *--input=* argument. That one-line command combines the map with the topics, processing the hierarchies and relationships established by the topic

```
<?xml version="1.0" encoding="UTF-8"?>
<!DOCTYPE topic PUBLIC "-//OASIS//DTD DITA Topic//EN" "topic.dtd">
      <topic id="about">
       <title>About Chef Pedro</title>
       <shortdesc>Executive Chef, Yucatec-International Fusion Alchemist,
Marketing Architect.</shortdesc>
       <body>
      <p>Self-taught and persistent in the kitchen and marketing aspects of
the restaurant business, Chef Pedro has established himself a key player in
the new scene of Mexican gastronomy, particularly in the tradition of dishes
and flavors from the Yucatan peninsula.</p>
      <p>From an early age, Pedro learned the craft in the always-open
kitchen of his mother, Doña Raquel, among aromas of truly mestizo gastronomy.
Original top notes of condiments and herbs mixed with traditional Spanish
middle notes of saffron and olive oil built on ancient Yucatec base notes of
roasted tomato and hot peppers salsa inspired him to experiment with his own
style of cooking.</p>
       </body>
      </topic>
```

FIGURE 5.4 DITA topic including biographical information about Chef Pedro. The topic's elements include simple structures like a title, a short description, and a body containing paragraphs.

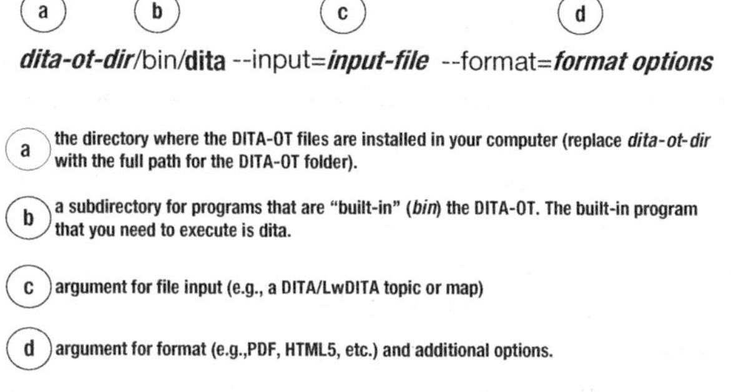
a
b
c
d
dita-ot-dir/bin/dita --input=input-file --format=format options
a the directory where the DITA-OT files are installed in your computer (replace dita-ot-dir with the full path for the DITA-OT folder).
b a subdirectory for programs that are "built-in" (bin) the DITA-OT. The built-in program that you need to execute is dita.
c argument for file input (e.g., a DITA/LwDITA topic or map)
d argument for format (e.g.,PDF, HTML5, etc.) and additional options.

FIGURE 5.5 General structure for a command that builds DITA (and LwDITA) deliverables with the DITA-OT.

references. The resulting HTML5 files should appear automatically (after a few minutes) in the DITA-OT *out* folder, although you can specify an alternative folder in the build command with the *--output* option.

If something goes wrong during the transformation process (maybe one of your files had an extra tag, or there was a missing component in your version of the DITA-OT), the Toolkit will report an error. To be honest, error messages from the DITA-OT can be complex and ambiguous. There are jokes in DITA circles about the draconian nature of DITA-OT error messages. Therefore, a DITA-aware tool with a graphical user interface (GUI) can be a better experience for novice DITA authors.

If you want to try a DITA-aware tool with a GUI, you can download a 30-day trial of Oxygen XML Editor from the website https://www.oxygenxml.com/xml_editor. In Oxygen XML Editor, a basic DITA transformation process requires just one click on the "Apply Transformation Scenario(s)" button (it

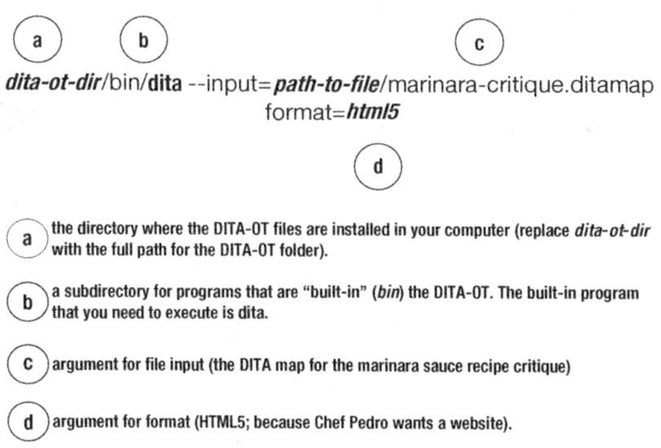
a
b
c
dita-ot-dir/bin/dita --input=path-to-file/marinara-critique.ditamap --format=html5
d
a the directory where the DITA-OT files are installed in your computer (replace dita-ot-dir with the full path for the DITA-OT folder).
b a subdirectory for programs that are "built-in" (bin) the DITA-OT. The built-in program that you need to execute is dita.
c argument for file input (the DITA map for the marinara sauce recipe critique)
d argument for format (HTML5; because Chef Pedro wants a website).

FIGURE 5.6 Command for the DITA-OT to generate a web deliverable from the marinara sauce critique DITA map.

looks like a wrench tool with a play button) on the main toolbar while a map is open in the editor window. If no transformation scenario has been selected, the dialog box will direct you to the "Configure Transformation Scenario(s)" window. As an alternative, you can enter the keyboard shortcut of *Ctrl* + *Shift* + *T* (for Windows) or *Command* + *Shift* + *T* (for macOS). The resulting files appear automatically (after a few minutes) in a folder named *out* that Oxygen will create in the same folder where the map is located. You can specify an alternate folder in the transformation scenario dialog window.

Chef Pedro can work with an information architect or web designer and create a stylesheet to format the default web transformation from the DITA-OT. Figure 5.7 shows a screen capture of the navigation menu for the marinara sauce recipe critique website without custom formatting.

Transforming LwDITA Maps

The process for generating end user deliverables from DITA maps is the same for transforming LwDITA maps (regardless of XDITA, HDITA, or MDITA authoring format). The examples included in the following sections, and continued in Chapter 6, are based on this scenario:

Chef Pedro has been quite successful with his chain of restaurants *Sensei Sushi* and he has decided to franchise the brand. The content needs of the company now are many: they will need guides for workers in the corporate-owned restaurants, guidelines and expectations for franchise owners, and because of the nature of this business (restaurants), they will also require collections of recipes and acceptable ingredients that can be reused in end-user products like a menu for print and online channels.

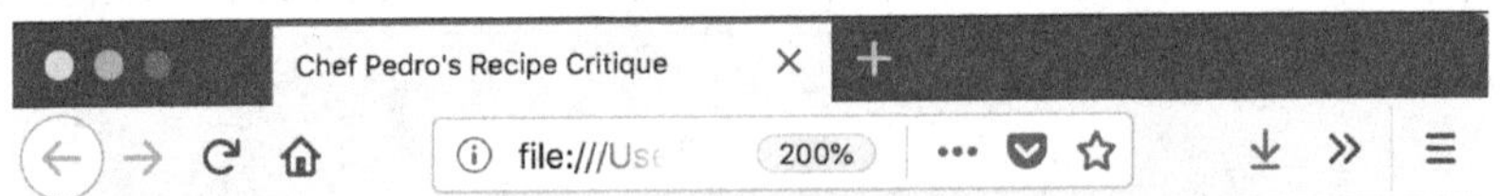

FIGURE 5.7 Navigation menu for a web transformation of Chef Pedro's recipe critique project. The DITA-OT generated the menu and took care of basic layout for this web deliverable.

The *Sensei Sushi* content repository includes many files that provide information for different audiences and contexts. Those files include topics with instructions for the corporate staff, restaurant operators, franchise owners, recipes for kitchen workers, and even maintenance guidelines for the engineering team. Those topics can be present in several combinations grouped in maps. In this specific example, the map will only reference those topics that are needed to build a promotional brochure for the *Sensei Sushi* franchise opportunity. The brochure will include the following sections (each section will be in a separate LwDITA topic):

- Introduction to the franchise opportunity
- Details about the franchise offer
- Legal terms of the franchise agreement
- An action plan for potential franchise owners
- A sample sushi recipe from the restaurant's cookbook.

The LwDITA map to create the *Sensei Sushi* brochure can be represented in the three initial LwDITA authoring formats, as I explain in the following sections.

The XDITA Map

In Chapter 3 I introduced the components of a LwDITA map, and those are expressed in XDITA as follows:

- Map (**<map>**) - describes the relationships among a set of resources, such as LwDITA topics
- Navigation title (**<navtitle>**) - provides an alternate title for a topic that becomes a part of navigation resources or tables of contents in deliverables
- Topic metadata (**<topicmeta>**) - defines the metadata that applies to a topic when it appears in a map
- Topic reference (**<topicref>**) - identifies and links to a topic or external content source.

Figure 5.8 shows the XDITA version of the map.

You can create the XDITA map from Figure 5.8 in any text editor or in a LwDITA-aware tool like Oxygen XML Editor. Then, you can save the file as *sensei-brochure.ditamap*. Of course, you will also need all the topics that the map references (inside each **<topicref>** tag), but we will work with those in the next chapter. At this point we still won't have any actual topics with content; however, you can download these sample files from the *Creating Intelligent Content with Lightweight DITA* GitHub repository (https://github.com/carlosevia/lwdita-book) and generate deliverables following the steps and examples from this chapter.

```
<?xml version="1.0" encoding="UTF-8"?>
<!DOCTYPE map PUBLIC "-//OASIS//DTD LIGHTWEIGHT DITA Map//EN" "lw-map.dtd">
<map id="sensei-brochure">
  <topicmeta>
    <navtitle>Sensei Sushi Franchise Opportunity</navtitle>
  </topicmeta>
  <topicref href="franchise-intro.dita"/>
  <topicref href="franchise-offer.dita"/>
  <topicref href="franchise-terms.dita"/>
  <topicref href="franchise-plan.dita"/>
  <topicref href="fancy-roll.dita"/>
  </topicref>
</map>
```

FIGURE 5.8 XDITA version of the map to create the Sensei Sushi promotional brochure. The **<map>** element works as a parent for **<topicref>** elements that reference specific topics. The **<topicmeta>** element at the map level (in bold font) provides the main title (**<navtitle>**) for deliverables produced with this specific map.

Figure 5.9 shows the DITA-OT command for processing an XDITA map and producing a PDF deliverable, which looks very similar to the one used for the DITA map transformation.

In Oxygen XML Editor, the XDITA map would be processed through the same steps as the DITA map: by clicking on the "Apply Transformation Scenario(s)" button on the main toolbar.

The HDITA Map

Chef Pedro's team could alternatively create the map for the *Sensei Sushi* brochure in HDITA. The core components of a LwDITA map that can be

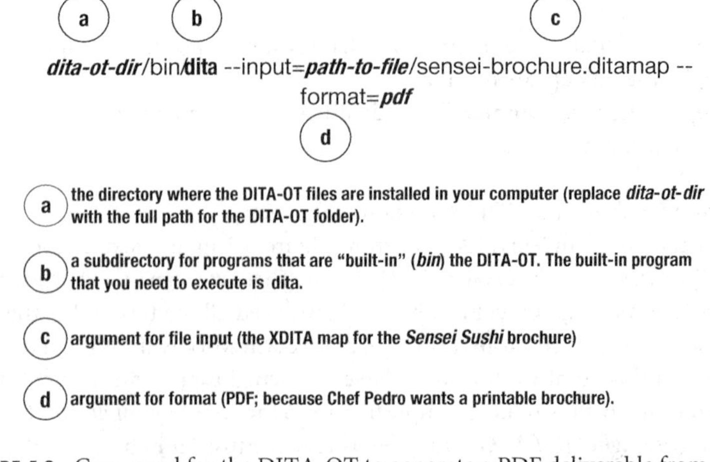
a
b
c
dita-ot-dir/bin/dita --input=path-to-file/sensei-brochure.ditamap --format=pdf
d
a the directory where the DITA-OT files are installed in your computer (replace dita-ot-dir with the full path for the DITA-OT folder).
b a subdirectory for programs that are "built-in" (bin) the DITA-OT. The built-in program that you need to execute is dita.
c argument for file input (the XDITA map for the Sensei Sushi brochure)
d argument for format (PDF; because Chef Pedro wants a printable brochure).

FIGURE 5.9 Command for the DITA-OT to generate a PDF deliverable from the XDITA version of the *Sensei Sushi* brochure.

represented in HDITA are the navigation element (<**nav**>) for opening a map environment, the title (<**title**> and <**h1**>[5]) to label the map and its deliverables, and a hyper reference inside a list item (<**a href**> inside a <**li**>) to express a topic reference.

Figure 5.10 shows the HDITA version of the map for creating the brochure.

Chef Pedro and his team can use any text editor to create the HDITA version of the map. They could also use a more advanced HTML editor, including WYSIWYG editors (as long as they allow users to save content as standards-compliant HTML5), or a LwDITA-aware tool like Oxygen XML Editor. Then, they can save the file as *sensei-brochure.html*. A conventional HTML editor probably will not be able to process the file as an HDITA map, and that's when the authors would need a LwDITA-aware tool or the DITA-OT. However, because HDITA files are valid HTML5 files, they can be opened in a web browser and produce an instant deliverable. If all Chef Pedro needed were a basic web version of the brochure, and if all the topics referenced in the map were also created in HDITA, this version of the map could provide the navigation structure for it. Additionally, Chef Pedro could link the HDITA topics to an external CSS file for formatting. Figure 5.11 shows a simple web view of the HDITA map, without any content processing or formatting, as seen on a browser.

```
<!DOCTYPE html>
<title>Sensei Sushi Franchise Opportunity</title>
<nav id="sensei-brochure">
  <h1>Sensei Sushi Franchise Opportunity</h1>
  <ul>
    <li>
      <p><a href="franchise-intro.html">Introduction</a>
        <p>
    </li>
    <li>
      <p><a href="franchise-offer.html">Our offer</a></p>
    </li>
    <li>
      <p><a href="franchise-terms.html">Legal terms</a></p>
    </li>
    <li>
      <p><a href="franchise-plan.html">Plan your franchise</a></p>
    </li>
    <li>
      <p><a href="fancy-roll.html">Sample recipe</a></p>
    </li>
  </ul>
</nav>
```

FIGURE 5.10 HDITA version of the map to create the *Sensei Sushi* promotional brochure. The <**nav**> element works as a parent for <**li**> elements that reference specific topics. The <**h1**> element at the map level (in bold font) provides the main title for deliverables produced with this specific map.

Sensei Sushi Franchise Opportunity

- Introduction
- Our offer
- Legal terms
- Plan your franchise
- Sample recipe

FIGURE 5.11 Quick web deliverable created by the HDITA version of the *Sensei Sushi* brochure map. When opened on a browser, the map creates a navigation menu for the topic collection. This web version does not include any single sourcing or content reuse features and is only for presentational purposes.

In this scenario, however, the simple website from Figure 5.11 would not be enough for the printed *Sensei Sushi* brochure. To create a PDF deliverable from the HDITA map, or if the project had any single-sourcing or content reuse requirements, Chef Pedro and his team would need to process it through a LwDITA-aware tool. Figure 5.12 shows the DITA-OT command for processing an HDITA map and producing a PDF deliverable, which looks very similar to the one used for the XDITA map transformation.

(a) (b) (c)

dita-ot-dir/bin/**dita** --input=***path-to-file***/sensei-brochure.html --format=***pdf***

(d)

(a) the directory where the DITA-OT files are installed in your computer (replace ***dita-ot-dir*** with the full path for the DITA-OT folder).

(b) a subdirectory for programs that are "built-in" (*bin*) the DITA-OT. The built-in program that you need to execute is dita.

(c) argument for file input (the HDITA map for the *Sensei Sushi* brochure)

(d) argument for format (PDF; because Chef Pedro wants a printable brochure).

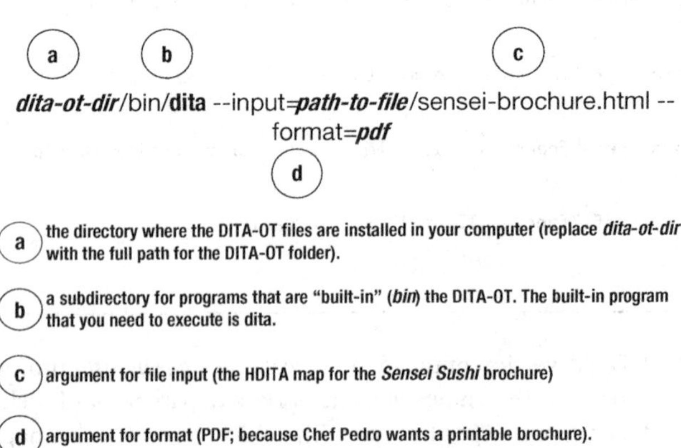

FIGURE 5.12 Command for the DITA-OT to generate a PDF deliverable from the HDITA version of the *Sensei Sushi* brochure.

In Oxygen XML Editor, the HDITA map would be processed through the same steps as the XDITA map: by clicking on the "Apply Transformation Scenario(s)" button on the main toolbar. The resulting PDF should look very similar to the one produced with the XDITA map, as the end users do not need to know which LwDITA authoring format was used to create the brochure.

The MDITA Map

The map for creating the *Sensei Sushi* brochure can also be coded in MDITA. As we will frequently see when examining the LwDITA map and topic components, the MDITA syntax is by far the easiest of the three initial authoring formats. The only components included in an MDITA version of the brochure map would be a title (represented by a Markdown *atx* heading of # in this case) and list items (-) that include links to each topic and its navigation title. Figure 5.13 shows a version of the brochure map created in MDITA.

You can save the file from figure 5.13 as *sensei-brochure.md* and then use a LwDITA-aware tool to produce the PDF deliverable.

Figure 5.14 shows the DITA-OT command for processing an MDITA map and producing a PDF deliverable, which looks very similar to the one used for the transformations in XDITA and HDITA.

In Oxygen XML Editor, the HDITA map would be processed through the same steps as the XDITA and HDITA maps: by clicking on the "Apply Transformation Scenario(s)" button on the main toolbar. The resulting PDF should look very similar to the one produced with the XDITA and HDITA maps, as the end users do not need to know which LwDITA authoring format was used to create the brochure.

The following chapter introduces the main topic components available in LwDITA. It continues the brochure scenario in the different LwDITA authoring formats.

```
# Sensei Sushi Franchise Opportunity

-    [Introduction](franchise-intro.html)

-    [Our offer](franchise-offer.html)

-    [Legal terms](franchise-terms.html)

-    [Plan your franchise](franchise-plan.html)

-    [Sample recipe](fancy-roll.html)
```

FIGURE 5.13 MDITA version of the map to create the *Sensei Sushi* promotional brochure. The list items reference specific topics, and the heading one (in bold font) provides the main title for deliverables produced with this specific map.

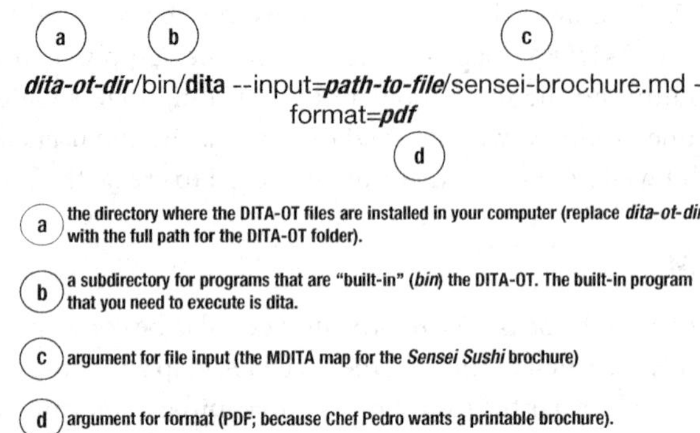

a
b
c
dita-ot-dir/bin/dita --input=path-to-file/sensei-brochure.md --
format=pdf
d
a the directory where the DITA-OT files are installed in your computer (replace dita-ot-dir with the full path for the DITA-OT folder).
b a subdirectory for programs that are "built-in" (bin) the DITA-OT. The built-in program that you need to execute is dita.
c argument for file input (the MDITA map for the Sensei Sushi brochure)
d argument for format (PDF; because Chef Pedro wants a printable brochure).

FIGURE 5.14 Command for the DITA-OT to generate a PDF deliverable from the MDITA version of the *Sensei Sushi* brochure.

Notes

1 Available at www.learningdita.com
2 https://youtu.be/rCH1OQqBBB8
3 https://youtu.be/p_eBj6e0gBU
4 https://www.dita-ot.org/3.0/topics/output-formats.html
5 In Chapter 6 I will address the redundant need for both a **<title>** and a **<h1>** in HDITA maps and topics.

References

Bellamy, L., Carey, M., & Schlotfeldt, J. (2012). *DITA best practices: A roadmap for writing, editing, and architecting in DITA*. Upper Saddle River, NJ: IBM Press.

Evia, C., Eberlein, K., & Houser, A. (2018). *Lightweight DITA: An introduction*. Version 1.0. OASIS.

6

THE LwDITA TOPIC COMPONENTS

In the previous chapter I analyzed the LwDITA document type of map, which works as a collection and organization mechanism for content units. Those content units are represented in the document type of topic. Although in Chapter 3 I introduced the main content components available in LwDITA, here I focus on how to represent each of those topic components in the authoring formats of XDITA, HDITA, and MDITA. Keep in mind that LwDITA is a work in progress and some elements in this chapter might change between the publication of this book and the actual release of the Lightweight DITA standard.

The examples included in this chapter continue the scenario of Chef Pedro's content requirements for the promotional *Sensei Sushi* brochure. The sample files are available for download from the *Creating Intelligent Content with Lightweight DITA* GitHub repository (https://github.com/carlosevia/lwdita-book).

I have organized this chapter according to the following classification of LwDITA content components:

- Basic topic components
- Table components
- Highlight components
- Metadata components
- Multimedia components.

In the last section of this chapter I highlight one of the most promising LwDITA features: the ability to create coherent and consistent user deliverables from cross-format sources developed by diverse groups of content creators.

Basic topic components

Topic

XDITA

The essential unit of content in LwDITA is a topic, which is represented in XDITA with the XML tag **<topic>** . The generic topic is the only document type available for creating content in the initial release of the LwDITA specification. For Chef Pedro's content needs, a very simple topic would look as the example in Figure 6.1.

You can type the code from Figure 6.1 in any text editor, but working in a LwDITA-aware application like Oxygen XML Editor brings benefits like auto-completion of tags and templates, which can reduce spelling errors and typos. The first line of code in the example is the XML declaration, which announces to the computer processor that this is an XML file and should be treated as such. The second line indicates that this is not just any XML file, and that it must be validated against the document type definition (DTD) of *lw-topic.dtd*, which is a grammar file that includes the XDITA syntax rules and was created by the Lightweight DITA subcommittee at OASIS. Another benefit of using an LwDITA-aware app to create content is that it will probably include the grammar files and provide validation as you type. This second line of code enforces the XDITA authoring format. Without it, the topic would just be a regular XML file (like the first marinara sauce recipe from Chapter 1), and would need its own stylesheets and schemas to produce deliverables for end users.

In XDITA, the attribute for a unique identifier at the topic level (the **id** portion of the **<topic id="franchise-intro">** line) is required. Without it, the topic will not validate as standards-based XDITA content. I am a fan of using the same text for the topic identifier attribute and the file name: e.g., the **@id** of this topic is "franchise-intro," and I would save it as *franchise-intro.dita* (XDITA topics can be saved with the file extensions *.xml* or *.dita*). The next line of code in the

```
<?xml version="1.0" encoding="UTF-8"?>
<!DOCTYPE topic PUBLIC "-//OASIS//DTD LIGHTWEIGHT DITA Topic//EN" "lw-topic.dtd">
<topic id="franchise-intro">
  <!-- Some content will go here -->
</topic>
```

FIGURE 6.1 Minimal XDITA topic. The opening and closing XML tags for topic (in bold font) create an environment for content. In this example, the only content is a placeholder XML comment (marked by the characters <!-- and -->).

Some content will go here

[Title] [Short Description] [Prolog] [Body]

FIGURE 6.2 Validation error reported by Oxygen XML Editor. Oxygen validates the XDITA topics as the authors develop them. In this case, the "red squiggly of doom" error tells the authors that the topic is not valid and must be fixed.

example is an XML comment (enclosed within the characters <!-- and -->) that I am using as a temporary placeholder for actual content.

At this point, an author new to structured content should resist the urge to preview the topic in a deliverable. The "format free" characteristic of intelligent content (Rockley et al., 2015) depends on the separation of content and presentation; after all, this sample topic can be transformed to different deliverables with a variety of formats and stylesheets. The concept of "what you see is what you get" (WYSIWYG) from many web developing editors does not translate to topic-based authoring in XML because a topic is just a component in a larger collection of chunks that need to be processed to create deliverables. Furthermore, this sample topic stub is not yet valid XDITA. A LwDITA-aware tool like Oxygen XML would inform the author that the topic is incomplete. Some of my students call the Oxygen validation error notifier the "red squiggly of doom" (Figure 6.2).

Before I fix the XDITA topic to remove the error messages, I will present the mapping of the XDITA element of topic to the HDITA and MDITA authoring formats.

HDITA

The HTML5 semantic tag of **<article>** provides a content environment similar to the **<topic>** component from XDITA. In HDITA, **<article>** has a required **@id**, that could have the same value as the file's name. In the following example, the **@id** attribute on **<article>** is *"franchise-intro"*, and the file can be saved as *franchise-intro.html* (Figure 6.3). The first line of code in the file is establishing that the HDITA topic should be validated as HTML.

You can create this HDITA topic in any text editor, a more advanced HTML editor, or a LwDITA-aware tool like Oxygen XML. The validation process of an HTML5 file as an HDITA topic will be application-specific, as HTML does not have a customizable document type definition or schema syntax.

```
<!DOCTYPE html>
<article id="franchise-intro">
  <!-- Some content will go here -->
</article>
```

FIGURE 6.3 Minimal HDITA topic. This topic needs the HTML5 element of **<article>** to create an environment for content. This file, however, is not valid HTML5. Just like the XDITA example in Figure 6.1, the HDITA topic requires a **<title>** element, which I will add in the following section.

MDITA

In MDITA core profile, any structure saved as Markdown format can work as a basic topic. Figure 6.4 reproduces the essential topic with a placeholder comment for content. In Markdown, a title is not required, so this one-line example can work as a valid basic (but useless for practical reasons) topic, even if its content is just a commented annotation. You can create this file in any text editor or a LwDITA-aware tool, and save it as *franchise-intro.md*.

In XDITA and MDITA, a topic requires an **@id**, which is provided as an attribute of the components **<topic>** and **<article>**, respectively. In MDITA, the required **@id** should be automatically generated when the topic is saved, through a "slug"-generation process. Therefore, the **@id** for *franchise-intro.md*, if needed for future topic linking and reuse, will be *franchise-intro*. In MDITA extended profile, authors can specify an **@id** for the topic that overrides the "slugify" process. The assigned **@id** should be included in an optional YAML[1] front matter header. In *Lightweight DITA: An Introduction,* we wrote the following about the optional YAML header for MDITA topics:

> This YAML header can supply a direct value for the @id attribute that is required on the root element of a DITA topic; it can also include prolog metadata about who authored the DITA topic. If included in a topic, the YAML front matter header must be the first thing in the MDITA file and must be set between triple-dashed lines.
>
> (Evia et al., 2018, p.19)

Figure 6.5 shows the *franchise.intro.md* topic with an assigned **@id** of *sensei-intro* that would override the **@id** generated with the file's name.

```
<!-- Some content will go here -->
```

FIGURE 6.4 Minimal MDITA topic. This topic does not need a body element. It does not need a title either, and it could only include a placeholder comment for future content.

```
---
id: sensei-intro
---

<!-- Some content will go here -->
```

FIGURE 6.5 Sample MDITA extended profile topic with an assigned **@id** in a YAML header. The assigned **@id** will be attached to the topic even if the authors rename the source file (with the default "slugify" process of MDITA core profile, renaming a file will change its automatically-generated **@id**).

The validation of Markdown files as MDITA topics will also be application-specific. The Lightweight DITA subcommittee at OASIS will release recommendations and standards for that validation, but will not produce tools or files to enforce it, leaving the implementation to interested vendors and developers.

Title

XDITA

The "red squiggly of doom" from Figure 6.2 indicates that, according to the XDITA grammar rules, a topic cannot be empty. A valid XDITA topic needs, at least, a title, which is represented by the XML element **<title>**. The new version of the basic XDITA topic should look as Figure 6.6.

The title component in this revised example includes the XML tags that represent the **<title>** element and the actual content for human users that appears inside the tags. The content embraced by the XML tags requires proper capitalization and correct spelling according to any style guide developed or adopted by Chef Pedro and his team. With this new title component, the topic stub now can clear validation warnings in a LwDITA-aware tool like Oxygen XML Editor, and it can be seen in *author* mode, which *hides* the XML code and allows editing in an environment similar to a WYSIWYG editor (Figure 6.7).

```
<?xml version="1.0" encoding="UTF-8"?>
<!DOCTYPE topic PUBLIC "-//OASIS//DTD LIGHTWEIGHT DITA Topic//EN" "lw-topic.dtd">
<topic id="franchise-intro">
  <title>An innovative, attractive, and out of the ordinary concept</title>
</topic>
```

FIGURE 6.6 Minimal XDITA topic with a title component. The file will now clear validation in LwDITA-aware apps and also shows actual content for human readers.

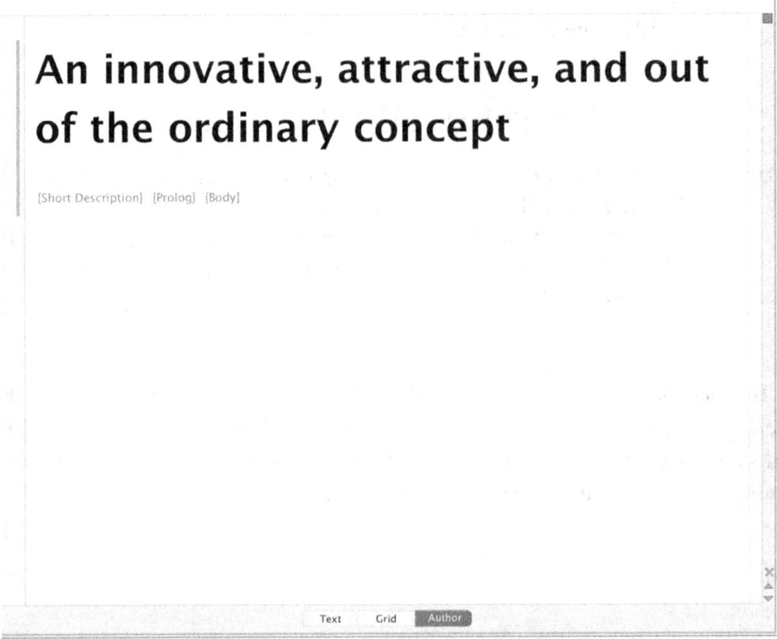

FIGURE 6.7 Author mode in Oxygen XML Editor. This mode provides a quick preview of a topic, similar to a WYSIWYG editor. With its title element, the sample XDITA topic now cleared Oxygen error messages.

HDITA

According to the W3C recommendation for HTML5, the "document's title is often different from its first heading, since the first heading does not have to stand alone when taken out of context." (W3C, 2017). Therefore, whereas a valid HTML5 file requires a **<title>** element, this component won't perform as the topic's first heading. As a result, HDITA topics need both a title (**<title>**) element and a heading 1 (**<h1>**) element to signal the document's first heading. Redundantly, both elements should contain the same information in order to comply with syntax rules from HTML5 and LwDITA. LwDITA-aware tools could automate the process of generating a **<h1>** from a **<title>** and reduce repetition for human authors. Figure 6.8 shows the franchise introduction topic with a title and a heading 1.

MDITA

The level-one heading that provides a title for an MDITA topic can be expressed, according to the GitHub Flavored Markdown (GFM) spec, both with an *atx*

```
<!DOCTYPE html>
<title>An innovative, attractive, and out of the ordinary concept</title>
<article id="franchise-intro">
  <h1>An innovative, attractive, and out of the ordinary concept</h1>
</article>
```

FIGURE 6.8 Sample HDITA topic with the required title component. In order to be valid as an HDITA topic and HTML5 file at the same time, the topic requires a title and a heading 1, which should hold the same content.

("the true structured text format")[2] or *setext* (Structure Enhanced Text)[3] heading. Figure 6.9 shows the franchise introductory topic in MDITA core profile with an *atx* heading for its title.

In Figure 6.10, an MDITA extended profile with an assigned **@id** of "*franchise-intro*" uses a *setext* heading for its title component.

Short description

XDITA

An optional topic component that I have addressed in previous chapters is the multipurpose short description (**<shortdesc>** in XDITA), which performs a staging move (see Table 2 in Chapter 2) before a topic goes into detail about a specific subject. Figure 6.11 shows a short description in the introductory XDITA topic for the *Sensei Sushi* franchise brochure.

```
# An innovative, attractive, and out of the ordinary concept

<!-- Some content will go here -->
```

FIGURE 6.9 Sample MDITA core profile topic with a title component. The title is marked by a heading 1 in *atx* syntax.

```
---
id: franchise-intro
---

An innovative, attractive, and out of the ordinary concept
==========================================================

<!-- Some content will go here -->
```

FIGURE 6.10 Sample MDITA extended profile topic with a title component. The title is marked by a heading 1 in *setext* syntax.

```
<?xml version="1.0" encoding="UTF-8"?>
<!DOCTYPE topic PUBLIC "-//OASIS//DTD LIGHTWEIGHT DITA Topic//EN" "lw-topic.dtd">
<topic id="franchise-intro">
  <title>An innovative, attractive, and out of the ordinary concept</title>
  <shortdesc>Are you interested in investing with us? Welcome to our franchise
information package.</shortdesc>
</topic>
```

FIGURE 6.11 XDITA topic with a short description component. The opening and closing tags of **<shortdesc>** hold content that the authors can use as a staging rhetorical move in the topic.

HDITA and MDITA

In HDITA and MDITA topics, the optional short description is implied in the first paragraph of content. Figure 6.12 shows the introductory topic with a short description paragraph in HDITA.

Figure 6.13 presents the same topic in MDITA extended profile, which includes the YAML header with an assigned **@id**, an *atx* heading for the title, and the short description implied in the first paragraph.

```
<!DOCTYPE html>
<title>An innovative, attractive, and out of the ordinary concept</title>
<article id="franchise-intro">
  <h1>An innovative, attractive, and out of the ordinary concept</h1>
  <p>Are you interested in investing with us? Welcome to our franchise
information package.</p>
</article>
```

FIGURE 6.12 HDITA topic with a short description component. The short description defaults to the first paragraph in an HTML file. If authors need more structure and their workflows require identifying a first paragraph as a short description, they should use the XDITA syntax instead.

```
---
id: franchise-intro
---

# An innovative, attractive, and out of the ordinary concept

Are you interested in investing with us? Welcome to our franchise information
package.
```

FIGURE 6.13 MDITA topic with a short description component. The short description is implied in the first paragraph of a Markdown file.

Body and Paragraph

The previous examples did not have much content but are all valid LwDITA topics. Maybe Chef Pedro only needs a brief blurb for this information. If so, the topics could end here and join a content collection to produce deliverables for end users. Nevertheless, despite the potential uses of such a content blurb, the component that contains the majority of conventions for content is the body – represented in XDITA and HDITA by the tag **<body>**. The following section introduces additional topic components that can be included inside the body environment.

Inside the body component, the most common unit for small pieces of content is a paragraph (**<p>**). The example in Figure 6.14 adds a body component, with a paragraph, to the franchise introduction topic in XDITA:

The HDITA version of the paragraph, seen in Figure 6.15, looks pretty similar to its XDITA counterpart.

```
<?xml version="1.0" encoding="UTF-8"?>
<!DOCTYPE topic PUBLIC "-//OASIS//DTD LIGHTWEIGHT DITA Topic//EN" "lw -topic.dtd">
<topic id="franchise-intro">
  <title>An innovative, attractive, and out of the ordinary concept</title>
  <shortdesc>Are you interested in investing with us? Welcome to our franchise
  information package.</shortdesc>
  <body>
    <p>We offer more than 30 exclusive creations of original rolls, from the
California roll to sushi with BBQ chicken or grilled steak.</p>
  </body>
</topic>
```

FIGURE 6.14 XDITA topic with a body component. In XDITA, the body environment can hold several topic components. The primary component inside a body is a paragraph, which should be represented by opening and closing **<p>** tags.

```
<!DOCTYPE html>
<title>An innovative, attractive, and out of the ordinary concept</title>
<body>
  <article id="franchise-intro">
    <h1>An innovative, attractive, and out of the ordinary concept</h1>
    <p>Are you interested in investing with us? Welcome to our franchise
information package.</p>
    <p>We offer more than 30 exclusive creations of original rolls, from the
California roll to sushi with BBQ chicken or grilled steak.</p>
  </article>
</body>
```

FIGURE 6.15 HDITA topic with paragraph components. In HDITA, a paragraph is also represented by opening and closing **<p>** tags, and paragraphs should be inside a body environment.

The GFM spec defines paragraph as a "sequence of non-blank lines" (GitHub Flavored Markdown Spec, 2017). Thus, an MDITA paragraph does not require any tags, as seen in Figure 6.16.

Lists

The body of a LwDITA topic can also contain topical conventions for lists. LwDITA includes components for representing the following types of lists:

- Definition lists
- Ordered lists
- Unordered lists.

In XDITA, the definition list (<**dl**>) is a content environment that includes a definition list entry (<**dlentry**>), a definition term (<**dt**>), and a definition description (<**dd**>). In this example (Figure 6.17), Chef Pedro and his team use a definition list to describe the terms that apply to franchise owners of *Sensei Sushi*.

The previous example shows the "minimize mixed content" rule in action. Whereas in DITA 1.3 a definition description can contain character data or additional XML elements, in XDITA it must include a paragraph (<**p**>) housing any text. Without a doubt, the definition list is one of the most verbose XDITA environments. The tags required for declaring the list, its entries, terms, and descriptions do not look extremely lightweight. In cases like this one, an LwDITA-aware editor can help with tag autocompletion and authorial guidance.

The W3C recommendation for HTML explains the <**dl**> element as a "description list of zero or more term-description groups. Each term-description group consists of one or more terms (represented by <dt> elements), and one or more descriptions (represented by <dd> elements)" (W3C, 2017). Thus, in HDITA the definition list environment looks as shown in Figure 6.18. Note that the "minimize elements that allow mixed content" also applies to HDITA topics.

```
---
id: franchise-intro
---

# An innovative, attractive, and out of the ordinary concept

Are you interested in investing with us? Welcome to our franchise information
package.

We offer more than 30 exclusive creations of original rolls, from the California
roll to sushi with BBQ chicken or grilled steak.
```

FIGURE 6.16 MDITA topic with paragraph components. In MDITA, a paragraph is a sequence of non-blank lines and should be visually separated from other content components by a return or enter.

```
<?xml version="1.0" encoding="UTF-8"?>
<!DOCTYPE topic PUBLIC "-//OASIS//DTD LIGHTWEIGHT DITA Topic//EN" "lw -topic.dtd">
<topic id="franchise-terms">
  <title>Profit, fun, and flavor under the same brand</title>
  <body>
    <dl>
      <dlentry>
        <dt>Initial investment:</dt>
        <dd><p>$700 (includes initial franchise fee)</p></dd>
      </dlentry>
      <dlentry>
        <dt>Franchise fee:</dt>
        <dd><p>$200</p></dd>
      </dlentry>
    </dl>
  </body>
</topic>
```

FIGURE 6.17 Definition list environment in XDITA. The component includes one or more definition list entries, each with a definition term and a definition description.

There is no direct equivalent for a definition list in MDITA core profile, although some Markdown flavors do have a way to represent this component. If an author needs to include a definition list in MDITA, the recommendation is to take advantage of the MDITA extended profile and express the definition list with a raw code block of HDITA syntax. The following example (Figure 6.19) shows the definition list in MDITA extended profile with an HDITA code snippet.

```
<!DOCTYPE html>
<title>Profit, fun, and flavor under the same brand</title>
<body>
  <article id="franchise-terms">
    <h1>Profit, fun, and flavor under the same brand</h1>
    <dl>
      <dt>Initial investment:</dt>
      <dd>
        <p>$700 (includes initial franchise fee)</p>
      </dd>
      <dt>Franchise fee:</dt>
      <dd>
        <p>$200</p>
      </dd>
    </dl>
  </article>
</body>
```

FIGURE 6.18 Definition list environment in HDITA. Unlike its counterpart in XDITA, this definition list does not need the holding definition entry environment to contain pairs of definition term and definition description.

```
---
id: franchise-terms
---

# Profit, fun, and flavor under the same brand

<dl>
     <dt>Initial investment:</dt>
     <dd>
       <p>$700 (includes initial franchise fee)</p>
     </dd>
     <dt>Franchise fee:</dt>
     <dd>
       <p>$200</p>
     </dd>
</dl>
```

FIGURE 6.19 Definition list environment in an MDITA extended profile topic. The definition list element does not exist in GitHub Flavored Markdown syntax. Thus, if authors need a definition list in MDITA, they should express it with a raw HDITA code block.

In XDITA and HDITA, the ordered list (**<ol>**) is a much simpler environment than the definition list, and it only requires one or more instances of a list item (**<li>**). Figure 6.20 includes an ordered list in XDITA giving steps that a potential investor should go through to obtain the franchise license.

The "minimize mixed content" rule in LwDITA wraps content from the list items in paragraphs. Authors coming to XDITA from HTML5 might find that unusual, but this can simplify content reuse in more advanced situations.

The ordered list would look as follows (Figure 6.21) in HDITA:

The unordered list (**<ul>**) is a very similar component. Figure 6.22 shows an unordered, or bulleted, list with features of the *Sensei Sushi* franchise in an XDITA topic.

```
<?xml version="1.0" encoding="UTF-8"?>
<!DOCTYPE topic PUBLIC "-//OASIS//DTD LIGHTWEIGHT DITA Topic//EN" "lw-topic.dtd">
<topic id="franchise-plan">
  <title>Make a plan! Start your future today!</title>
  <body>
    <ol>
      <li><p>Contact one of our franchise advisors</p></li>
      <li><p>Pick a location for your restaurant</p></li>
      <li><p>Follow our franchise guide</p></li>
    </ol>
  </body>
</topic>
```

FIGURE 6.20 Ordered list environment in XDITA. The "minimize mixed content" rule forces authors to wrap the content of each list item in paragraphs.

```
<!DOCTYPE html>
<title>Make a plan! Start your future today!</title>
<body>
  <article id="franchise-plan">
    <h1>Make a plan! Start your future today!</h1>
    <ol>
      <li>
        <p>Contact one of our franchise advisors</p>
      </li>
      <li>
        <p>Pick a location for your restaurant</p>
      </li>
      <li>
        <p>Follow our franchise guide</p>
      </li>
    </ol>
  </article>
</body>
```

FIGURE 6.21 Ordered list environment in HDITA. The component follows the same structure as its counterpart in XDITA.

Figure 6.23 shows the same topic in HDITA syntax.

To express ordered and unordered lists in MDITA, you should follow the recommendations from the GFM spec, which specify that "a list is an ordered list if its constituent list items begin with ordered list markers, and a bullet list if its constituent list items begin with bullet list markers" (GitHub Flavored Markdown Spec, 2017). The spec adds that "an ordered list marker is a sequence of 1–9 arabic (*sic*) digits (0–9), followed by either a . character or a) character." (GitHub Flavored Markdown Spec, 2017) Figure 6.24 shows the list for potential investors in MDITA syntax.

```
<?xml version="1.0" encoding="UTF-8"?>
<!DOCTYPE topic PUBLIC "-//OASIS//DTD LIGHTWEIGHT DITA Topic//EN" "lw-topic.dtd">
<topic id="franchise-offer">
  <title>What we offer</title>
  <body>
    <ul>
      <li><p>"Know-how" license</p></li>
      <li><p>Warranty of exclusive territory</p></li>
      <li><p>Initial training</p></li>
      <li><p>Support through online, email, and telephone channels</p></li>
    </ul>
  </body>
</topic>
```

FIGURE 6.22 Unordered list environment in XDITA. Each list item will create, when the topic is processed, a bulleted entry.

```
<!DOCTYPE html>
<title>What we offer</title>
<body>
  <article id="franchise-offer">
    <h1>What we offer</h1>
    <ul>
      <li>
        <p>"Know-how" license</p>
      </li>
      <li>
        <p>Warranty of exclusive territory</p>
      </li>
      <li>
        <p>Initial training</p>
      </li>
      <li>
        <p>Support through online, email, and telephone channels</p>
      </li>
    </ul>
  </article>
</body>
```

FIGURE 6.23 Unordered list environment in HDITA. The component follows the same structure as its counterpart in XDITA.

Unordered list markers can be a -, +, or * character, as shown in Figure 6.25 of an MDITA topic with a list of what the *Sensei Sushi* franchise package offers.

Image and Figure

XDITA

In XDITA, non-textual topical conventions start with an image (**<image>**). The image component is always treated as an inline element: its appearance will not begin on a new line in publications generated from topics that contain it. The

```
---
id: franchise-plan
---

# Make a plan! Start your future today!

1.  Contact one of our franchise advisors
2.  Pick a location for your restaurant
3.  Follow our franchise guide
```

FIGURE 6.24 Ordered list environment in MDITA. When the topic is processed, the list items will be automatically numbered in a logical sequence established by the number assigned to the first list item.

```
---
id: franchise-offer
---

# What we offer

-    "Know-how" license
-    Warranty of exclusive territory
-    Initial training
-    Support through online, email, and telephone channels
```

FIGURE 6.25 Unordered list environment in MDITA. The GFM spec allows the use of the characters -, +, or * as unordered list item markers.

figure (<**fig**>) environment provides a wrap for the image. A figure is treated as a block element in XDITA. Figure 6.26 includes both an inline image and a block figure.

Notice that the images, both in inline and block mode, can include a component for alternate text (<**alt**>), which provides a behind-the-scenes textual description for human users and machine processors that cannot perceive images or require additional information. The figure environment includes a description (<**desc**>) that functions as a caption or label for the image. To put the previous example in context, the *author* mode in Oxygen XML can provide a simple "preview" of the topic and its visual elements (Figure 6.27).

```
<?xml version="1.0" encoding="UTF-8"?>
<!DOCTYPE topic PUBLIC "-//OASIS//DTD LIGHTWEIGHT DITA Topic//EN" "lw-topic.dtd">
<topic id="franchise-intro">
  <title>An innovative, attractive, and out of the ordinary concept</title>
  <shortdesc>Are you interested in investing with us? Welcome to our franchise
information package.</shortdesc>
  <body>
    <p>We offer <image href="images/plus-sign.jpg"><alt>Icon for a plus sign
</alt></image>than 30 exclusive creations for original rolls, from the
California roll to sushi with BBQ chicken or grilled steak.</p>
    <fig>
      <desc>This is love!</desc>
      <image href="images/sushi-love.jpg">
        <alt>Sensei Sushi logo</alt>
      </image>
    </fig>
  </body>
</topic>
```

FIGURE 6.26 Image and figure components in an XDITA topic. Both contain alternate text for human or machine readers that cannot process a visual element.

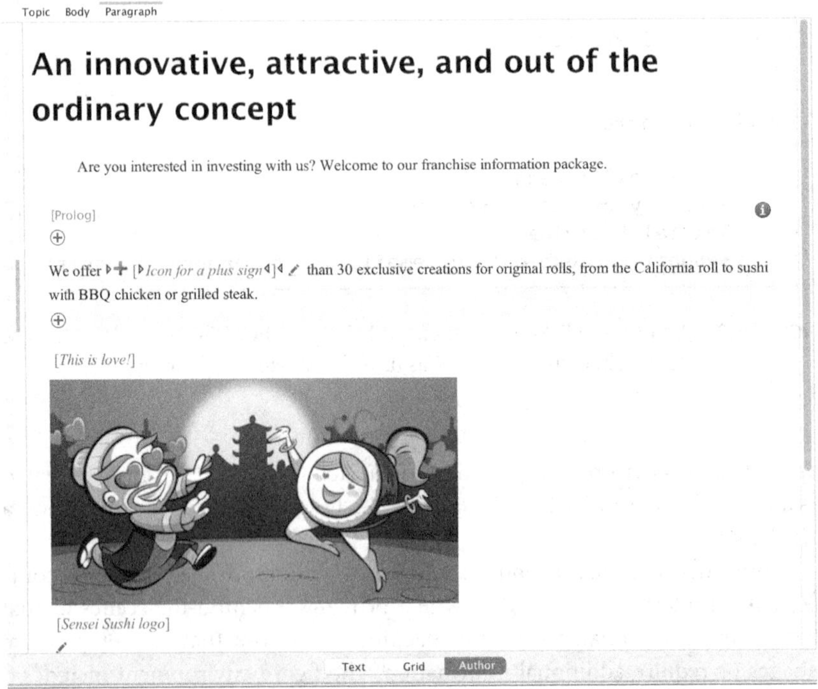
Topic
Body
Paragraph
An innovative, attractive, and out of the ordinary concept
Are you interested in investing with us? Welcome to our franchise information package.
[Prolog]
We offer [Icon for a plus sign] than 30 exclusive creations for original rolls, from the California roll to sushi with BBQ chicken or grilled steak.
[This is love!]
[Sensei Sushi logo]
Text
Grid
Author

FIGURE 6.27 Preview of the XDITA topic with image and figure environments in Oxygen XML *author* mode. The image is in line with its containing paragraph, whereas the figure is its own block environment.

HDITA

In HDITA, the inline image is represented with the HTML tag <**img**>, which requires the attribute of **@src** to specify the source file for the image. The block image should be included in the <**figure**> environment, and it can include a title (<**title**>) element to provide a description. The **@alt** attribute works just like it does in XDITA syntax. The HDITA topic in Figure 6.28 includes the inline image for the plus sign and the block figure with the *Sensei Sushi* logo.

You can save the HDITA topic from the previous example as *franchise-intro.html* and open in it a web browser to see the difference between an inline and block image. Figure 6.29 shows a browser view of the HDITA topic.

MDITA

In MDITA, the syntax to represent an inline image includes the label for alternate text and the link to the image file in the following structure:

```
<!DOCTYPE html>
<title>An innovative, attractive, and out of the ordinary concept</title>
<body>
  <article id="franchise-intro">
    <h1>An innovative, attractive, and out of the ordinary concept</h1>
    <p>Are you interested in investing with us? Welcome to our franchise
information package.</p>
    <p>We offer <img src="images/plus-sign.jpg" alt="Icon for a plus sign" />
than 30 exclusive creations for original rolls, from the California roll to
sushi with BBQ chicken or grilled steak.</p>
    <figure>
      <figcaption>This is love!</figcaption>
      <img src="images/sushi-love.jpg" alt="Sensei Sushi logo" />
    </figure>
  </article>
</body>
```

FIGURE 6.28 Image and figure components in an HDITA topic. Both need the HTML5 tag of **<img>** with the attribute of **@src** for the source file of an image.

```
![Alternate text](path-to-image-file.jpg)
```

The image can become a block element if it is treated as a paragraph (i.e., it is separated from other elements with a return or enter), and it can include an optional title or description in the following structure:

```
![Alternate text](path-to-image-file.jpg "Optional title")
```

Figure 6.30 shows the franchise introductory topic in MDITA syntax with the inline image for the plus sign and the block figure, with a title, for the *Sensei Sushi* logo.

An innovative, attractive, and out of the ordinary concept

Are you interested in investing with us? Welcome to our franchise information package.

We offer + than 30 exclusive creations for original rolls, from the California roll to sushi with BBQ chicken or grilled steak.

This is love!

FIGURE 6.29 Preview of the HDITA topic with image and figure environments in a web browser. The image is in line with its containing paragraph, whereas the figure is its own block environment.

```
---
id: franchise-intro
---

# An innovative, attractive, and out of the ordinary concept

Are you interested in investing with us? Welcome to our franchise
information package.

We offer ![Icon for a plus sign](images/plus-sign.jpg) than 30
exclusive creations for original rolls, from the California roll to
sushi with BBQ chicken or grilled steak.

![Sensei Sushi logo](images/sushi-love.jpg "This is love!")
```

FIGURE 6.30 Image and figure components in an MDITA topic. The exclamation point before the link text notifies processors that an image element is included in the topic.

Cross-reference

XDITA

A cross-reference (<**xref**>) component in XDITA allows the creation of links to internal and external resources. A topic can include cross-references to other topics in the same collection or to external sources like a PDF file or a website. In Figure 6.31, the topic with the bulleted list of franchise features now includes a hyper reference (**@href**) to an external website hosting the *Sensei Sushi* knowledge base for technical support.

```
<?xml version="1.0" encoding="UTF-8"?>
<!DOCTYPE topic PUBLIC "-//OASIS//DTD LIGHTWEIGHT DITA Topic//EN" "lw -topic.dtd">

<topic id="franchise-offer">
  <title>What we offer</title>
  <body>
    <ul>
      <li><p>"Know-how" license</p></li>
      <li><p>Warranty of territory exclusivity</p></li>
      <li><p>Initial training</p></li>
      <li><p>Support through online, email, and telephone channels</p></li>
      <li><p>Access to our <xref href="http://senseisushico.com/kb"
 scope="external" format="html">knowledge base</xref></p></li>
    </ul>
  </body>
</topic>
```

FIGURE 6.31 XDITA topic with a cross-reference to an external website. The <**xref**> tags embrace the phrase “knowledge base,” which will become active and clickable on deliverables produced from this topic.

The attributes for **@scope** and **@format** inside the cross-reference are optional. The scope attribute, if used, must have a value of "external", "local", or "peer".

HDITA

In HTML5, a cross-reference is represented with a combination of the anchor (**<a>**) element and the hyper reference (**@href**) attribute. This interactive content structure can also include attributes for relationship (**@rel**) and type (**@type**) that correspond to the DITA/XDITA attributes of scope (**@scope**) and format (**@format**), respectively. Figure 6.32 features an HDITA topic with the cross-reference component linking to the external HTML files that contain the *Sensei Sushi* knowledge base.

MDITA

In MDITA, a cross-reference is represented with a Markdown link structure that includes a link text and link destination in the following format:

```
[link text](link destination).
```

Figure 6.33 shows an MDITA version of the franchise offer topic with the cross-reference link to the external *Sensei Sushi* knowledge base.

```
<!DOCTYPE html>
<title>What we offer</title>
<body>
  <article id="franchise-offer">
    <h1>What we offer</h1>
    <ul>
      <li>
        <p>"Know-how" license</p>
      </li>
      <li>
        <p>Warranty of territory exclusivity</p>
      </li>
      <li>
        <p>Initial training</p>
      </li>
      <li>
        <p>Support through online, email, and telephone channels</p>
      </li>
      <li>
        <p>Access to our <a href="http://senseisushico.com/kb" rel="external"
type="text/html">knowledge base</a></p>
      </li>
    </ul>
  </article>
</body>
```

FIGURE 6.32 HDITA topic with a cross-reference to an external website. Compared to the XDITA example, the **<a>** tags replace the **<xref>** to embrace the phrase "knowledge base."

```
---
id: franchise-offer
---

# What we offer

-   "Know-how" license

-   Warranty of territory exclusivity

-   Initial training

-   Support through online, email, and telephone channels

-   Access to our [knowledge base](http://senseisushico.com/kb)
```

FIGURE 6.33 MDITA topic with a cross-reference to an external website. The GFM structure of link text + link destination does not require additional attributes for scope or type of link.

Footnote

XDITA

The cross-reference component also enables the inclusion of footnotes (<**fn**>) in XDITA topics. In Figure 6.34, the list of franchise terms includes a cross-reference to a footnote providing information about the initial fee paid by franchise owners.

The footnote component is composed of two elements: the cross-reference that calls it, and the actual footnote content. In the previous example, the cross-reference is calling a footnote with the **@id** value of "*initial-fee*" located in the topic with the **@id** value of "*franchise-terms*". The actual footnote contains a paragraph with text.

HDITA and MDITA

A cross-reference also provides the foundation for footnotes in HDITA. The HTML5 division element (<**div**>) with the custom data attribute of **@data-class**="**fn**" creates a section for the footnote content. The footnote division should have a unique **@id**. In the body of the text, where the footnote is called from, an internal cross-reference in the form of <**a href**="**#footnote-id**"> should embrace the text you want to make clickable for the footnote. In Figure 6.35, the clickable text is a number 1 with the superscript (<sup>) format. I will talk more about superscript text in the section about highlighting components.

In MDITA extended profile, a footnote can be represented with an HDITA code block following the structure from Figure 6.35. There is no equivalent for the footnote component in MDITA core profile.

```
<?xml version="1.0" encoding="UTF-8"?>
<!DOCTYPE topic PUBLIC "-//OASIS//DTD LIGHTWEIGHT DITA Topic//EN" "lw-topic.dtd">
<topic id="franchise-terms">
  <title>Profits, fun, and flavor under the same brand</title>
  <body>
    <dl>
      <dlentry>
        <dt>Initial investment:</dt>
        <dd>
          <p>$700<xref href="#franchise-terms/initial-fee"/></p>
        </dd>
      </dlentry>
      <dlentry>
        <dt>Franchise fee:</dt>
        <dd><p>$200</p></dd>
      </dlentry>
    </dl>
    <fn id="initial-fee">
      <p>The initial investment price includes the first franchise fee payment
      </p>
    </fn>
  </body>
</topic>
```

FIGURE 6.34 Footnote in an XDITA topic. The cross-reference component links to an internal section in the topic. The link requires the **@id** of the topic (preceded by a # character) and the **@id** of the footnote element (preceded by a / character).

The Lightweight DITA subcommittee at OASIS expects that, as more developers start adopting the proposed standard, software applications will automate processes such as the insertion of footnotes.

Note

XDITA

The topical component for note (<**note**>) in XDITA gives authors a tool to make block-level content stand out from regular paragraphs. The attribute for note type (**@type**) is optional, but if used it must take a value from the following: "caution", "warning", "danger", "trouble", "notice," or "note". Example 32 has a note, with a "notice" type attribute, replacing the footnote from Figure 6.36.

HDITA and MDITA

In HDITA, the note component is expressed with an HTML division (<**div**>) environment with the custom data attribute of **@data-class="note"**. The attribute for note type (**@data-type**) is optional, but if used it must take a value from the following: "caution", "warning", "danger", "trouble", "notice," or "note".

```
<!DOCTYPE html>
<title>Profits, fun, and flavor under the same brand</title>
<body>
  <article id="franchise-terms">
    <h1>Profits, fun, and flavor under the same brand</h1>
    <dl>
      <dt>Initial investment:</dt>
      <dd>
        <p>$700<a href="#initial-fee"><sup>1</sup></a></p>
      </dd>
      <dt>Franchise fee:</dt>
      <dd>
        <p>$200</p>
      </dd>
    </dl>
    <div id="initial-fee" data-class="fn" data-type="notice">
          <p>The initial investment price includes the first franchise
fee payment</p>
    </div>
  </article>
</body>
```

FIGURE 6.35 Footnote in an HDITA topic. The cross-reference component links to an internal division in the topic. HDITA footnote references need a clickable text component (a superscript number 1 in this example).

Figure 6.37 includes the HDITA version of the franchise terms topic with the "notice" note explaining the initial franchise payment.

The content component for note is not available in MDITA. If needed, you can include a note in an MDITA extended profile topic with an HDITA code block using the syntax of `<div data-class="note">` seen in figure 6.37.

Phrase

XDITA

If you need to make inline-level text stand out, a phrase (<**ph**>) component can do that inside a paragraph. In Figure 6.38, the first list item includes the term

```
<?xml version="1.0" encoding="UTF-8"?>
<!DOCTYPE topic PUBLIC "-//OASIS//DTD LIGHTWEIGHT DITA Topic//EN"
"lw-topic.dtd">
<topic id="franchise-terms">
  <title>Profits, fun, and flavor under the same brand</title>
  <body>
    <dl>
      <dlentry>
        <dt>Initial investment:</dt>
        <dd>
          <p>$700</p>
          <note type="notice">
            <p>The initial investment price includes the first franchise fee
payment</p>
          </note>
        </dd>
      </dlentry>
      <dlentry>
        <dt>Franchise fee:</dt>
        <dd><p>$200</p></dd>
      </dlentry>
    </dl>
  </body>
</topic>
```

FIGURE 6.36 Note environment in an XDITA topic. The note includes a paragraph with content that will stand out from the topic's other elements in deliverables produced from this source.

```
<!DOCTYPE html>
<title>Profits, fun, and flavor under the same brand</title>
<body>
  <article id="franchise-terms">
    <h1>Profits, fun, and flavor under the same brand</h1>
    <dl>
      <dt>Initial investment:</dt>
      <dd>
        <p>$700</p>
        <div data-class="note" data-type="notice">
          <p>The initial investment price includes the first franchise fee
             payment</p>
        </div>
      </dd>
      <dt>Franchise fee:</dt>
      <dd>
        <p>$200</p>
      </dd>
    </dl>
  </article>
</body>
```

FIGURE 6.37 Note environment in an HDITA topic. The note is created in HTML5 with a division element and custom data attributes to specify its class of "note" and an optional type.

```
<?xml version="1.0" encoding="UTF-8"?>
<!DOCTYPE topic PUBLIC "-//OASIS//DTD LIGHTWEIGHT DITA Topic//EN"
"lw-topic.dtd">
<topic id="franchise-offer">
  <title>What we offer</title>
  <body>
    <ul>
      <li><p><ph translate="no">Know-how</ph> license</p></li>
      <li><p>Warranty of territory exclusivity</p></li>
      <li><p>Initial training</p></li>
      <li><p>Support through online, email, and telephone channels</p></li>
    </ul>
  </body>
</topic>
```

FIGURE 6.38 XDITA topic with a phrase component. The **@translate** attribute has a value of "no", which indicates to machine processors and human editors that the marked phrase should not be translated.

"know-how." As Chef Pedro and his team prepared to translate materials for the *Sensei Sushi* operations in Mexico, they realized that "know-how" does not need to be translated for audiences reading Mexican Spanish. In business-speak, "know-how" means the same for their audiences in English and Spanish. Thus, the author can flag the phrase-level content with a **<ph>** and an attribute for **@translate** with the value of "*no*". This flag will tell human authors who can see the code and machine processors that this specific phrase should not be translated from the source language.

HDITA and MDITA

The inline component to flag a phrase should be expressed in HDITA with the HTML5 span (**<span>**) element. Figure 6.39 shows the "know-how" phrase with a do not translate attribute in an HDITA topic.

MDITA

Although there is no direct equivalent for phrase or span in Markdown, you can flag phrase-level content in MDITA extended profile using an HDITA code snippet. Figure 6.40 includes the HDITA **<span>** environment in an MDITA extended profile topic to select the phrase that should not be translated.

Preformatted Text

XDITA and HDITA

In a publishing environment using DITA or LwDITA, the *Sensei Sushi* staff has little to no control over the appearance of text in user deliverables. In the

```
<!DOCTYPE html>
<title>What we offer</title>
<body>
  <article id="franchise-offer">
    <h1>What we offer</h1>
    <ul>
      <li>
        <p><span translate="no">"Know-how"</span> license</p>
      </li>
      <li>
        <p>Warranty of territory exclusivity</p>
      </li>
      <li>
        <p>Initial training</p>
      </li>
      <li>
        <p>Support through online, email, and telephone channels</p>
      </li>
    </ul>
  </article>
</body>
```

FIGURE 6.39 HDITA topic with a phrase component. The phrase is expressed with the HTML5 **<span>** element.

process of transformation, the content sources will be linked to stylesheets and templates with rules that most likely will be outside of a casual author's control. However, in some cases authors might want to control the look of some textual elements regardless of transformation and deliverable rules. Figure 6.41 shows how the preformatted text component (**<pre>**) in XDITA preserves the stanza or set of lines in the promise creed of *Sensei Sushi*. Because the text is wrapped in the preformatted environment, the lines will appear separated in any deliverable and won't be affected by external templates or stylesheets.

```
---
id: franchise-offer
---

# What we offer

-   <span translate="no">"Know how"</span> license

-   Warranty of territory exclusivity

-   Initial training

-   Support through online, email, and telephone channels
```

FIGURE 6.40 MDITA topic with a phrase component. If you are working in MDITA and need to mark a specific phrase, you should use a raw HDITA code snippet and create an HTML5 span.

```
<?xml version="1.0" encoding="UTF-8"?>
<!DOCTYPE topic PUBLIC "-//OASIS//DTD LIGHTWEIGHT DITA Topic//EN"
"lw-topic.dtd">
<topic id="sensei-promise">
  <title>The Sensei Sushi Promise</title>
  <body>
    <pre>
      Sensei Sushi cares about tradition
      Sensei Sushi cares about the customer
      Sensei Sushi cares about fun.
     </pre>
  </body>
</topic>
```

FIGURE 6.41 Preformatted text in XDITA. The **<pre>** environment preserves line breaks as determined by the author.

Figure 6.42 shows a preview of the preformatted text in Oxygen XML's *author* mode.

The **<pre>** component performs the same function in HDITA topics, as shown in Figure 6.43.

A quick view of the HDITA topic from Figure 6.43 on a web browser shows the preformatted text with the line structure set in the source code (Figure 6.44).

MDITA

You can express the LwDITA content component of preformatted text in MDITA via indented or fenced code blocks in Markdown. The GFM spec describes indented code blocks as "composed of one or more indented chunks separated by blank lines. An indented chunk is a sequence of non-blank lines, each indented four or more spaces" (GitHub Flavored Markdown Spec, 2017). The spec also explains that a fenced code block begins with a code fence, indented no more than three spaces, and then defines code fence as "a sequence of at least three consecutive backtick characters (`) or tildes (~). (Tildes and backticks cannot be mixed.)" (GitHub Flavored Markdown Spec, 2017).

Figure 6.45 includes an MDITA topic with the *Sensei Sushi* promise preformatted via the indented code blocks method.

Section

XDITA and HDITA

The section (**<section>**) component gives authors a resource to create content separations inside a topic. Each section can contain its own title under the same parent topic. In this example, the legal team will add content to a section labeled "Terms and conditions" inside the franchise offer topic. Figure 6.46 shows the "Terms and conditions" section in XDITA, where the section's title is provided by a **<title>** tag immediately placed after the opening **<section>** tag.

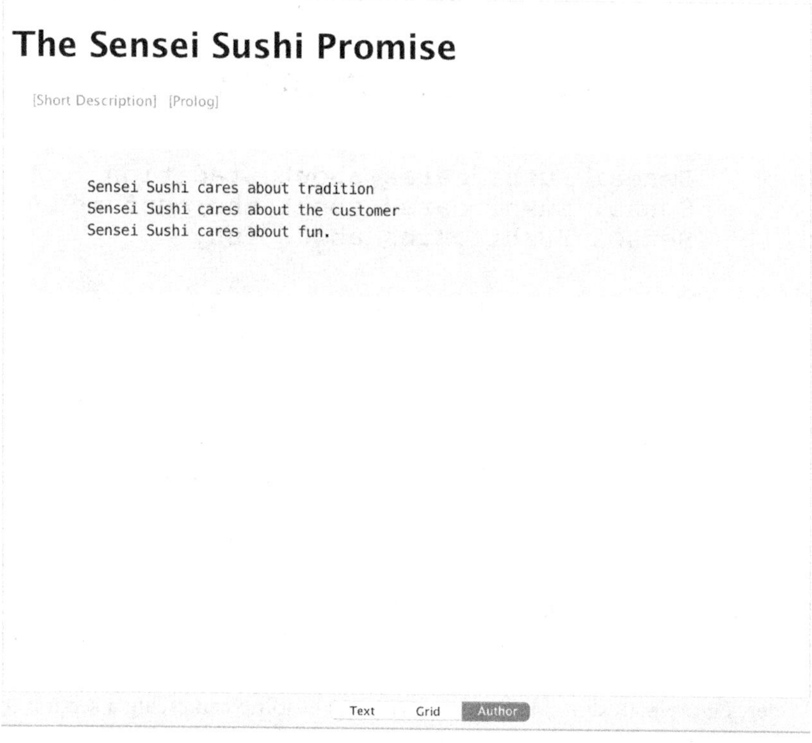

The Sensei Sushi Promise
[Short Description] [Prolog]
Sensei Sushi cares about tradition
Sensei Sushi cares about the customer
Sensei Sushi cares about fun.
Text
Grid
Author

FIGURE 6.42 Preview of an XDITA topic with a preformatted text environment in Oxygen XML's *author* mode. The line breaks inside the **<pre>** tags appear as the author wrote them.

```
<!DOCTYPE html>
<title>The Sensei Sushi Promise</title>
<body>
  <article id="sensei-promise">
    <h1>The Sensei Sushi Promise</h1>
    <pre>
      Sensei Sushi cares about tradition
      Sensei Sushi cares about the customer
      Sensei Sushi cares about fun.
    </pre>
  </article>
</body>
```

FIGURE 6.43 Preformatted text in HDITA. The syntax is identical to its counterpart in XDITA.

The Sensei Sushi Promise

```
Sensei Sushi cares about tradition
Sensei Sushi cares about the customer
Sensei Sushi cares about fun.
```

FIGURE 6.44 Web browser view of the preformatted text example in HDITA. The browser respects the line breaks established in the topic.

Figure 6.47 reproduces the franchise offer topic in HDITA syntax. In HDITA, the section component is also represented with the tag **<section>**. However, the section's title should be included in an HTML heading 2 (**<h2>**) element.

MDITA

If you are working in MDITA, you should use a Markdown heading 2 to create a content division similar to a section in XDITA and HDITA. You can represent the heading 2 with an *atx* (##) or *setext* (with underline from the character -) header. Figure 6.48 shows how a level-two *atx* heading can create a section in an MDITA topic.

If you need to make a direct link to a specific section inside an MDITA topic, the **@id** attribute for the section will be automatically generated as a slug.

```
---
id: sensei-promise
---

# The Sensei Sushi Promise


          Sensei Sushi cares about tradition

          Sensei Sushi cares about the customer

          Sensei Sushi cares about fun.
```

FIGURE 6.45 Preformatted text in MDITA. According to the GFM spec, preformatted lines can be indented or fenced by backtick characters or tides. In this example, the text is preformatted with indents.

```
<?xml version="1.0" encoding="UTF-8"?>
<!DOCTYPE topic PUBLIC "-//OASIS//DTD LIGHTWEIGHT DITA Topic//EN"
"lw-topic.dtd">
<topic id="franchise-offer">
  <title>What we offer</title>
  <body>
    <ul>
      <li><p><ph translate="no">"Know-how"</ph> license</p></li>
      <li><p>Warranty of territory exclusivity</p></li>
      <li><p>Initial training</p></li>
      <li><p>Support through online, email, and telephone channels</p></li>
    </ul>
    <section id="terms">
      <title>Terms and conditions</title>
      <!--  Some legal content here -->
    </section>
  </body>
</topic>
```

FIGURE 6.46 Example of a section component in XDITA. The section has its own **@id** and **<title>**, functioning as a separate (but related) environment inside a larger topic.

Therefore, the **@id** for the "Terms and conditions" section from Figure 6.48 would be "*terms-and-conditions*".

Table components

XDITA

In DITA 1.3, you can represent a tabular environment in more than one way. Probably the most common is through the CALS[4] table format, which also comes with a collection of tags and options that make it a rather heavy

```
<!DOCTYPE html>
<title>What we offer</title>
<body>
  <article id="franchise-offer">
    <h1>What we offer</h1>
    <ul>
      <li>"Know-how" license</li>
      <li>Warranty of exclusive territory</li>
      <li>Initial training</li>
      <li>Support through online, email, and telephone channels</li>
    </ul>
    <section id="terms">
      <h2>Terms and conditions</h2>
      <!--  Some legal content here -->
    </section>
  </article>
</body>
```

FIGURE 6.47 Section component in HDITA. The title for the section should be provided in a heading 2 following HTML5 syntax.

```
---
id: franchise-offer
---

# What we offer

-    "Know-how" license
-    Warranty of exclusive territory
-    Initial training
-    Support through online, email, and telephone channels

## Terms and conditions

<!--  Some legal content here -->
```

FIGURE 6.48 Section component in MDITA. The section environment opens with a heading 2, which in this example is represented by ## in *atx* syntax.

environment for casual content contributors. In XDITA, the only allowed table model is a simple table (<**simpletable**>), which also exists in DITA 1.3. As its name implies, simple table is "simpler" than the CALS model and contains the following components:

- Table header (<**sthead**>)
- Table row (<**strow**>)
- Table entry (<**stentry**>).

Figure 6.49 includes a simple table that presents the ingredients and quantities needed to prepare the "Fancy Roll" – a signature *Sensei Sushi* product.

Figure 6.50 shows a preview of the simple table environment in Oxygen's *author* mode.

HDITA

In HDITA, you should represent the components of a LwDITA table with the following HTML5 elements:

- Table (<**table**>)
- Table header (<**th**>)
- Table row (<**tr**>)
- Table entry (<**td**>).

```
<?xml version="1.0" encoding="UTF-8"?>
<!DOCTYPE topic PUBLIC "-//OASIS//DTD LIGHTWEIGHT DITA Topic//EN"
"lw-topic.dtd">
<topic id="fancy-roll">
  <title>Fancy Roll</title>
  <body>
    <simpletable>
      <sthead>
        <stentry>
          <p>Ingredient</p>
        </stentry>
        <stentry>
          <p>Amount</p>
        </stentry>
        <stentry>
          <p>Unit shipped</p>
        </stentry>
      </sthead>
      <strow>
        <stentry>
          <p>Gohan rice</p>
        </stentry>
        <stentry>
          <p>140 gms.</p>
        </stentry>
        <stentry>
          <p>14 kgs.</p>
        </stentry>
      </strow>
      <strow>
        <stentry>
          <p>Soya paper sheet</p>
        </stentry>
        <stentry>
          <p>1 pc.</p>
        </stentry>
        <stentry>
          <p>10 pcs.</p>
        </stentry>
      </strow>
    </simpletable>
  </body>
</topic>
```

FIGURE 6.49 Table inside an XDITA topic. To keep the inevitably verbose nature of a tabular environment in XML, XDITA uses the **<simpletable>** format instead of the more elaborate CALS table.

Figure 6.51 shows the HDITA code for the topic including a table with the ingredients, amounts, and units shipped for franchise owners interested in preparing the "Fancy Roll."

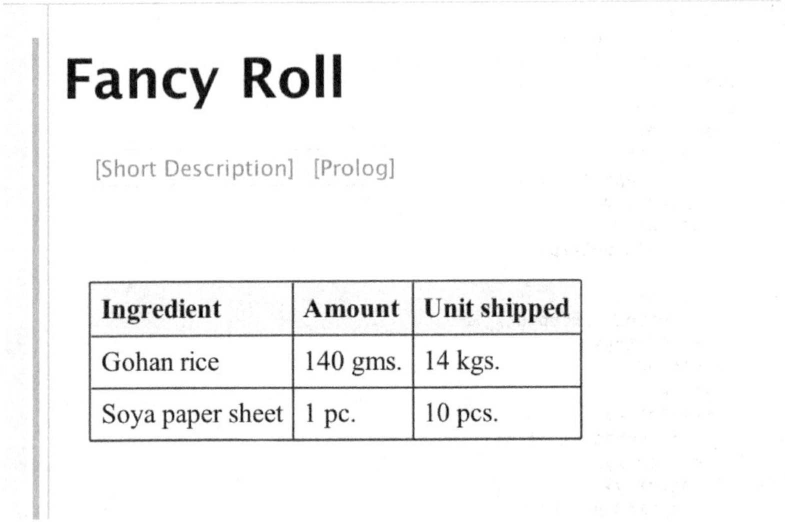

Fancy Roll

[Short Description] [Prolog]

Ingredient	Amount	Unit shipped
Gohan rice	140 gms.	14 kgs.
Soya paper sheet	1 pc.	10 pcs.

FIGURE 6.50 Preview of an XDITA table with the ingredients and shipped units for the Fancy Roll in Oxygen's *author* mode.

MDITA

The MDITA table component is based on the tabular extension included in GitHub Flavored Markdown. The table should contain a header row, a delimiter row, and zero or more rows with entries. Table entries inside a row should be separated by pipes (|), and the delimiter should contain hyphens (-), "and optionally, a leading or trailing colon (:), or both, to indicate left, right, or center alignment respectively" (GitHub Flavored Markdown Spec, 2017).

Figure 6.52 shows the topic with the "Fancy Roll" table in MDITA format.

Highlighting Components (Available in Both Topic and Map)

In LwDITA, authors have the following components to highlight sections of a text:

- Bold
- Italics
- Subscript
- Superscript
- Underline.

```
<!DOCTYPE html>
<title>Fancy Roll</title>
<body>
  <article id="fancy-roll">
    <h1>Fancy Roll</h1>
    <table>
      <tr>
        <th>
          <p>Ingredient</p>
        </th>
        <th>
          <p>Amount</p>
        </th>
        <th>
          <p>Unit shipped</p>
        </th>
      </tr>
      <tr>
        <td>
          <p>Gohan rice</p>
        </td>
        <td>
          <p>140 gms.</p>
        </td>
        <td>
          <p>14 kgs.</p>
        </td>
      </tr>
      <tr>
        <td>
          <p>Soya paper sheet</p>
        </td>
        <td>
          <p>1 pc.</p>
        </td>
        <td>
          <p>10 pcs.</p>
        </td>
      </tr>
    </table>
  </article>
</body>
```

FIGURE 6.51 Table inside an HDITA topic. Deliverable-specific formatting should be added when the topic is processed by a LwDITA-aware software tool.

```
---
id: fancy-roll
---

# Fancy Roll

| Ingredient        | Amount    | Unit shipped |
| ----------------- | --------- | ------------ |
| Gohan rice        | 140 gms.  | 14 kgs.      |
| Soya paper sheet  | 1 pc.     | 10 pcs.      |
```

FIGURE 6.52 Table inside an MDITA topic. MDITA takes advantage of the table extension in GitHub Flavored Markdown to represent tabular content.

In this section, I present those components with their corresponding mappings in the three initial LwDITA authoring formats and a brief example.

XDITA

- Bold (<**b**>): <li><p>Warranty of <**b**> exclusive territory </**b**> </p></li>
- Italics (<**i**>*): <p>We offer more than 30 exclusive creations of original rolls, from the* <**i**> *California* </**i**> *roll* to sushi with BBQ chicken or grilled steak.</p>
- Subscript (<**sub**>): <p>One serving of sushi rice requires 2 cups of H<**sub**>2</**sub**>O.</p>
- Superscript (<**sup**>): <p>Franchised restaurants should be located in areas of at least 200 ft<**sup**>2</**sup**>.</p>
- Underline (<**u**>): <p>Franchise owners <**u**>must</**u**> pay their fees on the first week of each calendar month.</p>

HDITA

- Bold (<**strong**>): <li><p>Warranty of <**strong**>exclusive territory </**strong**></p></li>.
- Italics (<**em**>): <p>We offer more than 30 exclusive creations of original rolls, from the <**em**>California roll</**em**> to sushi with BBQ chicken or grilled steak.</p>
- Subscript (<**sub**>): <p>One serving of sushi rice requires 2 cups of H<**sub**>2</**sub**>O .</p>
- Superscript (<**sup**>): <p>Franchised restaurants should be located in areas of at least 200 ft<**sup**>2</**sup**>.</p>
- Underline (<**u**> [5]): <p>Franchise owners <**u**>must</**u**> pay their fees on the first week of each calendar month.</p>

MDITA

- Bold (text wrapped with ** or with __): Warranty of **exclusive territory** or Warranty of __exclusive territory__.
- Italics (text wrapped with * or with _): a) We offer more than 30 exclusive creations of original rolls, from the *California roll* to sushi with BBQ chicken or grilled steak Or b) We offer more than 30 exclusive creations of original rolls, from the _California roll_ to sushi with BBQ chicken or grilled steak.
- Subscript (<**sub**>): <p>One serving of sushi rice requires 2 cups of H<**sub**>2</**sub**>O .</p>
- Superscript (<**sup**>): <p>Franchised restaurants should be located in areas of at least 200 ft<**sup**>2</**sup**>.</p>
- Underline (<**u**> in an HDITA code snippet): <p>Franchise owners <**u**>must</**u**> pay their fees on the first week of each calendar month.</p>

Metadata Components

The semantically rich nature of intelligent content described by Rockley et al. (2015; p. 5) depends on solid metadata capabilities. In LwDITA, those capabilities are represented in components that do not necessarily appear in end-user deliverables, but give human content managers and machine processors information for computing and automation.

XDITA

At the topic level, metadata components are housed inside the prolog (<**prolog**>) environment and represented with the data (<**data**>) component, which depends on pairs of the **@name** and **@value** attributes. Those attributes can provide information like the language of a topic, critical dates for a topic (creation, last revision, expiration, etc.), and much more. In Figure 6.53, a data component provides information about the topic's author. In deliverables produced by LwDITA-aware tools, readers most likely will not see Victoria's name as the author, but the information will be there for human supervisors tracking writers' contributions and machine processors organizing content by author.

HDITA

Topic-level metadata should be included in a <**meta**> tag inside a <**head**> environment. The metadata entries should be expressed in pairs of name (**@name**) and value (**@content**), according to the W3C recommendation for HTML5 metadata[6].

Figure 6.54 places the author metadata on an HDITA topic, which labels the file as written by Victoria Fernando.

```
<?xml version="1.0" encoding="UTF-8"?>
<!DOCTYPE topic PUBLIC "-//OASIS//DTD LIGHTWEIGHT DITA Topic//EN"
"lw-topic.dtd">
<topic id="franchise-intro">
  <title>An innovative, attractive, and out of the ordinary concept</title>
  <shortdesc>Are you interested in investing with us? Welcome to our franchise
information package.</shortdesc>
  <prolog>
    <data name="author" value="Victoria Fernando"/>
  </prolog>
  <body>
    <p>We offer more than 30 exclusive creations for original rolls, from the
California roll to sushi with BBQ chicken or grilled steak.</p>
 </body>
</topic>
```

FIGURE 6.53 Metadata component to identify the author of an XDITA topic. Readers of the Sensei Sushi brochure most likely won't know who created the introductory topic, but the information is embedded in the topic for human authors and machine processors with access to the XDITA source.

MDITA

So far in this chapter, I have only used the YAML header in MDITA extended profile to assign an **@id** to some topics. The YAML header can also house metadata pairs in the form of *name: value*. Figure 6.55 uses the YAML header to embed metadata that identifies Victoria Fernando as author of the topic.

Multimedia Components

LwDITA includes multimedia components that did not make it to the original release of the DITA 1.3 standard. Those components originated in LwDITA but will be included in a DITA 1.3 addendum and in the planned DITA 2.0 standard.

```
<!DOCTYPE html>
<head>
  <title>An innovative, attractive, and out of the ordinary concept</title>
  <meta name="author" content="Victoria Fernando">
</head>
<body>
  <article id="franchise-intro">
    <h1>An innovative, attractive, and out of the ordinary concept</h1>
    <p>Are you interested in investing with us? Welcome to our franchise
information package.</p>
    <p>We offer more than 30 exclusive creations for original rolls, from the
California roll to sushi with BBQ chicken or grilled steak.</p>
  </article>
</body>
```

FIGURE 6.54 Metadata component to identify the author of an HDITA topic. The metadata element is the only HDITA component that requires an HTML5 **<head>** element.

```
---
id: franchise-intro
author: Victoria Fernando
---

# An innovative, attractive, and out of the ordinary concept

Are you interested in investing with us? Welcome to our franchise
information package.

We offer more than 30 exclusive creations for original rolls, from the
California roll to sushi with BBQ chicken or grilled steak.
```

FIGURE 6.55 Metadata component to identify the author of an MDITA topic. The metadata information, provided in an optional YAML header, is only available in the MDITA extended profile.

The LwDITA multimedia components are organized around the audio (<**audio**>) and video (<**video**>) elements.

Audio in XDITA

In XDITA, audio can include the following components:

- Description (<**desc**>; previously mentioned in the figure environment)
- Controls (<**media-controls**>)
- Autoplay (<**media-autoplay**>)
- Loop (<**media-loop**>)
- Muted (<**media-muted**>)
- Source (<**media-source**>)
- Track (<**media-track**>).

Figure 6.56 shows an XDITA topic with an audio element that features the *Sensei Sushi* jingle. This audio-enhanced topic won't make it to the printed brochure for potential franchise owners, but can be included on the company's website.

The <**media-source**> component has an attribute of **@value**, which provides the path for the actual audio file that includes the recorded jingle.

Audio in HDITA and MDITA

In HDITA and MDITA extended profile, audio can include the following components:

- Description (**@title**)
- Controls (**@controls**)
- Autoplay (**@autoplay**)
- Loop (**@loop**)
- Muted (**@muted**)

```
<?xml version="1.0" encoding="UTF-8"?>
<!DOCTYPE topic PUBLIC "-//OASIS//DTD LIGHTWEIGHT DITA Topic//EN"
"lw-topic.dtd">
<topic id="sensei-jingle">
  <title>The Sensei Sushi Jingle</title>
  <body>
    <audio>
      <desc>Recording of the Sensei Sushi jingle</desc>
      <media-controls value="true"/>
      <media-autoplay value="false"/>
      <media-loop value="true"/>
      <media-muted value="true"/>
      <media-source value="sensei-audio.mp3"/>
      <media-track value="sensei-audio.vtt" type="captions"/>
    </audio>
  </body>
</topic>
```

FIGURE 6.56 Audio content environment in XDITA. The components for source and track should be present; all others are optional.

- Source (**<source>**)
- Track (**<track>**).

Figure 6.57 shows an HDITA topic with the audio environment. The same environment, in an HTML5 code block, can be used in an MDITA extended profile topic if needed.

Video in XDITA

In XDITA, video can contain the following components:

- Description (**<desc>**; previously mentioned in the figure environment)
- Poster (**<video-poster>**)

```
<!DOCTYPE html>
<title>The Sensei Sushi Jingle</title>
<body>
  <article id="sensei-jingle">
    <h1>The Sensei Sushi Jingle</h1>
<audio title="Recording of the Sensei Sushi jingle" controls autoplay
loop muted>
  <source src="sensei-audio.mp3"/>
  <track src="sensei-audio.vtt" kind="captions"/>
</audio>
  </article>
</body>
```

FIGURE 6.57 Audio content environment in HDITA. In HTML5, many media components represented with elements in XDITA are expressed with attributes instead. Pay attention to the element-to -attribute correspondence in some multimedia components.

- Controls (<**media-controls**>)
- Autoplay (<**media-autoplay**>)
- Loop (<**media-loop**>)
- Muted (<**media-muted**>)
- Source (<**media-source**>)
- Track (<**media-track**>).

In Figure 6.58, the topic features a video component about the *Sensei Sushi* promise.

Video in HDITA and MDITA

In HDITA and MDITA extended profile, video can include the following components:

- Description (@**title**)
- Poster (@**poster**)
- Controls (@**controls**)
- Autoplay (@**autoplay**)
- Loop (@**loop**)
- Muted (@**muted**)
- Source (<**source**>)
- Track (<**track**>).

```
<?xml version="1.0" encoding="UTF-8"?>
<!DOCTYPE topic PUBLIC "-//OASIS//DTD LIGHTWEIGHT DITA Topic//EN"
"lw-topic.dtd">
<topic id="sensei-promise">
  <title>The Sensei Sushi Promise</title>
  <body>
    <video>
      <desc>Video about the Sensei Sushi promise</desc>
      <video-poster value="sensei-video.jpg"/>
      <media-controls value="true"/>
      <media-autoplay value="false"/>
      <media-loop value="true"/>
      <media-muted value="true"/>
      <media-source value="sensei-video.mp4"/>
      <media-track value="sensei-video.vtt" type="captions"/>
    </video>
  </body>
</topic>
```

FIGURE 6.58 Video content environment in XDITA. The main difference from the audio-enhanced example is the <**video-poster**> component, which provides an optional image for transformations, such as the PDF brochure, that cannot display a video.

Figure 6.59 shows an HDITA topic with the video environment. The same environment, in an HTML5 code block, can be used in an MDITA extended profile topic if needed.

The examples included in this chapter have featured topics for the *Sensei Sushi* brochure created in parallel XDITA, HDITA, and MDITA versions. Ignoring the experimental nature of this scenario, you might wonder now who would need different authoring formats to create the same file (e.g., why would Chef Pedro need XDITA, HDITA, and MDITA versions of the franchise offer topic?). The answer is one of the strongest selling points of LwDITA: the proposed standard allows authors to produce content in their preferred authoring format (XML, HTML5, or Markdown) with the benefit that those formats will be compatible with each other. If the promotional brochure were a real deliverable, Chef Pedro would not need three versions of the same topic. However, the legal team could author the franchise terms topic in HDITA, the kitchen manager could write the sample recipe in XDITA, and the marketing editor could create the introductory topic in MDITA. Those files, produced in different languages, would live together in LwDITA maps and produce cross-format deliverables, and that is the focus of the next section.

All Together Now: Cross-format Authoring in LwDITA

Charlotte Robidoux's article "Rhetorically Structured Content: Developing a Collaborative Single-Sourcing Curriculum" has become a timeless call to embrace structured authoring as a unifier of academia and industry practices in technical communication. Robidoux, director of digital content at Cognizant, authored that article when she was a content strategist and publications manager at Hewlett-Packard. Reporting on the practices of content developers at HP, Robidoux wrote the following about the existence of content silos:

```
<!DOCTYPE html>
<title>The Sensei Sushi Promise</title>
<body>
  <article id="sensei-promise">
    <h1>The Sensei Sushi Promise</h1>
    <video title="Video about the Sensei Sushi promise" controls autoplay
loop muted poster="sensei-video.jpg">
  <source src="sensei-video.mp4"/>
  <track src="sensei-video.vtt" kind="captions"/>
</video>
  </article>
</body>
```

FIGURE 6.59 Video content environment in HDITA. In HTML5 syntax, many of the video components that are represented with XML elements in XDITA are attributes of the **<video>** tag.

> We also observed how common it is for writers to adopt their own favorite practices when working on books independently. Working in "silos," as Rockley (2002) indicated, gave rise to inconsistency, which was difficult for editors to overcome across many thousands of pages of product documentation. Yet, when we systematically implemented structured writing guidelines from the ground up within a document set, as suggested by Ament (2002), we began to see clarity and improved consistency.
>
> (Robidoux, 2008, p.121)

Robidoux cited the first edition of Ann Rockley's *Managing Enterprise Content: A Unified Content Strategy*, which in its second edition still contains a strong warning about the development or content silos or, as Rockley described the problem, the silo trap. According to Rockley, silos are equivalent to "plaque in your arteries, inhibiting the blood flow to your vital organs. If silos hinder the flow of information, the organization is unable to function effectively or respond rapidly to threats and opportunities" (Rockley & Cooper, 2012, p.6).

Even the most "intelligent" content written in properly-structured DITA XML cannot communicate by itself with related files that were created in HTML or Markdown. The Lightweight DITA subcommittee at OASIS posits that content silos could finally communicate in a common language regardless of file format if they adopt the proposed LwDITA standard.

The Cross-format Sensei Sushi Brochure

I retake the scenario of Chef Pedro and the *Sensei Sushi* content needs in this section. As the business grows, so do its communication problems. The *Sensei Sushi* content could be easily siloed according to different teams' practices and preferred authoring languages. Let's revisit the *Sensei Sushi* content silos,

- The legal team wrote the franchise terms topic in HTML
- The kitchen manager had help from a technical writing intern who authored some recipes and procedures in XML
- The marketing editor had been creating introductory information in Markdown.

In a desktop publishing tool or word processor, you would have to copy and paste from one format to the other, making the source files instantly obsolete and taking the content out of the authors' preferred working environments. Using the DITA 1.3 standard, you could incorporate those files as external resources; i.e., a DITA map could reference the diverse authoring formats and produce a deliverable. However, each section would have its own formatting and there would be no consistency in presentation. Furthermore, in DITA

XML you cannot reuse content from, say, an HTML file in an XML topic. With LwDITA, the map could be processed to generate consistent deliverables that, regardless of authoring format, look and feel the same to end users. And, as we will see in Chapter 8, the cross-format capabilities of LwDITA allow seamless content reuse at the topic, section, paragraph, or even phrase level among XDITA, HDITA, and MDITA content files.

This means that the *Sensei Sushi* brochure designer can use a LwDITA map to aggregate and collect pieces of content, while the legal, kitchen, and marketing teams create their content in whatever LwDITA (or DITA XML) format they prefer. All those topics would live on the same intelligent content repository and produce deliverables that, to an end user, would look like coherent units without differences in style or format.

For this example, let's bring back three sample topics from earlier in this chapter. We will use the following files:

- The franchise introductory topic created in MDITA (Figure 6.16) by the marketing team (saved as *franchise-intro.md*)
- The franchise terms topic created in HDITA (Figure 6.37) by the legal team (saved as *franchise-terms.html*)
- The sample recipe for the "Fancy Roll" created in XDITA (Figure 6.49) by the kitchen staff and the technical writing intern (saved as *fancy-roll.dita*).

A map created in XDITA (Figure 6.60) could reference those topics as follows:

The brochure developer can save this map as *crossformat-brochure.ditamap*. The **@format** attribute inside each topic reference (**<topicref>**) instructs the processor on how to treat each file linked from the map. To produce a PDF deliverable from this map, the one-line command for the DITA-OT would be similar to the one we used to process an XDITA map in Chapter 5 (Figure 6.61).

```
<?xml version="1.0" encoding="UTF-8"?>
<!DOCTYPE map PUBLIC "-//OASIS//DTD LIGHTWEIGHT DITA Map//EN" "lw-map.dtd">
<map id="sensei-brochure">
  <topicmeta>
    <navtitle>Sensei Sushi Franchise Opportunity</navtitle>
  </topicmeta>
  <topicref href="franchise-intro.md" format="mdita"/>
  <topicref href="franchise-terms.html" format="hdita"/>
  <topicref href="fancy-roll.dita" format="xdita" />
    </map>
```

FIGURE 6.60 XDITA map for the cross-format version of the *Sensei Sushi* brochure. The topic reference components include attributes for format (in bold font), which take the value ("xdita", "hdita", or "mdita") corresponding to each file's authoring language.

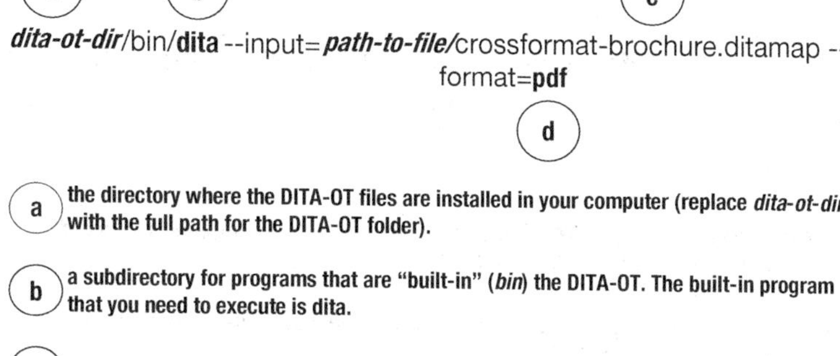

FIGURE 6.61 Command for the DITA-OT to generate a PDF deliverable from the cross-format *Sensei Sushi* XDITA map.

Figure 6.62 displays the HDITA version of the cross-format map to produce the *Sensei Sushi* introductory brochure.

The HDITA map can be saved as *crossformat-brochure.html*. Figure 6.63 shows the DITA-OT command to produce a PDF deliverable from the HDITA map.

Lastly, Figure 6.64 shows the MDITA version of the cross-format map for the *Sensei Sushi* brochure.

```
<!DOCTYPE html>
<title>Sensei Sushi Franchise Opportunity</title>
<nav id="crossformat-brochure">
  <h1>Sensei Sushi Franchise Opportunity</h1>
  <ul>
    <li>
      <p><a href="franchise-intro.md" type="text/markdown">Introduction</a>
        <p>
    </li>
    <li>
      <p><a href="franchise-terms.html" type="text/html">Legal terms</a></p>
    </li>
    <li>
      <p><a href="fancy-roll.dita" type="text/xml">Sample recipe</a></p>
    </li>
  </ul>
</nav>
```

FIGURE 6.62 HDITA map for the cross-format version of the *Sensei Sushi* brochure. To make the file valid HTML5, the attribute for format in each topic reference is **@type**, and the values are "text/markdown" for MDITA, "text/html" for HDITA, and "text/xml" for XDITA.

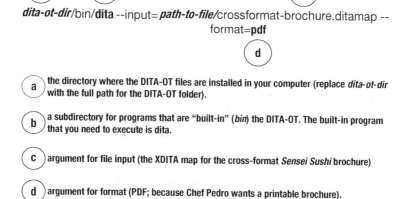

a b c

```
dita-ot-dir/bin/dita --input=path-to-file/crossformat-brochure.html --
format=pdf
```

d

a — the directory where the DITA-OT files are installed in your computer (replace *dita-ot-dir* with the full path for the DITA-OT folder).

b — a subdirectory for programs that are "built-in" (*bin*) the DITA-OT. The built-in program that you need to execute is dita.

c — argument for file input (the HDITA map for the cross-format *Sensei Sushi* brochure)

d — argument for format (PDF; because Chef Pedro wants a printable brochure).

FIGURE 6.63 Command for the DITA-OT to generate a PDF deliverable from the cross-format *Sensei Sushi* HDITA map.

Figure 6.65 shows the DITA-OT command to generate a PDF deliverable from the MDITA map in Figure 6.64.

A LwDITA-aware software application like Oxygen XML Editor can also process the XDITA, HDITA, and MDITA versions of the cross-format map. The "Apply Transformation Scenario(s)" dialog box in Oxygen would present the user with options to produce deliverables from each of these LwDITA maps. Figure 6.66 shows the table of contents of a PDF built in Oxygen XML from the XDITA version of this cross-format map.

```
# Sensei Sushi Franchise Opportunity

-    [Introduction](franchise-intro.md)

-    [Legal terms](franchise-terms.html)

-    [Sample recipe](fancy-roll.dita)
```

FIGURE 6.64 MDITA map for the cross-format version of the *Sensei Sushi* brochure. In Markdown syntax there is no need for attributes specifying file types or formats.

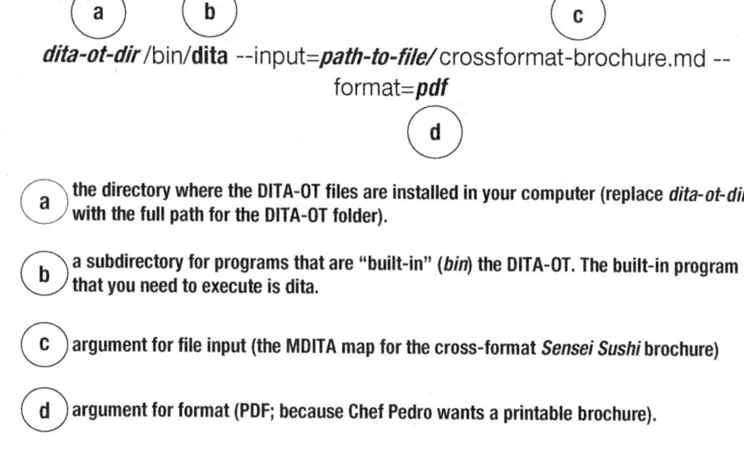
a
b
c
dita-ot-dir/bin/dita --input=path-to-file/crossformat-brochure.md --format=pdf
d
a the directory where the DITA-OT files are installed in your computer (replace dita-ot-dir with the full path for the DITA-OT folder).
b a subdirectory for programs that are "built-in" (bin) the DITA-OT. The built-in program that you need to execute is dita.
c argument for file input (the MDITA map for the cross-format Sensei Sushi brochure)
d argument for format (PDF; because Chef Pedro wants a printable brochure).

FIGURE 6.65 Command for the DITA-OT to generate a PDF deliverable from the cross-format *Sensei Sushi* MDITA map.

So, Is My Content Intelligent Now?

This chapter introduced you to the main components available in LwDITA to structure and present information. Becoming familiar with these content structures and how to represent them in the initial LwDITA authoring formats is an important step in preparing intelligent content deliverables. However, LwDITA alone will not make any content intelligent. In order to take advantage of the LwDITA proposed standard and make content stand out from the millions of dead pages created in word processors and desktop publishing tools, we need to

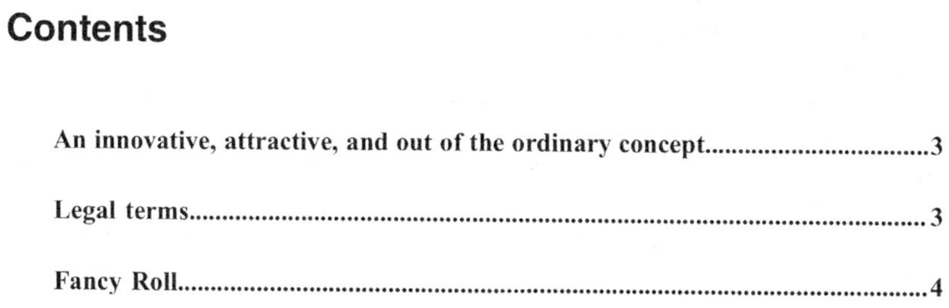

Contents

An innovative, attractive, and out of the ordinary concept........3

Legal terms........3

Fancy Roll........4

FIGURE 6.66 Table of contents of a PDF deliverable produced from the XDITA version of the cross-format map. End users will not know which topic was created in which authoring format. The effect of content silos is minimized when the final product presents each topic with the same format and appearance.

go back to a concept I discussed in Chapter 1 and prepare to combine content structured with LwDITA with principles of computational thinking.

In the following chapter, I revisit the concept of abstraction as a starting point of computational thinking. I also set the foundations used in Chapter 8 to examine an author's role in intelligent content workflows, expanding a series of abstractions (Evia et al., 2015) based on thinking processes recommended for technical writers. Then, I will connect those abstractions and models to LwDITA.

Notes

1 http://yaml.org/
2 https://github.github.com/gfm/#atx-heading
3 https://github.github.com/gfm/#setext-heading
4 Continuous Acquisition and Lifecycle Support
5 Although the W3C recommendation for HTML5 treats the <u> element as "unarticulated" (https://www.w3.org/TR/html5/textlevel-semantics.html#the-u-element), HDITA gives it a semantic meaning of underline to map the <u> component usage in DITA and XDITA
6 https://www.w3.org/TR/html50/document-metadata.html#attr-meta-name

References

Evia, C., Sharp, M. R., & Perez-Quiñones, M. A. (2015). Teaching structured authoring and DITA through rhetorical and computational thinking. *IEEE Transactions on Professional Communication*, 58(3), 328–343.

Evia, C., Eberlein, K., & Houser, A. (Eds.) (2018). *Lightweight DITA: An introduction.* Version 1.0. OASIS.

GitHub Flavored Markdown Spec. (2017, August 1). Retrieved from https://github.github.com/gfm/

Robidoux, C. (2008). Rhetorically structured content: Developing a collaborative single-sourcing curriculum, *Technical Communication Quarterly*, 17(1), 110–135.

Rockley, A. (2002). *Managing enterprise content: A unified content strategy.* Indianapolis, IN: New Riders.

Rockley, A. & Cooper, C. (2012). *Managing enterprise content: A unified content strategy.* (2nd ed.). Berkeley, CA: New Riders.

Rockley, A., Cooper, C., & Abel, S. (2015). *Intelligent Content: A Primer.* Laguna Hills, CA: XML Press.

W3C. (2017, December 14). HTML 5.2: W3C recommendation. Retrieved from https://www.w3.org/TR/html52

7

THE ABSTRACTIONS BEHIND INTELLIGENT CONTENT

The April 4, 2017 edition of The New York Times featured a story titled "Learning to Think Like a Computer," which contributed to introducing the concept of computational thinking to mainstream audiences. The article acknowledged that computational thinking is not necessarily a new term, and that it was used by educator and mathematician Seymour Papert "in 1980 to envision how children could use computers to learn" (Pappano, 2017). The article went on to mention that Jeannette Wing "gets credit for making it fashionable" (Pappano, 2017). Wing's model of computational thinking, which I introduced in Chapter 1, highlights the importance of abstractions over numerical processes and algorithms. Based on that model, this chapter explores the layers of abstraction behind the process of authoring intelligent content.

Hayakawa & Hayakawa explain the concept of abstraction through the example of "Bessie the cow," which is described in their influential work on semantics as a dynamic process (with respiratory, nervous, digestive and other systems "constantly changing") and not just a static object. In the Hayakawas' abstraction ladder, the word "Bessie" "is the lowest verbal level of abstraction," which leaves out the characteristics that Bessie the cow could have in common with other animals, other farm assets, other general assets, and eventually other sources of wealth for a farmer, omitting further characteristics (Hayakawa & Hayakawa, 1990; p. 84). Applying this concept to content development or technical communication, we can place a deliverable (e.g., a standard operating procedure or a webpage) at that lowest level of abstraction, not as a static object but as a dynamic process.

The concept of abstraction is also quite prevalent in the introductory literature to computing architecture. In his popular textbook *Structured Computer Organization*, Andrew S. Tanenbaum described computers "as a series of abstractions, each abstraction building on the one below it" (2006, pp. 1–2). Following that model, computing engineers can master the complexity of communicating high-level human needs and processes (e.g., check email messages, create a spreadsheet, watch a movie on Netflix) to the low-level electronic signals and components of a computer. Without levels or layers of abstraction, a developer would have to code, for example, a Twitter status update directly into a series of instructions for the computer's processor and memory. Abstraction allows humans to separate the "layers" of a particular problem and work on each one individually without concern for the others. Then, as the layers are recombined, they work together to solve the problem in a process that can be represented as a replicable algorithm.

Most authors probably will enter an intelligent content workflow unaware of the larger discussions on computational thinking and abstractions behind automating publication and filtering routines. The abstractions relevant to the creation of intelligent content with LwDITA introduced in this chapter are a combination of the semantic (process vs. object) model and the computer architecture levels. These abstractions hide the layers that authors do not need to know until they move to a more advanced layer. To a casual observer, the act of writing static content on a word processing application or a presentation-oriented web content management system might look similar to that of creating intelligent content (in both cases a person is typing on a computer), but the "mental" (abstraction) layers behind those processes go beyond the use of "metal" (automation) tools.

The layers of abstraction of authoring in a workflow with LwDITA are related to the stages on a content development lifecycle. However, whereas a fully-developed lifecycle requires detailed planning and evaluation stages, the specific recommendations from *Creating Intelligent Content with Lightweight DITA* focus on the deficit in content-development training and education. Concepts and practices from user experience research, content strategy, and usability have made it to the technical communication vocabulary in industry and academia, and undoubtedly paved the way for intelligent content. Yet in many technical communication academic programs the preferred authoring tools and workflows involve a word processor or a static website platform. Those teaching practices prevail despite decades of conversation about the benefits of intelligent content enablers like single-sourcing and reuse and industry best practices.

A very important disclaimer: Despite the benefits of adopting an intelligent content workflow with LwDITA, there are many situations and contexts that would be better off without it. Intelligent content requires dedication, commitment, and resources. Thus, a lone writer developing deliverables for an audience of one or two readers in one type of deliverable, could still find the ideal solution in a word processor. Having an understanding of the principles of authoring intelligent content with LwDITA, however, can benefit that lone writer in the near future, as even the smallest content unit (a Microsoft Word file today) can grow to become a complex repository (1000 pages of unstructured content with hundreds of tasks, frequently-asked questions, and product descriptions, for example). From a cautionary or preventive perspective, planning ahead can minimize the future impact of dealing with legacy content siloed in one platform. From an educational perspective, some authors mentioned in the next section claim that making computation, and its potential benefits, available to thinkers of all disciplines is a responsibility in academia.

Intelligent Content Needs Computational Thinking

Before implementing any computing tools or developing automation solutions, a user experimenting with a computational thinking methodology or exploring the benefits of intelligent content must break down the process in a series of abstractions. The "Learning to Think Like a Computer" article from The New York Times that I mentioned earlier in this chapter included a relevant example provided by Dan Garcia, from the University of California, Berkeley. Garcia explained abstraction as a foundational element in computational thinking with the following scenario:

> "There is a reason when you go to the 'Joy of Cooking' and you want to make a strawberry milkshake, you don't look under 'strawberry milkshake,'" he said. Rather, there is a recipe for milkshakes that instructs you to add ice cream, milk and fruit of your choice. While earlier cookbooks may have had separate recipes for strawberry milkshakes, raspberry milkshakes and boysenberry milkshakes, eventually, he imagines, someone said, "Why don't we collapse that into one milkshake recipe?"
>
> (Pappano, 2017)

Applying that example to the world of intelligent content, Garcia's versatile milkshake recipe represents the type of authoring process that cannot be achieved with a word processor or a presentational web platform. The process of seeing the milkshake flavor as a variable in one layer, with additional ingredients as constants in another layer, the placement of specific requirements and steps in a third layer, and computing rules to create a unique recipe for readers in yet another layer requires, like Chef Pedro's content needs for the *Sensei Sushi* publications from previous chapters, a different kind of thinking from the author. And that process is not about tools; actually, only a few of those layers require a computing tool, and some happen inside the author's mind before going to a computing device. That authors can view content as non-linear and envision more than one outcome based on principles of reuse and single-sourcing might sound like a major innovation to professionals in academia and industry accustomed to using a word processor as their main tool. Yet, this process is not new in the world of technical communication: it has been more than 17 years since Hart-Davidson (2001) asked scholars and practitioners to see the content chunks of single-sourcing projects as rhetorical objects and not just mere information. Nine years later, Hart-Davidson (2010) noted that the technical communication literature focused narrowly on the concept of single-sourcing, to the detriment of other aspects of a content management (CM) workflow that involve technical authors. Evaluating the coverage of topics related to CM in academic work, Andersen lamented that technical communication "scholarship on CM to date has almost exclusively taken an academic perspective; when articulating and theorizing trends, methods, and technologies, we tend to situate our discussions within the existing scholarship rather than the larger CM discourse that is actively shaping CM practice" (Andersen, 2014, p. 117). This deficiency presents a unique opportunity for implementing an approach based on principles of computational thinking. The mandate of "go learn about intelligent content and then bring it back to your classroom and research agenda" has been ineffective for many years as a way to convince technical communication faculty and graduate students about the importance of industry practices. Much like separating the layers of computing architecture so engineers can focus on one problem at a time, seeing the process behind intelligent content with LwDITA as a series of layers involving important, but separate, abstractions can provide a more navigable path for adoption.

In previous chapters, I have highlighted the role of LwDITA code as an important component of a content-development workflow built on principles of computational thinking. Nevertheless, this is not a "learn code qua code" manifesto, and in some instances (like the use of Oxygen XML Editor as an authoring tool in Chapters 5 and 6) the actual code behind an implementation of LwDITA can be hidden in a layer of abstraction that shows a graphical user interface to a writer.

Abstractions for content creators are ways of thinking before structuring information and seeing its future applications. A computer programmer would take the sum of those abstractions to design an algorithm and automate a routine, but for an author the final outcome is to think and see what the content can accomplish once it is liberated from the word processing or web presentational models.

Automation "is the mapping of computation to physical systems that perform them" (Perković et al., 2010, p. 124). Rockley explains that mapping process as it pertains to content development with the example of a company hosting a webinar. If the webinar is transcribed into text, and if that text is processed through the layers of abstraction needed to have it structured and tagged for human readers and machine processors, "the main work is done; everything else can be automated" (Rockley, 2016). She provides potential automated outcomes such as extracting questions and answers from the webinar transcription and turning them into blog posts, compiling "the blog posts into a digest post of the top 'X' things you need to know," extracting "key quotes and tweet them," and taking "the same questions, post them to Facebook, and start a conversation" (Rockley, 2016).

Across industries and professions, just mentioning the word "automation" can strike fear of humans (and/or their jobs) becoming obsolete, and technical communication is no exception. Gu & Pullman hypothesized that "a systems-based approach to content management may very well result in a devaluing of technical writers and editors and reduce their roles to those of assembly workers, where they are concerned only with producing discrete information chunks" (Gu & Pullman, 2009, p. 5). Gu & Pullman presented that scenario in 2009, and technical writing jobs have not become assembly-line positions (at least not yet). I argue that in a model of intelligent content with LwDITA built on principles of computational thinking, *machine automation cannot happen without human abstraction*. The workplace still needs thinkers and curators of automated content, and technical communication programs in academia should be preparing students for those positions and for conducting research that will advance and improve intelligent content concepts and practices. Rockley & Gollner, writing about intelligent content as a key step in developing a sustainable content strategy, mention that:

> Automation can be used to minimize the time, effort and money needed to apply a good content strategy. However, automation doesn't just happen. Content must be consciously designed to support it. An intelligent content strategy establishes a coherent plan under which content will be designed, developed and deployed so as to achieve maximum benefit to the customer and the organization while minimizing the cost to the organization.
>
> (Rockley and Gollner, 2011)

Rockley & Gollner's portrayal of content automation subject to human thinking structures bears resemblance to the model of computational thinking by Jeannette Wing that I mentioned in Chapter 1. In this model, automation can be implemented as a problem-solving approach, but only after abstractions are applied in the development of structures in algorithmic workflows. In sum, in order to achieve efficient automation routines for content, authors (and not necessarily programmers or developers) need to get involved in a structured process involving layers of abstraction and replicable rules.

On the academic side of technical communication (and in corporate training), we have the opportunity to fill this gap in knowledge and teach about the benefits and requirements of developing an intelligent content strategy based on principles and practices of computational thinking. Back in 2004, David Dayton identified "two major fault lines" creating tension in the profession of technical communication: one between academics and practitioners, and another among academics, with a camp focusing on rhetorical generalism and another identifying the field at the intersection of information technology and organizational communication (Dayton, 2004). Those fault lines are still threatening the field's foundation, and even prompted Carolyn Rude to pose the rhetorical question, "In trying to define our field as something more than adjunct to the computer industry engaged in vocational training, have we overcorrected?" (2015, p. 10). I see the blending of computational thinking and writing studies discussed in this chapter as a way to patch that fault line and find ways to teach computing principles in our domain without losing our academic and disciplinary identities.

From the perspective of computing education, Mark Guzdial provides a supporting statement for teaching computing principles outside of computer science courses:

> Computing professionals and educators have the responsibility to make computation available to thinkers of all disciplines. Part of that responsibility will be met through formal education. While a professional in another field may be able to use an application with little training, the metaphors and ways of thinking about computing must be explicitly taught.
> (Guzdial, 2008, p. 25)

Commenting on Wing's model of computational thinking, Guzdial identifies two sets of examples with different goals. One is about "applying computing ideas to facilitate computing work in other disciplines," and another is about "applying computing ideas in daily life, completely apart from any use of computing." He questions the ultimate promise of computational thinking and presents it as a problem of knowledge transfer. "If you learn to make a computer repeat steps, does that influence how you think about your co-workers, as Jeannette Wing suggests? If you learn how to sort numbers with recursion, do you also learn how to use recursion when developing a strategy for tiling your kitchen floor?" (Guzdial, 2016, p. 40). Guzdial adds that "achieving the goals of applying computing ideas to facilitate computing work in other disciplines is clearly achievable," but "applying computing ideas in daily life is less likely" (2016, p. 40). Lorena Barba has stronger doubts about the ambitious benefits of Wing's computational thinking. She points out that "most people don't want to be a computer scientist, but everyone can use computers as an extension of our minds, to experience the world and create things that matter to us" (Barba, 2016).

In this book, I follow Guzdial's and Barba's cautious philosophy: developing intelligent content with LwDITA grounded on principles of computational thinking will help communicators produce future-proof content that is ready for automation and is not restricted to one deliverable and one audience. It is possible that students introduced to LwDITA methodologies for creating content will be on an easier path for acquiring skills in programming and other advanced computing topics, or perhaps the students will only apply computing practices to work relevant to their identity as content creators. And I have not heard from DITA or LwDITA practitioners who used their intelligent content knowledge for tiling the kitchen floor. The recommendations and models presented in this book come from my experience teaching DITA and LwDITA at the college level and in industry workshops and conferences. They also come from my roles as co-chair of the Lightweight DITA subcommittee with OASIS and co-editor of the technical specification for the LwDITA standard.

Evaluating Content Developers as Computational Thinkers

When talking about covering concepts of computing outside of computer science courses, Perković et al. (2010) proposed a model for computational thinking across the curriculum. However, recent approaches look at specific disciplinary applications. Musaeus et al., for example, claim that computational thinking "as part of the medical curriculum could help educate novices (medical students and physicians in training) in the analysis and design of complex healthcare organizations, which increasingly rely on computer technology. Such teaching should engage novices in information practices where they learn to perceive practices of computer technology as directly involved in the provision of patient care" (Musaeus et al., 2017, p. 85). Likewise, Senske reported from an effort to teach computational thinking to architecture students, based on the idea that "understanding computation and being able to express oneself computationally is not optional" (2017, p. 525). If computational thinking should be taught for medical students in the context of provision of patient care, and for architects it should be presented in the context of design principles, for content professionals it should be in the processes, tools, and indicators required in an intelligent content workflow. LwDITA provides a low-barrier entry point for students in writing programs or humanities departments.

Guzdial also sees disciplinary application as an essential step in assessing computational thinking. He adds that demonstrating knowledge of computing is a necessary, but insufficient part of computational thinking assessment. He proposes that students "must be applying, connecting, or transferring the computing knowledge to other domains to be computational thinking" (Guzdial, 2016a).

For students and practitioners of content development or technical communication, demonstrating knowledge of computing in the context of their profession is, therefore, a goal when talking about computational thinking or computational literacy. A starting point to assess that knowledge can come from the International Society for Technology in Education (ISTE) Standards for Students, which include a rubric to standardize the assessment of computational thinking across the curriculum. The ISTE Standards for Students, which have the overall goal to "promote future-ready learning," focus on the following dimensions:

1. Empowered learner
2. Digital citizen
3. Knowledge constructor
4. Innovative designer
5. Computational thinker
6. Creative communicator
7. Global collaborator

I would argue that students working on an intelligent content workflow with LwDITA could fulfill many of those standards, but for the purpose of *Creating Intelligent Content with Lightweight DITA* I will focus on the "Computational thinker" standard. ISTE specifies that the "Computational thinker" dimension could be assessed if "students develop and employ strategies for understanding and solving problems in ways that leverage the power of technological methods to develop and test solutions" (ISTE, 2018).

The standard adds the following indicators for assessing students as computational thinkers:

- 5a. Students formulate problem definitions suited for technology-assisted methods such as data analysis, abstract models and algorithmic thinking in exploring and finding solutions.
- 5b. Students collect data or identify relevant data sets, use digital tools to analyze them, and represent data in various ways to facilitate problem-solving and decision-making.
- 5c. Students break problems into component parts, extract key information, and develop descriptive models to understand complex systems or facilitate problem-solving.
- 5d. Students understand how automation works and use algorithmic thinking to develop a sequence of steps to create and test automated solutions (ISTE, 2018).

The ISTE indicators for assessing the dimension of computational thinker can be related to the main characteristics of intelligent content and, eventually, to the layers of abstraction behind content developed in a LwDITA workflow. A modern content-development lifecycle is an important connector for establishing those relations, and that is the overarching topic of the following sections.

Abstractions in the Intelligent Content Process

I have mentioned a few times the definition of intelligent content provided by Rockley et al. in *Intelligent Content: A Primer*, which introduces important keywords that drive the development of those "more than templates" of structured authoring that allow writers to put into action thought structures built on solid abstractions that could lead to automated publishing workflows. The characteristics of intelligent content set the foundation for assessing computational thinking, based on the ISTE indicators, in the domains of technical communication and content authoring.

As I mentioned in Chapter 1, according to Rockley et al. intelligent content should present the following five characteristics:

1. **Modular** content is "intentionally designed for reuse." Instead of page-centric books, authors of intelligent content create modules or components of content (topics) "one at a time."
2. **Structured** content is "designed to be both human and machine readable." Enablers of that kind of dual readability are the behind-the-scenes labels and notes (i.e., tags and attributes) that made the formula of content + code result in a data source.
3. **Reusable** content uses "existing modular content components to develop new content products." In a word processing environment, an author can use copy and paste functions, but those eventually reach manual limitations. Reuse in intelligent content is automated and provides consistency across deliverables and sections, while also simplifying translation processes (and costs associated with them).
4. **Format-free** content "does not include presentation information, such as instructions about fonts, column widths, or text placement." The separation of format and content is essential for multichannel publishing, and the layer of abstraction provided by a desktop publishing application in this regard can be a dangerous one. A word processor successfully abstracts the process of separating computing rules for content and format, but as a result keeps the content locked in one deliverable. In most cases, human authors would have to modify font-sizes and paragraph structures manually.
5. **Semantically rich** content includes "added extra, machine-readable information that describes what the content is, what it's about, and more." This layer of metadata can specify the type of audience, platform (or cuisine, if we look back at the marinara sauce example from Chapter 1) for a whole topic of information or for specific paragraph or phrase level elements in that topic (Rockley et al., 2015, pp. 3–5).

I propose a sixth characteristic of *rhetorical effectiveness*. Intelligence applied to content development and delivery does not guarantee intelligence in reconciling the needs and perspectives of readers and writers. *Rhetorically effective* content can connect topical and authorial intentions with user responses regardless of a deliverable's format or context. If content production can be automated, it still depends on humans as authors, information architects, and experience evaluators in order to be rhetorically effective.

Rhetorical effectiveness plays an important role in the application of LwDITA as an agent of intelligent content. Rhetorical effectiveness establishes successful context and also helps to envision the future of a content repository. In some cases, LwDITA authors cannot control all the use and reuse cases of their content, but rhetorical effectiveness should be an aspirational value in intelligent content workflows at the planning, authoring and evaluating levels. In Chapter 8, I introduce a model for content development with LwDITA that fosters rhetorical effectiveness through context-setting metadata and human-in-the-loop (HITL) requirements for automation.

Developing intelligent content with LwDITA is, thus, the most straightforward application of computational thinking in structured authoring and technical communication. It can be used in workplace settings and it can also be taught in academic environments for workforce preparation, but also for advancing knowledge in this area. Scholars in writing programs and technical communication are positioned to conduct research in the intersection of computational thinking and content in ways that most computing professionals simply are not prepared or motivated to explore. Opportunities for practice and research abound across the spectrum of modern content-development lifecycles, which provide the foundation for the layers of abstraction behind authoring and publishing workflows with LwDITA.

Exploring Intelligent Content-development Lifecycles

I have identified the intended audiences of this book as a) students and instructors who have been hesitant to learn about intelligent content and DITA because they see those as technologies alien to their work as scholars of writing, and b) practitioners who are interested in DITA or LwDITA from an author perspective and not necessarily as tools developers. For both of these audience groups, the mandate of "go learn about intelligent content and then bring it back to your work" responds to the call for ways to better align education and research in technical communication with practice that Andersen (2014) categorizes as certainly not new but never so urgent. An appropriate reaction to this urgency should separate that mandate in manageable layers of abstraction that can be addressed individually by working on a progression of activities and ideas by focusing on some concepts while ignoring others that would be revealed after completing the current layer. In writing studies, the process vs. product debate has been pretty much settled since the days of Janet Emig (1977); thus, it is unfair to expect professionals from academia or industry to embrace intelligent content as a product or practice without a detailed process giving steps to achieve it.

Although there is no generally-adopted process or workflow for authoring intelligent content with DITA or LwDITA, some authors have proposed detailed models for content-development lifecycles that provide a solid foundation for the layers of abstraction that I will introduce in Chapter 8. These models go beyond traditional document-based lifecycles (which are more production-oriented) associated with technical communication practices that work mainly as straightforward maps in a line of progression. Andersen claims that "the era of document-based information development (ID), which has shaped all aspects of research on professional and technical communication, training, and practice since the field's inception, is coming to an end" (2014a, p. 10).

Recent models have proposed less linear and more iterative frameworks that focus on developing and implementing a recursive and overall content strategy. Bailie & Urbina's content lifecycle model, for example, is built on a structure of four quadrants that represent the stages of 1) analysis, 2) collection, 3) management, and 4) publication (which includes "post-publication maintenance") followed by a loop back to analysis for the next cycle. Each quadrant involves some decisions for humans behind the content-development process.

The quadrants, and related decisions, included in Bailie & Urbina's content lifecycle are as follows:

1. Analysis (Examining Business Drivers). Includes decisions about business requirements, user experience, governance, and budget.
2. Collection (Creating or Gathering Content). Includes decisions about the sources of content.
3. Management (Improving Production Efficiency). Includes decisions about the adoption of content standards and technologies.
4. Publication (More than Presentation). Includes decisions related to "all the aspects of content that happen after the authoring is done and the content is ready to be sent to its destination" (Bailie & Urbina, 2013, pp. 237–241).

Bailie & Urbina emphasize that their model is software-agnostic ("The stages of the lifecycle address a comprehensive set of issues that must be addressed no matter what software is adopted"), extensible ("The cycle is not limited to content within a silo, whether a departmental silo or genre silo), and iterative ("Content lives on through multiple iterations, whether the iteration is a translation, a revision, or other type of variant") (2013, p. 243).

Combining discourse from the academic and practitioner sides of technical communication, Andersen assembled a "composite and descriptions of the essential stages, key activities, and common deliverables in building a content strategy framework" (2014, p. 134). Andersen's framework covers the following stages and activities:

1. Analyzing customer needs: gather user requirements, define personas and scenarios, and identify device constraints.
2. Analyzing business needs: gather business requirements, analyze content lifecycle, conduct content audit, and analyze existing content.

3. Developing an information architecture (the content strategy road map): build content models and define metadata that describe the content, define reuse strategy, and define adaptive content strategy.
4. Creating unified processes (work flow and governance): define workflow and define governance.
5. Developing the technology strategy: define technology requirements, evaluate tool options, work with content management system (CMS) integrators to implement the content model, and implement tools.
6. Creating structured content: create new content or convert unstructured to structured content.
7. Managing change: create change-management plan, including a communication plan, enlist change agents and champions, and define new roles and modify existing ones (Andersen, 2014, pp. 135–136).

These models of a content-development process establish concrete stages, decisions, and activities that can be linked to the ISTE indicators for assessing computational thinking and describing the layers of abstraction in the process of creating intelligent content with LwDITA.

In a previous publication (Evia et al., 2015), I described the approach implemented in the undergraduate course *Creating User Documentation* at Virginia Tech to teach concepts of intelligent content, DITA, and computational thinking combined with rhetorical problem solving. That approach is based on a sequence of layers of abstraction that supersede (and actually include) a technical writing process focused on document production. Those original layers of abstraction for teaching content development with DITA to students in a department of English are the result of years of collaboration with my former colleagues Matthew Sharp, who is now assistant professor of communication at Embry-Riddle Aeronautical University, and Manuel Pérez-Quiñones, who is now professor and associate dean of computing and informatics at the University of North Carolina, Charlotte.

We developed those layers following the approach for teaching professional writing recommended by Linda Flower, which "acknowledges the importance of discourse conventions but concentrates on broader rhetorical strategies for analyzing the audience, planning, revising, and managing one's time and writing process" (1989, p.5). The "layers of abstraction identified to introduce concepts of component content management, structured authoring, and DITA from a computational thinking and genre theory perspective (Evia et al., 2015, p. 334)" represent those broader rhetorical strategies, and are as follows:

- Layer 1: Developing quality documentation. "The main objective in this layer is to introduce technical documentation as a process and not just a product."
- Layer 2: Separating content from design. "This layer requires (students) to relinquish control of format in order to create content within an XML and template-based environment."

- Layer 3: Authoring granular content with XML. "This layer has the objective of introducing component-based XML authoring and filtering with the purpose of presenting modules created in XML as equivalents of more traditional technical and professional writing genres."
- Layer 4: Authoring and linking Component Content Management modules with DITA. "The overall objective of this layer is to make students comfortable with topic-based writing and the functions and responsibilities of a DITA author."
- Layer 5: Single sourcing and content reuse. "In this layer, students write content once, and then create multiple deliverables for different audiences, using some unique topics and some reused topics" (Evia et al., 2015, pp. 335–339).

Those layers of abstraction focus, one by one, on practical and separate concepts related to the characteristics of intelligent content and competencies and skills that, based on industry conversation and formal interviews with practitioners and academics (see Evia et al., 2015 for details on the methodology), are expected of technical communicators working in content management environments. The layers of abstraction did not have the specific goal of assessing if students became computational thinkers; thus, they were not directly inspired by a strict rubric like the ISTE standards. However, they were loosely based on the College Board's AP Computer Science Principles "big ideas" (2017). That model also reflects our academic privilege as college professors whose students did not have real workplace expectations and deadlines: as we taught these layers in fictional scenarios, our students did not have the pressure from actual customers/users, managers, and subject matter experts that technical communicators face in the workplace. Therefore, instead of following a rigid content development workflow (e.g., Bailie & Urbina's model), students focused on the quadrant of *collection* (creating or gathering content), while we assumed that elements of information technology (tools support, processing), management (deadlines and supervision), and design (templates and stylesheets) were the instructors' responsibility and were just briefly discussed in class.

Furthermore, those layers of abstraction from the 2015 publication are XML-centric, because we used them to teach DITA XML. Michael Priestley and I created our first LwDITA demos and test files after that article was submitted for publication; as a result, those initial five layers of abstraction are all about DITA XML.

In the following chapter I introduce a revised version of the layers of abstraction for teaching intelligent content to technical communication students and trainees. The revised layers expand beyond the content acquisition stage and cover from planning to evaluation and revision. They are also based on the LwDITA authoring formats described in Chapter 4, which embrace the diversity of tools used by content creators across disciplines and professional silos. Furthermore, those revised layers are connected to specific stages in the content-development lifecycles introduced in this chapter and the ISTE standards for evaluating students as computational thinkers.

References

Andersen, R. (2014). Rhetorical work in the age of content management: Implications for the field of technical communication. *Journal of Business and Technical Communication*, 28(2), 115–157.

Andersen, R. (2014a). Toward a more integrated view of technical communication. *Communication Design Quarterly Review*. 2(2), 10–16.

Bailie, R.A. & Urbina, N. (2013). *Content strategy: Connecting the dots between business, brand, and benefits*. Laguna Hills, CA: XML Press.

Barba, L.A. (2016, March 5). Computational thinking: I do not think it means what you think it means [Blog post]. Retrieved from http://lorenabarba.com/blog/computational-thinking-i-do-not-think-it-means-what-you-think-it-means/

College Board. (2017). AP computer science principles. Retrieved from https://apcentral.collegeboard.org/pdf/ap-computer-science-principles-course-and-exam-description.pdf

Dayton, D. (2004). The future of technical communication according to those who teach it. *Paper presented at the conference of the Society for Technical Communication.*

Emig, J. (1977). Writing as a mode of learning. *College Composition and Communication*, 28(2), 122–128.

Evia, C., Sharp, M. R., & Perez-Quiñones, M. A. (2015). Teaching structured authoring and DITA through rhetorical and computational thinking. *IEEE Transactions on Professional Communication*, 58(3), 328–343.

Flower, L. (1989). Rhetorical problem solving: Cognition and professional writing. In M. Kogen (Ed.), *Writing in the business professions* (pp.3–36). Urbana, IL: NCTE.

Gu, B. & Pullman G. (2009). Introduction: Mapping out the key parameters of content management. In G. Pullman & B. Gu (Eds.), *Content management bridging the gap between theory and practice* (pp. 1–12). Amityville, NY: Baywood.

Guzdial, M. (2008). Education: Paving the way for computational thinking. *Communications of the ACM*. 51(8), 25–27.

Guzdial, M. (2016). *Learner-centered design of computing education: Research on computing for everyone*. New York, NY: Morgan & Claypool.

Guzdial, M. (2016a, January 13). What does it mean to assess computational thinking? [Blog post]. Retrieved from https://computinged.wordpress.com/2016/01/13/what-does-it-mean-to-assess-computational-thinking/

Hart-Davidson, W. (2001). Reviewing and rebuilding technical communication theory: Considering the value of theory for informing change in practice and curriculum. *Paper presented at the Society for Technical Communication conference.*

Hart-Davidson, W. (2010). Content management: Beyond single-sourcing. In R. Spilka (Ed.) *Digital literacy for technical communication: 21st century theory and practice* (pp. 128–143). New York, NY: Routledge.

Hayakawa, S. I. & Hayakawa, A.R. (1990). *Language in thought and action*. Orlando, FL: Harcourt.

ISTE. (2018). ISTE standards for students. Retrieved from http://www.iste.org/standards/for-students

Musaeus, P., Tatar, D., & Rosen, M. (2017) Medical computational thinking: Computer scientific reasoning in the medical curriculum. In P.J. Rich & C.B. Hodges (Eds.) *Emerging research, practice, and policy on computational thinking* (pp. 85–98), Springer.

Pappano, L. (2017, April 4). Learning to think like a computer. *The New York Times*, Retrieved from https://www.nytimes.com/2017/04/04/education/edlife/teaching-students-computer-code.html

Perković, L., Settle, A., Hwang, S., & Jones, J. (2010). A framework for computational thinking across the curriculum. *Proceedings of the fifteenth annual conference on innovation and technology in computer science education*, 123-127.

Rockley A. & Gollner, J. (2011, January 10). An intelligent content strategy for the enterprise. *Bulletin of the American Society for Information Science and Technology*. Retrieved from https://onlinelibrary.wiley.com/doi/full/10.1002/bult.2011.1720370211

Rockley, A. (2016, July 14). *Why automation is the future of content creation*. Retrieved from https://contentmarketinginstitute.com/2016/07/automation-future-content-creation/

Rockley, A., Cooper, C., & Abel, S. (2015). *Intelligent Content: A Primer*. Laguna Hills, CA: XML Press.

Rude, C. D. (2015). Building identity and community through research. *Journal of Technical Writing and Communication*, 45(4), 366–380.

Senske, N. (2017). Evaluation and impact of a required computational thinking course for architecture students. *Proceedings of the 2017 ACM SIGCSE Technical Symposium on Computer Science Education*, 525–530.

Tanenbaum, A.S. (2006). *Structured computer organization* (5th Ed.). Upper Saddle River, NJ: Pearson Prentice Hall.

8

ABSTRACTIONS IN THE LwDITA CONTENT LIFECYCLE

The scenario is pretty common in professional conferences: an instructor or trainer attends an event and is inspired by a presentation or visit to a vendor's booth that focuses on a new software application for automating content processes. The instructor requests a free demo or obtains departmental support to purchase an academic or trial license. The curriculum in the instructor's program is modified to include the selected tool, and then the tool developer releases a paid upgrade, which the instructor's department cannot afford. The result: rapid obsolescence and a failed experiment that keeps the department from exploring technologies for creating intelligent content.

Saul Carliner sees these choices of time and money in tools as a risky investment for practitioners and academics alike. For practitioners, "the primary issue is which technologies they should choose for investing their limited training dollars," based on the rapid changes in software applications. For academics, the risks include both "limited resources to purchase costly publishing software" (including enterprise-level content management systems), and the perishable nature of tools-based training, "often outdated within five years," for students (Carliner, 2010, p. 47).

Instead of purchasing a commercial software application and then building a curriculum around it, technical communication instructors and trainers can focus on the mental activities that lead to the development of intelligent content. Those activities are an implementation of the "broader rhetorical strategies for analyzing the audience, planning, revising, and managing one's time and writing process" proposed in Linda Flower's "Rhetorical Problem Solving: Cognition and Professional Writing" (1989, p. 5).

The thinking and working process that I propose in this book involves a series of layers of abstraction based on the model introduced at the end of Chapter 7. For the purpose of this chapter, a revised version of those layers, focusing on the flexibility about authoring formats allowed by LwDITA and inspired by the ISTE standards for evaluating students as computational thinkers (ISTE, 2018), looks as follows:

- Layer 1: Developing a content strategy
- Layer 2: Authoring modular content with LwDITA
- Layer 3: Separating content from design and context
- Layer 4: Linking topics and maps for collection and reuse
- Layer 5: Processing and producing deliverables
- Layer 6: Preparing for the future.

The "Learning to Think Like a Computer" article from The New York Times mentioned in Chapter 7 provides an appropriate example for looking at each layer of abstraction and its connections to the ISTE standards and the content-development lifecycles presented in this chapter. Dan Garcia's milkshake recipe from that article can be the inspiration for a fictional content project that can guide us through these revised layers of abstraction.

As I focus on each layer of abstraction, I attempt to connect it to stages in content-development lifecycles and the ISTE standards for evaluating computational thinkers. My objective, as I mentioned before, is to separate the intimidating mandate of learning about industry practices and then bringing them back to the classroom in manageable tasks that stay relevant to our profession and also relate to computing-for-all initiatives in the disciplinary context of content development and technical communication, as an alternative to learning about code and programming in introductory computer science courses (although I strongly believe that every student, regardless of academic major, can benefit from an introductory course in computer programming). The correspondence among these layers of abstraction and the indicators in the ISTE standard has not been evaluated empirically beyond my own assessment of students' writing and their progression towards completing the undergraduate degree in Professional and Technical Writing at Virginia Tech.

Layer 1: Developing a Content Strategy

Few concepts have such a strong potential for uniting and dividing, at the same time, opinions about the importance of planning for the development and management of content as *content strategy*. Clark (2016) notes that the idea of content strategy "can realize the interdepartmental possibilities" involving the adoption of reuse and single-sourcing outside of technical communication that authors have been promising for decades. However, Clark also analyzes the discrepancies in definition and implementation of content strategy in the realms of documentation, marketing, web development, and others. Clark's meticulous literature review on the term is eye-opening and inspiring to take the first step through the layers of abstraction behind developing intelligent content with

LwDITA. Authors must be guided by a content strategy, and its development and adoption processes require mental abstractions to defer further layers of the authoring lifecycle until a plan is ready to implement. Without a content strategy, a user cannot advance in the LwDITA process layers of abstraction. Andersen debunks the role of technology over strategy when she explains that while "high-speed networks and the evolution of content technologies (e.g., Web 2.0, CM systems) and their underlying standards (e.g., XML, HTML5, DITA) have made possible the emergence of intelligent content (. . .), its success depends on the content strategy that governs its life cycle" (2014, p. 133).

A simple and direct definition of content strategy, for those who do not have time to read Clark's excellent analysis of the term, comes from Rahel Anne Bailie, who is an active member of the Lightweight DITA subcommittee at OASIS. Bailie defines content strategy as "the analysis and planning to develop a repeatable system that governs the management of content throughout the entire content lifecycle" (2014, p. 14). Going back to the adaptive milkshake recipe from Dan Garcia's example, in a LwDITA workflow an author would need to (following Bailie's definition) analyze and plan before writing any content. The abundance of definitions and approaches to content strategy also creates a long list of potential deliverables related to this concept.

Let's assume that the overarching task is to develop a collection of soda fountain recipes and procedures. For the milkshake entry, the collection should include a versatile recipe with a list of ingredients and steps. The ingredients list should accommodate different flavors in one single template, instead of having separate recipes for each possible flavor. For the scope of this chapter, this layer is not a comprehensive collection of content strategy materials; instead, it focuses on the mental tasks that, at a minimum, authors should focus on before starting an intelligent content project with LwDITA.

1. Perform an audience analysis. Determine who will be the users of the milkshake recipe. If possible, conduct observations and interviews. Bailie & Urbina recommend developing personas and scenarios to understand the audience. Personas, they claim, "help you understand the behavioral characteristics of typical content consumers. From that information, it's possible to anticipate what the most common tasks will be and what information will be in highest demand" (2013, p. 20). Getto & St. Amant (2014) present an overview of personas and their usage at the intersection of user experience and technical communication. Through personas and scenarios, the author can identify the users' needs, expectations, and anticipated reactions to the recipe/collection of recipes. Then, those needs statements can be converted into specific topics and tasks for the recipes.
2. Conduct a content audit or inventory. The author could be creating original content for the recipes or collecting legacy documentation (in this case, as Dan Garcia mentioned, from the pages of an existing cookbook). If the

milkshake represents a truly revolutionary approach to frozen treats, the author should work with the soda fountain experts to document their ideas and tasks while identifying all sources of content. Traditionally, a content audit is based on a spreadsheet with columns representing bits of information and rows for each piece of content. Halvorson & Rach (2012) say that there "is no one perfect format, size, or timing for an audit; there are many different (and totally valid) ways to audit your content," and they recommend including at least the following columns:

- ID: Each content unit needs an identification number or code. A content unit can include a whole milkshake or root beer float recipe, but a picture illustrating how to use the mixer and a how-to video for making whipped cream are also content units that need their own row and ID.
- Title/Topics: Most recipes will have a clear title; other smaller units can use "a short description of the key topics or themes covered."
- URL: If the content units live on the web.
- Format: Explain if the content unit is a piece of "text, video, PDF, etc."
- Source: "Specify whether the content is created in-house, by a content partner (newsfeeds, articles, blog posts, and so on), or by your users."
- Technical home: The content units reside in computer files that are stored somewhere. If the soda fountain has several folders for recipes and images, the "home" for each unit should be specified to avoid missing pieces and duplication.
- Metadata: Lauren Creekmore defines metadata as "attributes of content you can use to structure, semantically define, and target content" (in Abel & Bailie, 2014, p. 28). These attributes are foundational for the filtering and processing of content that will take place in future layers. An example would be a context metadata for the milkshake recipe. The recipe could be the same, with some variations about available equipment and ingredients, for personnel preparing it in a restaurant or a food truck environment. The metadata, which end users do not see, can set specific rules for each of those environments. After processing, the resulting recipe will give the exact instructions for each context. Layer 3 provides more details about this sample use of metadata.
- Traffic/usage statistics: "If it's feasible, get the skinny on how people are using (or not using) each piece of content."
- Last update: "When was the last time somebody in your organization paid attention to this piece of content?"
- Language: "If you have content in multiple languages, you'll want to record the language or dialect used on each piece of content" (Halvorson & Rach, 2012, pp. 51–52).

3. Develop a content structure. Structured authoring can provide many benefits, including consistency of format and sections among recipes. The

recipe can be its own content type specific characteristics and headings. Sara Wachter-Boettcher (2012) actually includes the recipe in her list of common examples of content types, which also includes bios, blog posts, business listings, episodes, event listings, fact sheets, FAQs, feature articles, help/user assistance modules, podcasts, poems, press releases, products, reviews, short stories, testimonials, tips and lists, and tutorials. In Chapter 1 we saw how DITA XML is frequently associated in the world of technical communication with the content types of concept, task, and reference. Chapters 5 and 6 guided us through the role of content types in LwDITA, but for the purpose of the milkshake recipe we can think of a structured topic that includes sections for ingredients and tools, steps, and a result.

4. Compile or adopt a style guide and code of ethics. If the collection of recipes has more than one author, a style guide can keep all recipes consistent in punctuation, capitalization, word usage, and other editorial decisions. Adopting an existing style guide would be an easy decision, but maybe the owner has specific ideas about content formatting. Similarly, adopting a code of ethics can avoid leaving users at a disadvantage by establishing principles. Russell Willerton (2015) assembled a thorough overview of ethics in the technical and professional communication literature that includes a section on characteristics of available codes for the profession.
5. Create a diversity plan. Authors should acknowledge the diversity of their content users, which can include local issues such as including information for milkshakes that use non-dairy alternatives instead of milk. The diversity plan should also consider outlining a global content strategy, which Val Swisher defines as "a plan for managing content that is intended for people whose main language is something other than the source language" (2014). The plan should also acknowledge the diversity of content *authors*, which includes language but also covers the diverse departments or groups involved with the content. If the soda fountain project were to expand, authors could include professionals from the kitchen, technical writers in charge of instructions, and marketing writers developing promotional materials. Those groups have different communication styles, expectations, and structures that should be acknowledged and reconciled.
6. Make a technology plan considering human involvement. Following from the previous task, this one should identify the writing platforms, content standards, and tools used by the potential authors. The technology plan should also cover decisions about content management applications or services, and tools for processing of deliverables. The plan should also consider and accommodate a human-in-the-loop (HITL) strategy. Rothrock & Narayanan posit that traditional projects involving automation "regard human interaction as an external input to the system being considered. However, studies of complex systems in today's technological landscape must include humans as active participants" (2011, p. v). For this example,

the plan includes humans as content developers and curators working with a user experience team to produce end-user deliverables for the soda fountain. For the milkshake example, the selected standard will be LwDITA, authored in the following two options:

- Option a: With the text editor Atom by GitHub, with the DITA Open Toolkit as processing tool, and with content and source code stored and delivered in GitHub and GitHub Pages, respectively.
- Option b: With the LwDITA-aware application Oxygen XML, and with content and source code stored and delivered in GitHub and GitHub Pages, respectively.

The tasks involved in this layer are related to several stages of the content-development lifecycles featured in the previous chapter. Layer 1 tasks focus on Bailie & Urbina's *analysis* stage. They also cover some of the work included in Andersen's *Analyzing the customer and business needs* and *Developing an information architecture* stages. Contrasting layer 1 with the ISTE standards for assessing computational thinking in students, some of its tasks could comply with sections of standards 5a (*Students formulate problem definitions suited for technology-assisted methods such as data analysis, abstract models and algorithmic thinking in exploring and finding solutions*), 5b (*Students collect data or identify relevant data sets, use digital tools to analyze them, and represent data in various ways to facilitate problem-solving and decision-making*), and 5c (*Students break problems into component parts, extract key information, and develop descriptive models to understand complex systems or facilitate problem-solving*).

Layer 2: Authoring Modular Content with LwDITA

Probably the most important layer for readers of *Creating Intelligent Content with Lightweight DITA*, layer 2 involves content development tasks that can only happen after completing the first layer of abstraction. Following the model proposed by Flower (1989), this layer focuses on important discourse conventions that, regardless of their inherent importance, need the broader rhetorical conventions of the remaining layers. Once a content audit has identified all legacy documentation, and it has been prepared for update or migration, it's time for authors to produce text and/or multimedia content to address the users' needs identified in layer 1. For the milkshake example, let's assume that the soda fountain operator manual will include a few recipes, with the versatile milkshake being one of them, probably featured next to the root beer float and the banana split. The authors, after collecting information from any existing sources, conducting interviews with experts, and observing work in the kitchen, can start creating topics following the guidelines from the proposed LwDITA standard.

Focusing, for now, exclusively on the milkshake recipe and ignoring all other offerings from the fountain manual, we can identify more than one way to achieve with LwDITA the versatility required by Dan Garcia's example. One possible approach could be through *conditional content*, which Julio Vazquez defines as "content that has sufficient metadata to allow a processor to filter or flag that content in any output or format, using a profile to determine the exact output for a given context or format" (2016, p. 64). Layer 3 will look at conditional content, as we advance to connecting elements of the recipe to specific contexts. A second approach, which is more appropriate for layer 2, is provided by *content variables*, which Nancy Harrison defines as "variables that contain phrase-level content that needs to be in a topic no matter what document the topic is part of, but that changes depending on context, for example, a product name or a company name" (2016, p. 66).

The content variable *"icecream-flavor"* appears in a phrase-level element of the milkshake recipe (inside an ingredient item), but its value changes depending on the flavor established by the manager. If the milkshake today will be strawberry-flavored, the variable *"icecream-flavor"* will be set to the value of *"strawberry"*. If tomorrow the flavor needs to be vanilla, the variable can take that new value and keep the same content with only that variation. That variable should be part of the metadata specified in the previous layer, as the author identified elements that need to change in the recipes. Without that metadata, an author cannot produce the adaptive milkshake recipe required by Dan Garcia's example. The following sections show how to use a content variable in the three initial authoring formats of LwDITA.

XDITA

In XDITA, the LwDITA authoring format based on XML, a content variable is implemented on the phrase (**<ph>**) element using the **@keyref** attribute. Hackos explains the **@keyref** mechanism in DITA XML, as a process of "putting placeholders into your topics and then defining the content for those placeholders" elsewhere (2011, p. 272). The **@keyref** mechanism, Hackos adds, is comprised of two components:

- The referencing key (the **@keyref** attribute), which is "found in the topic where the content will be included," and
- The defining key (the **@keys** attribute), which uses the **<keydef>** element to "set the content to replace the placeholder" (Hackos, 2011, p. 273).

The referencing key is covered in this layer, and the defining key will be set in layer 4. Layer 5 addresses the processing tasks that will populate the content placeholders with the value established in the defining keys.

In the versatile milkshake recipe authored in XDITA, the referencing key will be inside the ingredient that specifies a pint of ice cream. The content placeholder will leave the ice cream flavor initially empty, and then it will adopt a value determined by the defining key in layer 4. Figure 8.1 shows a version of the XDITA code for the milkshake recipe. Like all code samples from previous chapters, the examples included in this section can be authored in any text editor (not in a word processor) or a LwDITA-aware software application, and can be downloaded from the *Creating Intelligent Content with Lightweight DITA* GitHub repository (https://github.com/carlosevia/lwdita-book).

The code from Figure 8.1 (let's call it a draft of the recipe) includes an unordered list (<**ul**>) with the identifier of "ingredients." This list of ingredients contains two list item (<**li**>) elements. The first one is straightforward text that specifies some milk (a more advanced recipe could even specify if the fountain attendant should use actual milk or a non-dairy milk alternative). An author working with this source code would be able to tell that step 1 is asking for ¼ cup of milk[1]. Step 1 does not require any abstraction beyond understanding text and the English language. The second list item, however, has an XDITA phrase (<**ph**>) element inside the list item. This phrase element has a **@keyref** attribute that works as a placeholder for variable text. The **@keyref** attribute

```
<?xml version="1.0" encoding="UTF-8"?>
<!DOCTYPE topic PUBLIC "-//OASIS//DTD LIGHTWEIGHT DITA Topic//EN"
"lw-topic.dtd">
<topic id="milkshake">
 <title>Easy Milkshake</title>
 <body>
   <p> The Easy Milkshake is our best-seller and a soda fountain tradition. We frequently
update the recipe to incorporate fresh flavors and ingredients.</p>
<ul id="ingredients">
   <li><p>1/4 cup of milk</p></li>
   <li><p>A pint of <ph keyref="icecream-flavor"/> ice cream</p></li>
  </ul>
  <ol id="steps">
<li><p>Combine all ingredients in the Blendimixx 3000</p></li>
<li><p>Mix for 30 seconds</p></li>
<li><p>Serve in a cold fountain glass</p></li>
  </ol>
</body>
</topic>
```

FIGURE 8.1 Recipe for a versatile milkshake in XDITA – following on an idea presented by Dan Garcia. In this example, the recipe was created in XDITA – the LwDITA authoring format based on a simplified version of DITA XML. The list item asking for a pint of ice cream includes a key reference with the value of *"icecream-flavor,"* which will be set at processing time in a different layer.

has the generic value of *"icecream-flavor"* . Ingredient 2, by itself, would be very confusing for a reader expecting a milkshake recipe. The **@keyref** attribute has to be established in this authoring layer, but it depends on the defining key to be specified in layer 4. As a result, the LwDITA topic for the milkshake recipe is not ready for processing in this layer. The author can save this recipe as *milkshake.dita*, but even a LwDITA-aware editor or the DITA Open Toolkit would indicate an error if the author attempts to build a deliverable at this stage.

HDITA

The same milkshake recipe can be created in HDITA, the LwDITA authoring format based on HTML5, with a similar mechanism for the content variable. In HDITA, the referencing key for variable content is expressed with the custom data attribute **@data-keyref**. In HTML5, phrase-level content can be included in the **<span>** element. Thus, the recipe in HDITA would look like the draft in Figure 8.2.

The unordered list element with the identifier of "ingredients" is in this version and it looks very similar to the one included in the XDITA recipe. The main

```
<!DOCTYPE html>
<title>Easy Milkshake</title>
<body>
<article id="milkshake">
 <h1>Easy Milkshake</h1>
 <p>The Easy Milkshake is our best-seller and a soda fountain tradition. We frequently update
the recipe to incorporate fresh flavors and ingredients.</p>
<ul id="ingredients">
   <li>
    <p>1/4 cup of milk</p>
   </li>
   <li>
    <p>A pint of <span data-keyref="icecream-flavor"></span> ice cream</p>
   </li>
</ul>
 <ol id="steps">
<li><p>Combine all ingredients in the Blendimixx 3000</p></li   >
<li><p>Mix for 30 seconds</p></li>
<li><p>Serve in a cold fountain glass</p></li>
 </ol>
</article>
</body>
```

FIGURE 8.2 Recipe for the versatile milkshake authored in HDITA. The ingredient asking for a pint of ice cream uses the HTML5 custom data attribute @data-keyref to set a placeholder for a value that will be processed in a more advanced layer.

differences are in the element holding the variable content (**<span>** in HDITA, whereas in XDITA it was **<ph>**) and the attribute setting the placeholder *"icecream-flavor"* for a flavor to be determined in a more advanced layer (**@data-keyref** in HDITA, whereas in XDITA it was **@keyref**). These differences keep the LwDITA authoring formats compliant with the HTML5 and DITA XML standards, respectively. The author can save this recipe as *milkshake.html*, and the resulting file can be viewed in a web browser, but the recipe won't make sense for end users because the content variable for "icecream-flavor" is not established in this layer of abstraction (Figure 8.3).

MDITA

The versatile milkshake recipe can be expressed, with some minor differences, in the MDITA core profile. MDITA uses the shortcut reference

Easy Milkshake
file:///User
Easy Milkshake
The Easy Milkshake is our best-seller and a soda fountain tradition. We frequently update the recipe to incorporate fresh flavors and ingredients.
• 1/4 cup of milk
• A pint of ice cream
1. Combine all ingredients in the Blendimixx 3000
2. Mix for 30 seconds
3. Serve in a cold fountain glass

FIGURE 8.3 HDITA version of the milkshake recipe as seen on a web browser. Note that the ingredient for a pint of ice cream does not have a flavor attached to it, which will come in a more advanced layer when the topic is processed through a LwDITA-aware software application.

link structure from CommonMark/GitHub Flavored Markdown (GFM) to establish content variables. The GFM spec explains shortcut reference links as consisting "of a link label that matches a link reference definition elsewhere in the document and is not followed by [] or a link label. The contents of the first link label are parsed as inlines, which are used as the link's text. The link's URI and title are provided by the matching link reference definition. Thus, [foo] is equivalent to [foo][]" (GitHub Flavored Markdown Spec, 2017).

The milkshake recipe authored in MDITA extended profile, with a GFM shortcut reference link setting the content placeholder for *"icecream-flavor"* , would look like Figure 8.4.

The unordered list item for ingredients is still in the recipe, and the second ingredient has the placeholder variable *"icecream-flavor"* , which will inherit a value in a more advanced layer of abstraction. The author can save this MDITA topic as *milkshake.md.*

The tasks involved in this layer are related to stages of the content-development lifecycles featured earlier in the previous chapter. Layer 2 tasks focus on Bailie & Urbina's *collect* stage. They also cover some of the work included in Andersen's *Creating structured content* stage. Contrasting layer 2 with the ISTE standards for assessing computational thinking in students, some of its tasks could comply with sections of standards 5a (*Students formulate problem definitions suited for technology-assisted methods such as data analysis, abstract models and algorithmic thinking in exploring and finding solutions*) and 5b (*Students collect data or identify relevant data sets, use digital tools to analyze them, and represent data in various ways to facilitate problem-solving and decision-making*).

```
# Easy Milkshake

The Easy Milkshake is our best -seller and a soda fountain tradition. We frequently update the
recipe to incorporate fresh flavors and ingredients.

- 1/4 cup of milk
-A pint of [icecream-flavor] ice cream

1. Combine all ingredients in the Blendimixx 3000
2. Mix for 30 seconds
3. Serve in a cold fountain glass
```

FIGURE 8.4 Recipe for the versatile milkshake authored in MDITA. The ingredient for ice cream uses a GitHub Flavored Markdown shortcut reference link to inherit a key reference from a map that will appear in a more advanced layer.

Layer 3: Separating Content from Presentation and Context

In a small soda fountain, the operators probably will have a printed manual as the only available documentation. In a larger operation, however, the content of a recipe collection could be used (or single-sourced) in the fountain's operation manual, website, social media presence, mobile app, and even conversational guidelines for a device like the Amazon Echo. In the first scenario, it makes sense to have an author in control of the manual's content and presentation to save time and money: one deliverable, one format, and one author. In the second scenario, however, an intelligent content solution to address all those potential deliverables depends on separating content from presentation. For years, I have taught in my courses the four levels of Pringle & O'Keefe's methodology for developing technical documents:

- Chaos ("there's no consistency in the presentation of content")
- Page consistency ("content looks the same on paper (or other delivery format," but there's no consistency in its source files)
- Template-based authoring (content follows "predetermined styles (and) writers don't spend time figuring out how to create particular formatting — they apply styles to add formatting")
- Structured authoring ("a publishing workflow that defines and enforces consistent organization of content") (2009, pp. 41–42).

In previous layers of abstraction, the milkshake recipe moved towards the structured authoring level. As it prepares for more advanced layers, the recipe must keep content and presentation separate. This separation "can create philosophical and cognitive dissonance for technical communicators trained to think of information as content that is inherently linked to presentation" (Clark, 2007, p. 36). Mark Baker warned about the difficulties of teaching this layer in the following statement:

> One of the hardest things about moving technical writers from desktop publishing to structured writing is persuading them to give up responsibility for how the final output looks. Writers will keep looking for ways to specify layout, even in markup languages specifically designed to remove layout concerns. They understand their jobs in terms of the responsibilities their old tools imposed on them.
>
> (Baker, 2013, p. 87)

The presentation rules and details for the milkshake recipe will be provided in a further layer of abstraction by an external tool and style sheet. After completing layer 2, the recipe topics look either like raw XML, HTML5, or Markdown code, depending on the LwDITA authoring format used to create them. In this layer, authors should focus on producing content (text, audio, videos, etc.) and letting the presentation be addressed elsewhere.

The fear of losing control over context is, however, real. According to some, writers separating content from presentation "will have no control over the context in which their information appears or the uses to which it may be put" (Gu & Pullman, 2009, p. 6). Those concerns echo a threat to the characteristic of rhetorical effectiveness, and DITA has tried to ameliorate that effect by giving authors control on the context of their content elements. Albers called for a similar dimension of rhetorical effectiveness when discussing the effects of single sourcing and XML in the careers of technical communicators: the real questions in documentation projects "should not revolve around technology but around whether the resulting documents effectively address a user's real-world information needs (Albers, 2003, p. 338). Swarts also expressed a need for content management systems that "suggest a rhetorical use of the content that writers have at their disposal" (Swarts, 2010, p. 159).

In a workflow like the one proposed in this chapter, authors and their supervisors take care of planning, authoring, organizing, and evaluating activities to prevent content-generation problems. When dealing with machine automation, there will always be the possibility of errors and the occasional misplaced component in a document, but those are more the exception than the rule. The human-in-the-loop strategy developed in layer 1 has the goal of refuting portrayals of writers as the lonely humans in a machine-dominated process of content automation, with the content products of their hard work being *arhetorically* assembled (borrowing a term from Bacha, 2009) by algorithms and machines without human control. The metadata and rules included in topics, phrases, and maps preserve the rhetorical effectiveness of intelligent content repositories.

LwDITA inherits the context-setting capability of DITA XML, which depends on rich metadata to filter or flag content. This type of context functions like a simple conditional statement in the "if-then" model of computer programming.

Taking this to our recipe example, let's give the soda fountain an official downtown location and also a mobile location with a food truck. Most processes are the same in both locations, but some change because of available equipment and ingredients. In the downtown location, the soda fountain operators have a professional *Blendimixx 3000* mixer, which they use for the milkshakes; however, in the food truck location they have a smaller *Blendilitte 200*. The sample recipe from layer 2 only mentions the professional mixer, but now that its content will also generate the operator manual for the food truck location, this same recipe should accommodate both cases while minimizing distractions for the users: in the downtown location, the manual should only mention the professional mixer, but in the food truck location it should only mention the smaller blender. The metadata attributes assigned in this layer will help filter out irrelevant information for each context in a future layer of abstraction.

DITA XML has several attributes that identify properties for conditional processing, which include **@audience**, **@plaftorm**, and **@product**. In LwDITA, the only conditional processing attributes are **@props** (in XDITA) or **@data-props** (in HDITA and MDITA extended profile). The DITA 1.3 spec defines **@props** (properties) as a "generic conditional processing attribute", and in LwDITA it can take different values based on authors' needs (2.2.4.2.1 Conditional processing attributes, 2018).

In XDITA, the recipe will look like Figure 8.5 with the added metadata for context,

The XDITA recipe, which can be saved as *milkshake.dita*, has a list item on the ordered list labeled "steps" that instructs the operator to combine all ingredients in a blender. The topic shows both options (the *Blendimixx 3000* and the *Blendilitte 200*), which have attached the corresponding metadata for each context with the conditional attribute **@props** inside a phrase element. In this layer of abstraction, the XDITA topic displays all available options for equipment and locations. The topic is written in valid XDITA (it conforms to the rules of the LwDITA standard) and can be processed in a software application to generate user deliverables. However, those user deliverables will be incorrect or redundant because the filters for specific context will be applied in a future layer. Figure 8.6 shows a PDF transformation of the XDITA milkshake recipe as it looks in layer 3.

```
<?xml version="1.0" encoding="UTF-8"?>
<!DOCTYPE topic PUBLIC "-//OASIS//DTD LIGHTWEIGHT DITA Topic//EN"
"lw-topic.dtd">
<topic id="milkshake">
 <title>Easy Milkshake</title>
 <body>
   <p>The Easy Milkshake is our best-seller and a soda fountain tradition. We frequently
update the recipe to incorporate fresh flavors and ingredients.</p>
<ul id="ingredients">
   <li><p>1/4 cup of milk</p></li>
   <li><p>A pint of <ph keyref="icecream-flavor"/> ice cream</p></li>
  </ul>

  <ol id="steps">
<li><p>Combine all ingredients in the <ph props="setting-downtown">Blendimixx
3000</ph> <ph props="setting-foodtruck">Blendilitte 200</ph></p></li>
<li><p>Mix for 30 seconds</p></li>
<li><p>Serve in a cold fountain glass</p></li>
  </ol>
</body>
</topic>
```

FIGURE 8.5 XDITA version of the milkshake recipe with two possible values for a setting condition. At processing time, the author can specify a filter and exclude the value that is not needed for a specific setting.

Easy Milkshake

The Easy Milkshake is our best-seller and a soda fountain tradition. We frequently update the recipe to incorporate fresh flavors and ingredients.

- 1/4 cup of milk
- A pint of ice cream

1. Combine all ingredients in the Blendimixx 3000 Blendilitte 200
2. Mix for 30 seconds
3. Serve in a cold fountain glass

FIGURE 8.6 PDF transformation of the XDITA milkshake recipe. Since no filters were applied during the transformation, the first step includes the values of both blenders without considering the setting where the recipe will be used. Also, there is no ice cream flavor set, as the content variable will be populated in a more advanced layer.

In HDITA, the conditional attribute **@data-props**, placed inside the HTML5 **<span>** element, can achieve similar results. An HDITA version of the milkshake recipe, with context information to specify the blender used in each location, would look like Figure 8.7.

The HDITA recipe, which can be saved as *milkshake.html*, is a valid HTML5 topic; therefore, it can be seen on a web browser at this stage. The resulting web

```
<!DOCTYPE html>
<title>Easy Milkshake</title>
<body>
<article id="milkshake">
 <h1>Easy Milkshake</h1>
 <p>The Easy Milkshake is our best-seller and a soda fountain tradition. We frequently update
the recipe to incorporate fresh flavors and ingredients.</p>
<ul id="ingredients">
  <li>
   <p>1/4 cup of milk</p>
  </li>
  <li>
   <p>A pint of <span data-keyref="icecream-flavor"></span> ice cream</p>
  </li>
</ul>
 <ol id="steps">
<li><p>Combine all ingredients in the <span data-props="setting-downtown">Blendimixx
3000</span> <span data-props="setting-foodtruck">Blendilitte 200</span></p></li>
<li><p>Mix for 30 seconds</p></li>
<li><p>Serve in a cold fountain glass</p></li>
 </ol>
</article>
</body>
```

FIGURE 8.7 HDITA version of the milkshake recipe with two possible values for a setting condition, which are specified with the HTML5 custom data attribute **@data-props**.

rendering (Figure 8. 8), however, shows both possible blender options in the same step and would be confusing for an actual human operator. In layer 5, processing the topic with the proper conditional code will produce correct deliverables for each location.

The context-aware recipe cannot be expressed in MDITA core profile. In order to use the conditional variable **@data-props**, a Markdown-based author would have to use a few code snippets of HDITA in MDITA extended profile. The recipe main elements are still in Markdown, but the available values for the conditional setting attribute are the same as those used in the HDITA topic, as shown in Figure 8.9. This MDITA version can be saved as *milkshake.md.*

The HDITA code snippets enable the MDITA topic to allow conditional content and let Markdown authors use DITA-like content filters. The MDITA topic, in this layer, would not make sense for human users, and it must be processed by a LwDITA-aware tool in layer 5.

The tasks involved in this layer are related to several stages of the content-development lifecycles featured earlier in the previous chapter. Layer 3 tasks focus on Bailie & Urbina's *manage* stage. They also cover some of the work

Easy Milkshake
file:///Users/ca
Easy Milkshake
The Easy Milkshake is our best-seller and a soda fountain tradition. We frequently update the recipe to incorporate fresh flavors and ingredients.
• 1/4 cup of milk
• A pint of ice cream
1. Combine all ingredients in the Blendimixx 3000 Blendilitte 200
2. Mix for 30 seconds
3. Serve in a cold fountain glass

FIGURE 8.8 HDITA version of the milkshake recipe seen through a web browser. Without advanced processing, the HTML file shows the values for both possible blenders in step 1.

```
# Easy Milkshake

The Easy Milkshake is our best-seller and a soda fountain tradition. We frequently update the
recipe to incorporate fresh flavors and ingredients.

- 1/4 cup of milk
- A pint of [icecream-flavor] ice cream

1.  Combine all ingredients in the <span data-props="setting-downtown">Blendimixx
3000</span> <span data-props="setting-foodtruck">Blendilitte 200</span>
2.  Mix for 30 seconds
3.  Serve in a cold fountain glass
```

FIGURE 8.9 MDITA version of the milkshake recipe with two possible values for a setting condition. To overcome Markdown's limitations as a language for structuring content, the conditional properties are expressed with HDITA code snippets.

included in Andersen's *Developing an information architecture* and *Creating structured content* stages. Contrasting layer 3 with the ISTE standards for assessing computational thinking in students, some of its tasks could comply with sections of standards 5a (*Students formulate problem definitions suited for technology-assisted methods such as data analysis, abstract models and algorithmic thinking in exploring and finding solutions*) and 5c (*Students break problems into component parts, extract key information, and develop descriptive models to understand complex systems or facilitate problem-solving*).

Layer 4: Linking Topics and Maps for Collection and Reuse

Linking Topics to Topics

In Chapter 6, we saw how to represent a cross-reference component in the LwDITA authoring formats. With that component, an author can link a topic to an external web resource, a file (an existing diagram in a PDF, for example), or another LwDITA topic. Cross-topic linking works regardless of authoring format: an XDITA topic can link to topics in HDITA and MDITA, and vice versa. However, the cross-reference component in LwDITA also enables one of DITA's strongest content reuse features: the content reference – or *conref* for short.

Layer 2 introduced the key reference attribute as a placeholder for content reuse. The conref is a related attribute that allows an author to bring content from one topic into another (without copying and pasting). The source element from the content reference can be updated and, after reprocessing the topic collection, all target topics that link to it will be automatically updated. Hackos describes the structure of the conref mechanism in the DITA standard as follows:

> The @conref attribute uses a unique @id attribute to identify the content unit you want to use. For example, if you want to use a <note> from one topic into another, you must add an @id attribute to the original note.
>
> (Hackos, 2011, p. 240)

In LwDITA, the structure of a conref should look like the following template: *path-to-file/file-name#topic-id/element-id*

For example, let's pretend that the LwDITA topic with the milkshake recipe includes a note component, with the type of warning, that tells the operator to unplug the blender after each use to prevent a fire hazard. That note should be presented in every recipe produced by the soda fountain. Instead of copying and pasting the note's content, an author can use a conref to link the topics. The milkshake topic, then, becomes the source for the conref, and in XDITA syntax it would look like Figure 8.10.

In HDITA syntax, the revised milkshake recipe would look like Figure 8.11.

The Lightweight DITA subcommittee at OASIS evaluated several approaches for including content references natively in Markdown syntax. However, some of them required changes to many other MDITA components or allowed content exchange exclusively among Markdown files. Therefore, there is no direct way to express a conref in MDITA core profile, and if authors want to take advantage of this reuse mechanism they would need to include a raw HDITA code snippet in an MDITA extended profile topic. Thus, the MDITA version of the milkshake topic with the warning note would look as Figure 8.12.

Keep in mind that all recipes included in the soda fountain manual will need the warning note. An author could copy and paste from the milkshake recipe into all the other recipes from the manual. However, what if the requirements change and a new type of blender does not require to be unplugged but needs to be descaled once a week? The author would need to update the note manually on every topic that includes it. With a conref, however, the only note that needs to be updated is the source in the milkshake topic, and all recipes that link to it will be updated automatically after re-processing the topics and their map (more about that in the next layer).

To continue with the example, let's look at the root beer float recipe, which is one of the many target topics that link to the warning note from the milkshake recipe. Figure 8.13 shows the XDITA version of the root beer float recipe.

Figure 8.14 shows the root beer float recipe in HDITA syntax.

Figure 8.15 shows the root beer float recipe in MDITA extended profile syntax. The content reference will be in a raw HDITA code block.

The **@conref** (in XDITA) or **@data-conref** (in HDITA and MDITA extended profile) attribute is available on the following LwDITA content components:

- Audio
- Definition description

```
<?xml version="1.0" encoding="UTF-8"?>
<!DOCTYPE topic PUBLIC "-//OASIS//DTD LIGHTWEIGHT DITA Topic//EN"
"lw-topic.dtd">
<topic id="milkshake">
 <title>Easy Milkshake</title>
 <body>
  <p>The Easy Milkshake is our best-seller and a soda fountain tradition. We frequently update
the recipe to incorporate fresh flavors and ingredients.</p>
  <ul id="ingredients">
   <li>
    <p>1/4 cup of milk</p>
   </li>
   <li>
    <p>A p  int of
     <ph keyref="icecream-flavor"/>
     ice cream</p>
   </li>
  </ul>
  <ol id="steps">
   <li>
    <p>Combine all ingredients in the
     <ph props="setting-downtown">Blendimixx 3000</ph>
     <ph props="setting-foodtruck">Blendilitte 200</ph>
    </p>
   </li>
   <li>
    <p>Mix for 30 seconds</p>
   </li>
   <li>
    <p>Serve in a cold fountain glass</p>
   </li>
  </ol>
  <note id="unplug" type="warning">
   <p>Unplug the blender after each use to prevent a fire hazard.</p>
  </note>
 </body>
</topic>
```

FIGURE 8.10 Milkshake recipe in XDITA syntax with the note component. The note has a unique **@id** with the value of unplug, and the optional @type for the note is set to "warning".

- Definition list
- Definition list entry
- Definition term
- Footnote
- List item
- Note
- Ordered list
- Paragraph
- Preformatted text
- Section
- Simple table

```
<!DOCTYPE html>
<title>Easy Milkshake</title>
<body>
 <article id="milkshake">
  <h1>Easy Milkshake</h1>
  <p>The Easy Milkshake is our best-seller and a soda fountain tradition. We frequently update
the recipe to incorporate fresh flavors and ingredients.</p>
  <ul id="ingredients">
   <li>
    <p>1/4 cup of milk</p>
   </li>
   <li>
    <p>A pint of <span data-keyref="icecream-flavor"></span> ice cream</p>
   </li>
  </ul>
  <ol id="steps">
   <li>
    <p>Combine all ingredients in the <span data-props="setting-downtown">Blendimixx
3000</span> <span data-props="setting-foodtruck">Blendilitte 200</span></p>
   </li>
   <li>
    <p>Mix for 30 seconds</p>
   </li>
   <li>
    <p>Serve in a cold fountain glass</p>
   </li>
  </ol>
  <div data-class="note" id="unplug" data-type="warning">
   <p>Unplug the blender after each use to prevent a fire hazard.</p>
  </div>
 </article>
</body>
```

FIGURE 8.11 Milkshake recipe in HDITA syntax with the note component. The HTML5 **<div>** element includes the **@id** with the value of "unplug" and custom data attributes to indicate that it is a LwDITA note with the type of "warning".

- Simple table entry
- Simple table header
- Simple table row
- Unordered list
- Video

Linking Maps to Topics

In this layer, we will work with maps as the main mechanism to organize topics and create information hierarchies. LwDITA maps are essential for some mental abstractions that take place in layer 4. The sample milkshake topics that have been evolving in previous layers must be collected in a map in order to produce deliverables for their intended human and algorithmic audiences (see

```
# Easy Milkshake

The Easy Milkshake is our best-seller and a soda fountain tradition. We frequently update the
recipe to incorporate fresh flavors and ingredients.


-1/4 cup of milk
-A pint of [icecream-flavor] ice cream


1.  Combine all ingredients in the <span data-props="setting-downtown">Blendimixx
3000</span> <span data-props="setting-foodtruck">Blendilitte 200</span>
2.  Mix for 30 seconds
3.  Serve in a cold fountain glass


<div data-class="note" id="unplug" data-type="warning">
<p>Unplug the blender after each use to prevent a fire hazard.</p>
</div>
```

FIGURE 8.12 Milkshake recipe in MDITA extended profile syntax with the note component. The conref is represented with a raw block of HDITA code.

Gallagher, 2017). In this section, we will look at an XDITA map that includes the milkshake recipe in a collection of topics that also includes recipes for a root beer float and a banana split. This map can be combined with the topics developed in earlier layers and advance to layer 5, where it will be processed by a LwDITA-aware tool and generate information products for the soda fountain operators. The map in the following example not only works as a collection mechanism for topics, it also provides the defining key for the *"icecream-flavor"* content variable created in layer 2. Figure 8.16 shows a sample XDITA map for the Soda Fountain Operator Manual.

```
<?xml version="1.0" encoding="UTF-8"?>
<!DOCTYPE topic PUBLIC "-//OASIS//DTD LIGHTWEIGHT DITA Topic//EN"
"lw-topic.dtd">
<topic id="float">
 <title>Root Beer Float</title>
 <body>
  <ul id="ingredients">
   <li><p>20 oz root beer</p></li>
   <li><p>A large scoop of vanilla ice cream</p></li>
  </ul>
 <ol id="steps">
   <li><p>Pour root beer in a large cold glass</p></li>
   <li><p>Scoop ice cream into the glass</p></li>
   <li><p>Serve float as it starts to fizzle</p></li>
  </ol>
  <note conref="milkshake.dita#milkshake/unplug" />
 </body>
</topic>
```

FIGURE 8.13 XDITA version of the root beer float recipe with a content reference. The conref links to the source note in the milkshake recipe. Note the syntax of **filename#topic-id/element-id**.

```
<!DOCTYPE html>
<title>Root Beer Float</title>
<body>
 <article id="float">
  <h1>Root Beer Float</h1>
  <ul id="ingredients">
   <li>
    <p>20 oz root beer</p>
   </li>
   <li>
    <p>A large scoop of vanilla ice cream</p>
   </li>
  </ul>
  <ol id="steps">
   <li>
    <p>Pour root beer in a large cold glass</p>
   </li>
   <li>
    <p>Scoop ice cream into the glass</p>
   </li>
    <li>
     <p>Serve float as it starts to fizzle</p>
   </li>
  </ol>
   <div data-conref="milkshake.dita#milkshake/unplug"></div>
 </article>
</body>
```

FIGURE 8.14 HDITA version of the root beer float recipe with a content reference. The conref links to the source note in the milkshake recipe.

The XDITA map in Figure 8.16 includes references (**<topicref>**) to the three hypothetical recipes in the manual. The author can save this file as *fountain. ditamap*, and in layer 5 a machine processor will parse the map and referenced topics in XDITA, HDITA, and MDITA. Following the discussion about content silos from layer 2, the map on Figure 8.16 includes topics created in the

```
# Root Beer Float

-20 oz of root beer
-A large scoop of vanilla ice cream

1.  Pour root beer in a large cold glass
2.  Scoop ice cream into the glass
3.  Serve float as it starts to fizzle

<div data-conref="milkshake.dita#milkshake/unplug"></div>
```

FIGURE 8.15 MDITA version of the root beer float recipe with a content reference. The conref links to the source note in the milkshake recipe. Authors can use an HDITA code block to express the content reference.

```
<?xml version="1.0" encoding="UTF-8"?>

<!DOCTYPE map PUBLIC "-//OASIS//DTD LIGHTWEIGHT DITA Map//EN" "lw-map.dtd">
<map>
<topicmeta>
 <navtitle>Soda Fountain Operator Manual</navtitle>
</topicmeta>
 <keydef keys="icecream-flavor">
   <topicmeta>
    <linktext>strawberry</linktext>
   </topicmeta>
</keydef>
 <topicref href="xdita-topics/milkshake.dita" format="xdita"/>
 <topicref href="hdita-topics/float.html" format="hdita"/>
 <topicref href="mdita-topics/bananasplit.md" format="mdita"/>
</map>
```

FIGURE 8.16 XDITA map for a soda fountain operator manual. The **<keydef>** environment declares the value for the "icecream-flavor" variable in any linked topics.

different LwDITA authoring formats (see the different values of **@format** in the **<topicref>** entries). This means that, for example, end users will not know what came from MDITA and what came from HDITA: they will just see a unified deliverable.

The XDITA map also has a navigation title (**<navtitle>**) that can specify the main heading for any user products created in the next layer of abstraction. The defining key for the *"icecream-flavor"* content variable is provided in the key definition (**<keydef>**) environment. Any LwDITA topics referenced in this map will inherit that key definition in layer 5, and all elements with a placeholder for *"icecream-flavor"* will display the key of, in this example, strawberry. If vanilla is the flavor of the day tomorrow, the author only needs to change that in the map key reference, and all the topics referenced will be updated automatically when the collection is processed in layer 5.

The tasks involved in this layer are related to several stages of the content-development lifecycles featured earlier in the previous chapter. Layer 4 tasks focus on Bailie & Urbina's *collect* and *manage* stages. They also cover some of the work included in Andersen's *Analyzing the customer and business needs* and *Developing an information architecture* stages. Contrasting layer 4 with the ISTE standards for assessing computational thinking in students, some of its tasks could comply with sections of standards 5b (*Students collect data or identify relevant data sets, use digital tools to analyze them, and represent data in various ways to facilitate problem-solving and decision-making*) and 5c (*Students break problems into component parts, extract key information, and develop descriptive models to understand complex systems or facilitate problem-solving*).

Layer 5: Processing and Producing Deliverables

Layer 5 addresses the "metal" tools in Wing's model of computational thinking. In this layer, developers would build applications based on the algorithms created in previous layers of abstraction. Authors in an intelligent content process based on principles of computational thinking do not need to build tools. Any author who is also a programmer and decides to build an automating solution to generate deliverables following the work on previous layers of abstraction deserves special recognition. However, most writing positions do not expect that kind of work. Most likely, authors will follow the tools strategy set in layer 1 and bring all the work developed in previous layers to the tool selected. This removes the emphasis from an actual software product and highlights the work performed by humans behind the automation.

The technical communication literature shows some waves of interests for technologies included in this layer, from single-sourcing (e.g, Ament, 2003; Carter, 2003) to content management (e.g., Hart-Davidson et al., 2007; Gu & Pullman, 2009), and most recently component content management (e.g, Andersen, 2014; Batova, 2014). The current topic of interest receives attention in conference presentations and journal articles for a while, and instructors evaluate ways to teach the technology *du jour*. If an authoring process or an academic curriculum lesson starts in this processing layer, it will probably end up being too complicated for anyone who is not a programmer or developer. And if the emphasis is placed on a specific software package instead of a methodology based on human tasks of abstractions, authors in industry and academia will face the tools' acquisition problems identified by Carliner that I mentioned in the introduction to this chapter.

The main automation tool that will take our milkshake example through layer 5 is the DITA Open Toolkit – the open source implementation of the DITA standard that we discussed in previous chapters. The same results can be achieved with many DITA-aware programs (open source and commercial) with a graphical user interface, and I will also show how to process the milkshake example in Oxygen XML.

The processing layer needs the files that we have created in previous layers of abstraction, which should include the following:

- Content strategy rules developed in layer 1
- LwDITA topics authored in layer 2
- Context filters added to LwDITA topics in layer 3
- Content references added to LwDITA topics in layer 4
- XDITA map to collect topics created in layer 4.

The fictional deliverable in this example is a web version of the soda fountain operator manual that can be accessed on a device at both soda fountain locations. In this first part, the processing tool will take the map and topics and populate the "*icecream-flavor*" variable with the **<key>** value established in the XDITA map.

On a given day, the author or a manager enters the **<key>** value on the map establishing the ice cream flavor for that day. After processing, the resulting deliverable will replace all *"icecream-flavor"* placeholders found in the topics with the actual content defined in the **<key>** element on the map. Figure 8.16 in layer 4, shows an XDITA map in which the **<key>** value has been established as *"strawberry"*.

Revisiting the reference information from Chapter 5, and according to the DITA-OT documentation, the general structure for a command that builds DITA (and LwDITA) deliverables from topics and maps is shown in figure 8.17.

To generate the web version of the soda fountain operator manual, you would need to enter the command shown on Figure 8.18 on a command-line environment *inside the directory or folder where you installed the DITA-OT.*

The command has the reference to the built-in (**bin**) subdirectory and the **dita** executable program, with the *fountain.ditamap* file created in layer 4 as input, and *html5* as the delivery format. The value for the **--input** argument needs to direct the DITA-OT to the specific folder where you stored the *fountain.ditamap* file (the *path-to-file* section of the command, which must be replaced by the actual path to the file in your computer). The easiest way to record the correct file location or path is to drag and drop the file into the command line interface immediately after the **--input=** argument. That one-line command combines the map with the topics, processing the hierarchies and relationships established by the topic references and also looking for and populating any variable content placeholders. The resulting HTML files will appear automatically in the DITA-OT **out** folder, although you can specify an alternative folder in the build command with the **--output** option. Figure 8.19 shows the resulting web version of the milkshake recipe after being processed with the DITA-OT.

(a) (b) (c) (d)

dita-ot-dir/bin/**dita** --input=***input-file*** --format=***format options***

(a) **the directory where the DITA-OT files are installed in your computer (replace *dita-ot-dir* with the full path for the DITA-OT folder).**

(b) **a subdirectory for programs that are "built-in" (*bin*) the DITA-OT. The built-in program that you need to execute is dita.**

(c) **argument for file input (e.g., a DITA/LwDITA topic or map)**

(d) **argument for format (e.g.,PDF, HTML5, etc.) and additional options.**

FIGURE 8.17 General structure for a command that builds DITA (and LwDITA) deliverables with the DITA-OT.

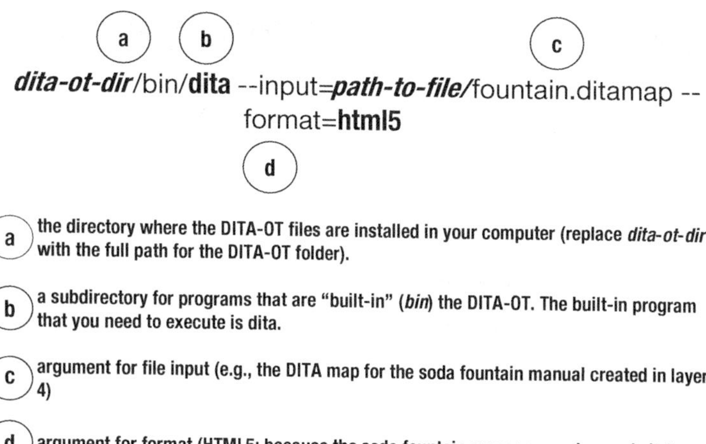
a
b
c
dita-ot-dir/bin/dita --input=path-to-file/fountain.ditamap --format=html5
d
a the directory where the DITA-OT files are installed in your computer (replace dita-ot-dir with the full path for the DITA-OT folder).
b a subdirectory for programs that are "built-in" (bin) the DITA-OT. The built-in program that you need to execute is dita.
c argument for file input (e.g., the DITA map for the soda fountain manual created in layer 4)
d argument for format (HTML5; because the soda fountain manager wants a website).

FIGURE 8.18 Command for the DITA-OT to generate a web deliverable from the soda fountain operator's manual XDITA map.

Figure 8.20 shows the resulting web version of the root beer float topic. The warning note about unplugging the blender appears in this recipe via the content reference mechanism.

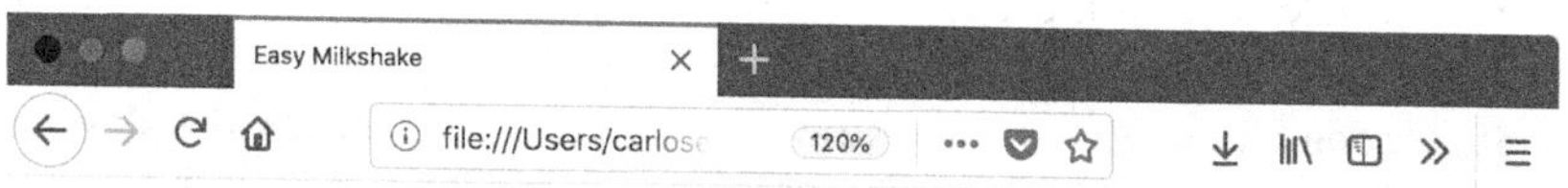
Easy Milkshake
file:///Users/carlos
120%

Easy Milkshake

The Easy Milkshake is our best-seller and a soda fountain tradition. We frequently update the recipe to incorporate fresh flavors and ingredients.

- 1/4 cup of milk
- A pint of strawberry ice cream

1. Combine all ingredients in the Blendimixx 3000 Blendilitte 200
2. Mix for 30 seconds
3. Serve in a cold fountain glass

Warning:

Unplug the blender after each use to prevent a fire hazard.

FIGURE 8.19 HTML5 transformation of the milkshake recipe processed with the XDITA map. The ice cream flavor inherited the value of "strawberry," but step 1 still shows both possible options for the blender to be used.

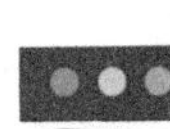
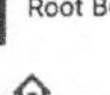

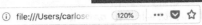

Root Beer Float

- 20 oz root beer
- A large scoop of vanilla ice cream

1. Pour root beer in a large cold glass
2. Scoop ice cream into the glass
3. Serve float as it starts to fizzle

Note:

Unplug the blender after each use to prevent a fire hazard.

FIGURE 8.20 HTML5 transformation of the root beer float recipe processed with the XDITA map. The "warning" note appears in this topic via the conref that reuses the original element from the milkshake recipe.

A LwDITA-aware software application like Oxygen can also produce the soda fountain manual. The "Apply Transformation Scenario(s)" dialog box in Oxygen would present the user with options to produce deliverables from this LwDITA map.

If the soda fountain runs out of strawberry ice cream and needs to update the manual to reflect that the default flavor is now vanilla, the author only needs to modify one line of code inside the XDITA map, as shown in Figure 8.21.

After saving the *fountain.ditamap* with the new ice cream flavor, you can run the same DITA-OT command from Figure 8.18 without any changes. Remember to replace the *path-to-file* segment with the actual path to the file in your computer.

Figure 8.22 shows the new web version of the milkshake recipe with vanilla as the ice cream flavor.

The web versions of the milkshake recipe in Figures 18 and 21, however, still show both blender options. These deliverables are not ready for the intended users of the soda fountain manual. The next step is to apply the *if-then* filter for conditional content. This stage involves adding a new file to the collection created in these layers of abstractions. The new file will be a DITAVAL (for DITA value), which "specifies which content is included or excluded based on condition definitions" (Bellamy et al, 2012, p. 171). This DITAVAL will specify the conditional arguments for applying filters to the processing stage. If the intended deliverable is exclusively for the operators working at the food truck setting of the soda fountain, then the filter

```
<?xml version="1.0" encoding="UTF-8"?>
<!DOCTYPE map PUBLIC "-//OASIS//DTD LIGHTWEIGHT DITA Map//EN" "lw-map.dtd">
<map>
<topicmeta>
 <navtitle>Soda Fountain Operator Manual</navtitle>
</topicmeta>
  <keydef keys="icecream-flavor">
   <topicmeta>
    <linktext>Vanilla</linktext>
   </topicmeta>
</keydef>
  <topicref href="xdita-topics/milkshake.dita" format="xdita"/>
  <topicref href="hdita-topics/float.html" format="hdita"/>
  <topicref href="mdita-topics/bananasplit.md" format="mdita"/>
</map>
```

FIGURE 8.21 XDITA map for the soda fountain operator manual with the "icecream-flavor" variable set to vanilla.

should follow the structure of *if* **@props**="setting-foodtruck", *then* exclude **@props**="setting-downtown". This is achieved in a DITAVAL that looks like Figure 8.23.

The same DITAVAL file can work for all LwDITA authoring formats with the **@props** attribute for XDITA and the **@data-props** attribute for HDITA and MDITA extended profile. You can save this new file as *setting.ditaval* and add it to the file collection, which now includes LwDITA topics, an XDITA map, and a DITAVAL filter.

Easy Milkshake

The Easy Milkshake is our best-seller and a soda fountain tradition. We frequently update the recipe to incorporate fresh flavors and ingredients.

- 1/4 cup of milk
- A pint of vanilla ice cream

1. Combine all ingredients in the Blendimixx 3000 Blendilitte 200
2. Mix for 30 seconds
3. Serve in a cold fountain glass

Warning:

Unplug the blender after each use to prevent a fire hazard.

FIGURE 8.22 HTML5 transformation of the milkshake recipe with vanilla as the ice cream flavor.

```
<?xml version="1.0" encoding="UTF-8"?>
<val>
  <prop action="exclude" att="props" val="setting-downtown"/>
  <prop action="exclude" att="data-props" val="setting-downtown"/>
</val>
```

FIGURE 8.23 DITAVAL file that excludes all references to the "downtown" setting when processing the map and topics. The two lines of code between the <val> and </val> tags reference the variables in XDITA and HDITA/MDITA extended profile syntaxes, respectively.

The marriage of the XDITA map with the DITAVAL in the DITA-OT takes place in the same one-line command but adding an option to indicate the filter location (Figure 8.24). You should also replace the *path-to-file* placeholders with the actual locations of the *fountain.ditamap* and *setting.ditaval* files in your computer.

The *filter* argument points the **dita** executable program in the direction of the DITAVAL, which will be processed with the XDITA map. The resulting web version of the milkshake recipe, which now excludes all references to the downtown location of the soda fountain, appears on Figure 8.26.

In Oxygen XML Editor, you can link a DITAVAL to a LwDITA map when configuring the transformation scenario by clicking on the *Filters* tab. The Oxygen user manual includes information on applying filters to DITA transformations[2].

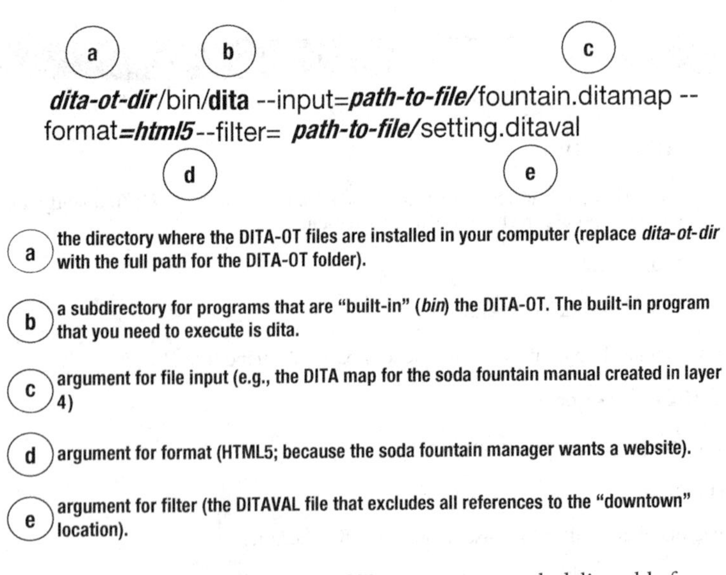
a
b
c
dita-ot-dir/bin/dita --input=path-to-file/fountain.ditamap --
format=html5--filter= path-to-file/setting.ditaval
d
e
a the directory where the DITA-OT files are installed in your computer (replace dita-ot-dir with the full path for the DITA-OT folder).
b a subdirectory for programs that are "built-in" (bin) the DITA-OT. The built-in program that you need to execute is dita.
c argument for file input (e.g., the DITA map for the soda fountain manual created in layer 4)
d argument for format (HTML5; because the soda fountain manager wants a website).
e argument for filter (the DITAVAL file that excludes all references to the "downtown" location).

FIGURE 8.24 Command for the DITA-OT to generate a web deliverable from the soda fountain operator's manual XDITA map that excludes references to the "downtown" location.

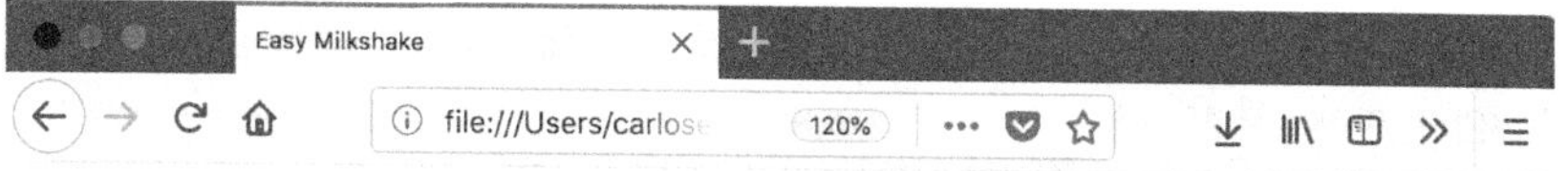

Easy Milkshake

The Easy Milkshake is our best-seller and a soda fountain tradition. We frequently update the recipe to incorporate fresh flavors and ingredients.

- 1/4 cup of milk
- A pint of vanilla ice cream

1. Combine all ingredients in the Blendilitte 200
2. Mix for 30 seconds
3. Serve in a cold fountain glass

Warning:

Unplug the blender after each use to prevent a fire hazard.

FIGURE 8.25 Filtered web deliverable of the milkshake recipe that excludes all references to the "downtown" setting.

If the setting needs to change, you only need to update the DITAVAL and process again with the same DITA-OT one-line command or applying the transformation scenario in Oxygen. For larger content repositories, this build process can be automated with scripts and algorithms, which are beyond the scope of *Creating Intelligent Content with Lightweight DITA* (aimed primarily at authors and instructors of introductory LwDITA workflows).

Building deliverables with the DITA-OT or LwDITA-aware tools is only one stage of this layer. The soda fountain will need a technology-based solution to store source code, enable authoring and processing, and deliver information products to end users (on web or print platforms). These layers of abstraction reflect the academic privilege behind their creation, as in a classroom environment my students do not have to deal with workplace clients and users with real needs. Even in client projects for internships or service learning purposes, deadlines and deliverables are flexible when they involve undergraduate students as content creators. Thus, this layer does not get involved with advanced software for component content management and presentation of deliverables. In my courses at Virginia Tech, students learn to host their source code and track versions of it with GitHub repositories, and their processing is automated with the DITA-OT or Oxygen XML. GitHub Pages is the default hosting service for web deliverables produced in this layer. Graduates of the Professional and Technical Writing program who work in industry, non-profits, or government agencies authoring for intelligent content workflows learn their worksite-specific tools as part of job training programs, and the layers of abstraction presented in this chapter make that learning process easier, particularly for graduates from a department of English. Teaching intelligent content (or even DITA) using a commercial CCMS, following its professionally-developed video tutorials and typing in a graphical user interface, is a professional skill that might benefit a handful of students and create limitations for many others who end up in environments that do not use that specific tool.

The tasks involved in this layer are related to stages of the content-development lifecycles featured earlier in the previous chapter. Layer 5 tasks focus on Bailie & Urbina's *publish* stage. They also cover some of the work included in Andersen's *Developing the technology strategy* and *Creating structured content*. Contrasting layer 5 with the ISTE standards for assessing computational thinking in students, some of its tasks could comply with sections of standard 5d (*Students understand how automation works and use algorithmic thinking to develop a sequence of steps to create and test automated solutions*) with limitations.

Layer 6: Preparing for the Future

Now that the soda fountain has an operator manual that adapts to different locations, reuses warning content among topics regardless of authoring format, and incorporates the ice cream flavor of the day to all its recipes with a one-line command, it's time to think about the future. LwDITA allows scalability as represented by additional publication channels, new audience and context requirements, and authors from different disciplines and writing traditions joining the process. Additional publication channels can include those already supported by the DITA-OT or other existing LwDITA-aware software applications (EPUB, mobile web devices, PDF, Microsoft Word, and others) or innovative approaches to user documentation like the conversational patterns for chatbots or agents like an Amazon Echo. New audience and context requirements can come from expert or novice fountain operators who need different levels of detail on their recipes, or additional settings for the soda fountain with different equipment and ingredients availability. Authors from different writing traditions can include those already represented in the initial LwDITA authoring formats (XML, HTML5, and Markdown) and those in formats considered for future releases of the LwDITA standard (e.g., JSON and Microsoft Word). This layer also includes a return to layer 1 for an iterative process of improvement and revision.

In general, this layer focuses on making the content and structures developed in previous layers as future-proof as possible. This is accomplished by the emphasis on open standards instead of proprietary software solutions. DITA, LwDITA, HTML5, and even CommonMark/GitHub Flavored Markdown are maintained by international standards' consortiums. Their continuous development guarantees applicability beyond the lifespan of a specific tool or app release. Furthermore, it also enables interoperability with new standards, like the International Standard for Intelligent Information Request and Delivery (iiRDS)[3], which has been heralded as the standard of Industry 4.0 and Internet of Things workflows.

The tasks involved in this layer are related to several stages of the content-development lifecycles featured earlier in the previous chapter. Layer 6 tasks focus on the characteristics of extensible and iterative from Bailie & Urbina's content model, which includes "a loop back to analysis for the next cycle" (2013, p. 236). The tasks in layer 6 also cover some of the work included in Andersen's *Managing change* stage. Contrasting layer 1 with the ISTE standards for assessing computational thinking in students, some of its tasks could comply with sections of standards 5a (*Students formulate problem definitions suited for technology-assisted methods such as data analysis, abstract models and algorithmic thinking in exploring and finding solutions*), 5c (*Students break problems into component parts, extract key information, and develop descriptive models to understand complex systems or facilitate problem-solving*), and even 5d (*Students understand how automation works and use algorithmic thinking to develop a sequence of steps to create and test automated solutions*) .

Notes

1 "1/4 cup of milk," as the XDITA version of the recipe presented in Figure 1 shows, is not really the same as "¼ (one quarter) cup of milk." Representing fractions in DITA can be properly achieved with snippets of the W3C standard MathML (https://www.w3.org/Math/). In order to keep this example as simple as possible, I avoided the complexity of adding MathML syntax to the XDITA topic.

2 https://www.oxygenxml.com/doc/versions/20.0/ug-author/topics/dita-map-edit-filters.html

3 https://www.parson-europe.com/en/knowledge-base/427-iirds-new-delivery-standard-technical-documentation.html

References

2.2.4.2.1 Conditional processing attributes (2018, June 19). Retrieved from http://docs.oasis-open.org/dita/dita/v1.3/errata02/os/complete/part3-all-inclusive/archSpec/base/conditional-processing-attributes.html#conditional-processing-attributes

Albers, M. J. (2003). Single sourcing and the technical communication career path. *Technical Communication*, 50(3), 335–344.

Ament, K. (2003). *Single sourcing: Building modular documentation*. Norwich, NY: William Andrew.

Andersen, R. (2014). Rhetorical work in the age of content management: Implications for the field of technical communication. *Journal of Business and Technical Communication*, 28(2), 115–157.

Bacha, J. (2009). Single sourcing and the return to positivism: The threat of plain-style, arhetorical technical communication practices. In G. Pullman & B. Gu (Eds.) *Content management: Bridging the gap between theory and practice* (pp. 143–159). Amityville, NY: Baywood.

Bailie, R.A. (2014). Content strategy. In S. Abel & R.A. Bailie (Eds.), *The language of content strategy* (pp. 14–15). Laguna Hills, CA: XML Press.

Bailie, R.A. & Urbina, N. (2013). *Content strategy: Connecting the dots between business, brand, and benefits.* Laguna Hills, CA: XML Press.

Baker, M. (2013). *Every page is page one: Topic-based writing for technical communication and the web.* Laguna Hills, CA: XML Press.

Batova, T. (2014). Component content management and quality of information products for global audiences: An integrative literature review. *IEEE Transactions on Professional Communication.* 57(4), 325–339.

Bellamy, L., Carey, M., & Schlotfeldt, J. (2012). DITA best practices: A roadmap for writing, editing, and architecting in DITA. Upper Saddle River, NJ: IBM Press.

Carliner, S. (2010). Computers and technical communication in the 21st century. In R. Spilka (Ed.), *Digital literacy for technical communication: 21st century theory and practice* (pp. 21–50). New York, NY: Routledge.

Carter, L. (2003). The implications of single sourcing on writers and writing. *Technical Communication,* 50(3), 1–4.

Clark, D. (2007). Content management and the separation of presentation and content. *Technical Communication Quarterly,* 17(1), 35–60.

Clark, D. (2016). Content strategy: An integrative literature review. *IEEE Transactions on Professional Communication,* 59(1), 7–23.

Creekmore, L. (2014). Metadata. In S. Abel & R.A. Bailie (Eds.), *The language of content strategy* (pp. 28–29). Laguna Hills, CA: XML Press.

Flower, L. (1989). Rhetorical problem solving: Cognition and professional writing. In M. Kogen (Ed.), *Writing in the business professions* (pp.3–36). Urbana, IL: NCTE.

Gallagher, J.R. (2017). Writing for algorithmic audiences. *Computers and composition.* 45, 25–35.

Getto, G. & St. Amant, K. (2014). Designing globally, working locally: Using personas to develop online communication products for international users. *Communication Design Quarterly.* 3(1), 24–46.

GitHub Flavored Markdown Spec. (2017, August 1). Retrieved from https://github.github.com/gfm/

Hackos, J. T. (2011). *Introduction to DITA: A user guide to the Darwin Information Typing Architecture including DITA 1.2* (2nd edition). Denver, CO: Comtech Services, Inc.

Halvorson, K. & Rach, M. (2012). *Content strategy for the web* (2nd Ed.). Berkeley, CA: New Riders.

Harrison, N. (2016). Content variables. In R. Gallon (Ed.), *The language of technical communication* (pp. 66–67). Laguna Hills, CA: XML Press.

Hart-Davidson, W. et al. (2007). Coming to content management: Inventing infrastructure for organizational knowledge work. *Technical Communication Quarterly.* 17(1), 10–34.

ISTE. (2018). ISTE standards for students. Retrieved from http://www.iste.org/standards/for-students

Pringle, A., & O'Keefe, S. (2009). *Technical writing 101: A real-world guide to planning and writing technical content.* Durham, NC: Scriptorium Press.

Rothrock, L. & Narayanan, S. (2011). *Human-in-the-loop simulations: Methods and practice*. London: Springer-Verlag.

Swarts, J. (2010). Recycled writing: Assembling actor networks from reusable content. *Journal of Business and Technical Communication*. 24(2), 127–163.

Swisher, V. (2014). *Global content strategy: A primer*. Laguna Hills, CA: XML Press.

Vazquez, J. (2016). Conditional content. In R. Gallon (Ed.), *The language of technical communication* (pp. 64–65). Laguna Hills, CA: XML Press.

Wachter-Boettcher, S. (2012). *Content everywhere: Strategy and structure for future-ready content*. Brooklyn, N.Y: Rosenfeld Media.

Willerton, R. (2015). *Plain language and ethical action: A dialogic approach to technical content in the 21st century*. New York, NY: Routledge.

CONCLUSION

Remaking the Future of Technical Communication with LwDITA

Congratulations! Your content is now intelligent! So intelligent that you should help it with those college applications for Ivy League schools. Wait a minute. . . actually, I have not seen any of *your* content. Unless your content consists of little stubs of topics about pasta sauce recipes, sushi restaurants, or ice cream-based treats, all the content samples in this book were my examples. Now it is your turn to apply some of the recommendations from *Creating Intelligent Content with Lightweight DITA* to your content. It does not have to be technical documentation, and it does not have to be cross-format in all three available LwDITA flavors. If you and your team are comfortable working in HTML and do not want to explore alternatives, you can use HDITA and ignore everything else. If Markdown works for you and you do not want to deal with tags, there is a lot you can accomplish with MDITA – even in its core profile.

My main recommendation for any plan for implementing ideas discussed in this book is the same for all scenarios: do not jump directly to writing code and copying all your existing content from, say, a word processor to a text editor or LwDITA-aware software application. Writing is a process regardless of medium; paper and pen, word processor, or cross-format LwDITA content repository. . . all these writing environments need a plan. Focus on the abstractions from Chapter 8 and develop a strategy that works for your content requirements. Maybe things in your world are complex and full DITA XML will be the way to go, or maybe you are not ready to adopt LwDITA and will just want some ideas about computational thinking to improve your process in a web content management system. As long as you keep in mind the abstractions behind the process and the structure that enables the production of discoverable, reconfigurable, and adaptable content, my job will be done.

If being an early adopter is not in your nature, and you would rather wait for LwDITA-aware apps that hide all instances of code (even Markdown) and offer a WYSIWYG-like environment, I do not blame you. The existing tool support for DITA is strong for its main target audience of technical communicators. Nevertheless, the Lightweight DITA subcommittee expects that the expanded audience of LwDITA (which ventures into marketing content and contributions from subject matter experts, among other groups) will attract a new wave of developers who were not interested in DITA XML.

We might need to be patient before we see a broad variety of LwDITA tools. The LwDITA standard is still a work in progress, and as of this writing we are evaluating some implementation ideas. You can always track the progress of LwDITA adoption on the website and materials produced by the Lightweight DITA subcommittee at OASIS.

What is in it for You?

In *Creating Intelligent Content with Lightweight DITA* I tried to place human authors at the center of intelligent content workflows. Human processes like thinking and abstraction should take place before any automation or machine processing, and authors should be at the center of a LwDITA-based publishing workflow, taking precedence over any software tools.

Creating Intelligent Content with Lightweight DITA recognizes the many shapes and backgrounds of those human authors. Bridging my roles as co-chair of the Lightweight DITA subcommittee and professor of technical communication is my identity as a Mexican-American researcher who came to the academic side of content development via computer science. I see the need for more inclusive writing technologies and methodologies from different perspectives, including disciplinary constraints, ethnicity, and language. Answering the call from Jones et al. (2016) for a more inclusive focus in technical and professional communication research, I actively pushed for the LwDITA authoring formats to move away from the prescriptive textual nature of DITA XML. Whereas, for example, a DITA task requires an author to be proficient enough in English to remember the spelling of **<shortdesc>**, **<steps>**, **<hazardstatement>**, or **<steptroubleshooting>**, in LwDITA an author can use more familiar HTML5 tags or the *atx* headers of Markdown. The MDITA topic type, which does not depend on tags written in English, makes LwDITA even more accessible to a variety of authors from diverse professional communities and cultural identities.

Those human authors are also shaped by their job titles and responsibilities, which also affect their expectations and next steps that I recommend after reading this book.

If you are a current DITA user, you should not panic and start a migration process to convert all your topics to LwDITA. The DITA standard is not going away, and LwDITA does not have the purpose of replacing it. If you are adventurous and have some time for experiments, you should give LwDITA a try and discuss your findings with your manager or IT department. If you are a content developer who is not a DITA user, give LwDITA a try by bringing your own tools, preferences, and workflows. Evaluate if a transition would be feasible and, above all things, do not expect miracles. LwDITA simplifies the production of intelligent content, but good content creation equals busy work in any tool or environment. Talk to your manager or IT department after exploring the LwDITA authoring formats.

If you are one of those managers or IT professionals, read the sentence about not expecting miracles. Read it a couple of times just to be sure. Then, determine if your users and processes can function in LwDITA. I have met many users who simply cannot be trusted to be in environments that do not enforce structure in sections or paragraphs. In some of those cases, the relaxed structure of LwDITA could create new problems. And we all have heard of companies of all sizes that have decades of content production stored in Microsoft Word or, even worse, PowerPoint files. Content conversion of hundreds of unstructured files will be busy work even if the new format is a LwDITA flavor.

If you are a developer, open source or commercial, please help the Lightweight DITA subcommittee create tools to lower the barrier for adoption of the proposed standard. We need apps for authoring, processing, migrating, and automating the content experience with XDITA, HDITA, and MDITA. We need tools to make the process of producing intelligent content with LwDITA as simple as possible. Reach out to the Lightweight DITA subcommittee at OASIS.

If you are in academia, develop a plan for teaching and practicing content strategy, experiment with the available LwDITA tools, and participate in public reviews of materials produced by the Lightweight DITA subcommittee[1]. All our work is open to the public and we depend on feedback. If the feedback only comes from industry, the fault lines get deeper. Bring your voice and interests to the process of producing information standards. Adopt principles of computational thinking in your teaching and research and contribute to redefining the quite annoying term of "traditionally non-computing discipline" that labels writing and communication.

Chapter 1 included a recap of the Adobe video on the future of tech comm, and you can now remake that future by expanding the possibilities of structured content without depending on one single authoring format. With LwDITA, XML is just one of the available agents, and content components for simple expressions of machine-ready metadata and multimedia elements that were not included in previous versions of the DITA standard are available out of the box. Brad Mehlenbacher predicted the future of technical communication as "uncertain and indeterminate" (2013, p. 205). The simple act of learning and implementing a standard for structuring content will not change that forecast. However, adopting the cross-silo collaboration built on principles of computational thinking that LwDITA enables surely will contribute to preparing technical communicators as the "rhetorically sensitive sociotechnical mediators" (Mehlenbacher, 2013, p. 206) that the future demands.

Note

1 https://www.oasis-open.org/committees/tc_home.php?wg_abbrev=dita-lightweight-dita

References

Jones, N. N., Moore, K. R., & Walton, R. (2016). Disrupting the past to disrupt the future: An antenarrative of technical communication. *Technical Communication Quarterly*, 25(4), 211–229. http://dx.doi.org/10.1080/10572252.2016.1224655

Mehlenbacher, B. (2013). What is the future of technical communication? In J. Johnson-Eilola & S.A. Selber (Eds.), *Solving problems in technical communication* (pp. 187–208). Chicago, IL: The University of Chicago Press.

INDEX